Periodization Training for Sports

by
Tudor O. Bompa, PhD
York University

Human Kinetics

Library of Congress Cataloging-in-Publication Data

Bompa, Tudor O.
    Periodization training for sports / by Tudor Bompa.
       p.   cm.
    Includes bibliographical references (p.) and index.
     ISBN 0-88011-840-7 (pbk. : alk. paper)
     1. Periodization training.   2. Weight training.   I. Title.
   GV546.B546   1999
   613.7'13--dc21   98-48169
                                         CIP

ISBN: 0-88011-840-7

Copyright © 1999 by Tudor O. Bompa

Acquisitions Editor: Martin Barnard; **Developmental Editor:** Sydney Slobodnik; **Managing Editor:** Cynthia McEntire; **Assistant Editors:** Chris Enstrom, Katy Patterson, Leigh Lahood; **Copyeditor:** Barbara Field; **Proofreader:** Kathy Bennett; **Indexer:** Gerry Lynn Messner; **Graphic Designer:** Robert Reuther; **Graphic Artist:** Kathleen Boudreau-Fuoss; **Photo Editor:** Amy Outland; **Cover Designer:** Keith Blomberg; **Photographer (cover):** Tom Roberts; **Photographer (interior):** Tom Roberts, except where otherwise noted. Photos on pages 99, 103, 107, 108, and 113 © Claus Andersen. Photos on pages 5, 102, 112, and 141 © Terry Wild Studio. Photo on page 101 © Barbara Dunn. Photo on page 105 © The Picture Desk/Robert Skeoch. Photo on page 111 © Anthony Neste; **Illustrator:** Titus Deac; **Mac Art:** Denise Lowry; **Printer:** Versa Press.

Human Kinetics books are available at special discounts for bulk purchase. Special editions or book excerpts can also be created to specification. For details, contact the Special Sales Manager at Human Kinetics.

Printed in the United States of America   10 9 8 7 6 5

Human Kinetics
Web site: www.HumanKinetics.com

United States: Human Kinetics, P.O. Box 5076, Champaign, IL 61825-5076
800-747-4457
e-mail: humank@hkusa.com

Canada: Human Kinetics, 475 Devonshire Road, Unit 100, Windsor, ON N8Y 2L5
800-465-7301 (in Canada only)
e-mail: orders@hkcanada.com

Europe: Human Kinetics, 107 Bradford Road, Stanningley
Leeds LS28 6AT, United Kingdom
+44 (0) 113 255 5665
e-mail: hk@hkeurope.com

Australia: Human Kinetics, 57A Price Avenue, Lower Mitcham, South Australia 5062
08 8277 1555
e-mail: liahka@senet.com.au

New Zealand: Human Kinetics, P.O. Box 105-231, Auckland Central
09-523-3462
e-mail: hkp@ihug.co.nz

Contents

PART I   Foundations of Strength Training

PART II   Periodized Strength Training

Preface

The market is nearly saturated with strength or weight training books, most of which are very traditional and have no appreciable differences. Nearly all discuss some basic physiology, describe various exercises, and suggest a few training methods. Planning is rarely discussed, and periodization—the structuring of training into phases—is seldom mentioned simply because few understand its importance. A unique strength training method is rarely offered.

Strength training is of paramount importance in the development of athletes, but it must consist of more than just lifting weights without a specific purpose or plan. The purpose of any training method or technique should be to prepare athletes for competition—the ideal test of their abilities, skills, and psychological readiness. To achieve the best results, athletes should be exposed to a planning-periodization program, or sport- and phase-specific variations of training. The term *periodization* emphasizes the unique nature of *Periodization of Strength,* the foremost concept in strength training.

This book demonstrates how to use Periodization of Strength in structuring a strength training program and specifies which training methods are best for each training phase. The phases are planned according to the competition schedule, with each having a specific goal. Ultimately, the entire training program aims at achieving peak performance for the most important competitions of the year.

Periodization of Strength designates the type of strength to be developed in each training phase to ensure reaching the highest levels of power or muscular endurance. Developing the required sport-specific combination of these abilities prior to the competitive phase is a must, because they form the physiological foundation on which athletic performance relies. The key element in organizing periodized strength training to develop power or muscular endurance is the sequence in which various types of strength training are planned. This sequence of specific training phases is the secret of the Periodization of Strength method.

Benefits of This Book

A major objective of this book is to demonstrate that strength training is more than just lifting as much weight as possible every day without regard for the goals of specific training phases. As such, it offers a methodology and concept to follow in reaching your training objectives for competition. Based on planning-periodization, this methodology is a basic guide for structuring strength training phases and establishing goals that normally lead to performance improvements.

The book is intended to benefit strength coaches, sports coaches, instructors, personal trainers, athletes, and college students by increasing their knowledge of Periodization of Strength and its physiological foundation. Once you apply this easy-to-understand concept, you will realize that it is the best way to organize a strength training program for improving your athletes' physiological adaptation, which ultimately produces better performance. Peak performance occurs because you plan for it!

How This Book Meets Your Strength Training Needs

As you read this book, you will recognize the superiority of Periodization of Strength over the methods you have used in the past. To help you apply this unique concept, you will learn the following:

- The dominant abilities required to achieve performance goals for each sport, such as maximum speed, power, or muscular endurance
- Strength training's essential role in overall development of the physiological abilities needed for athletes to reach the highest performance possible
- The concept of planning-periodization and its specific application to strength training for your sport
- Actual methods for dividing the annual plan into strength training phases, each with specific objectives
- How to develop several types of strength in a specific sequence to guarantee reaching the highest levels of power and/or muscular endurance possible in a particular year
- How to manipulate the load, force application, and number of repetitions during a workout, as well as the loading patterns in each phase, to create the specific physiological adaptation needed for athletes to reach peak performance

How the Book Is Organized

Part I of the book (chapters 1 through 6) reviews the main theories influencing strength training and explains that power and muscular endurance are a combined physical quality. It also explains why certain athletic movements require a certain type of strength and why simply lifting weights will not benefit your athletes' performance. A brief history of the concept of Periodization of Strength is also presented.

A successful strength training program depends on your level of knowledge in the area of strength physiology. The information in chapter 2, "How Muscles Respond to Strength Training," is presented simply so that people from all backgrounds can understand it. The broader your knowledge in this area, the easier it will be to design programs that result in transfer of strength training benefits to sport-specific skills.

A brief explanation of training principles and how they apply to strength training is followed by a discussion of the key elements in designing a strength training program. Both short- and long-term planning, focusing mainly on weekly and annual plans, and planning-periodization are explained in detail to help you comprehend this extremely important concept in training.

In part II, chapters 7 through 12 discuss in detail all the phases that make up Periodization of Strength. For each phase, the best training methods available for taking your athletes to the highest performance possible are presented. Chapter 13 underscores the importance of recovery in strength training and provides information on facilitating a faster recovery following workouts.

Acknowledgments

I would like to acknowledge the important contributions of the following individuals to the publication of this book.

I sincerely thank Patricia Galacher, my editor, for the hundreds of hours she worked with the text. Pat, without your important contribution, I would never have seen this book in print. I would also like to thank Titus Deac for the professional illustrations he has provided.

My thanks to the professionals at Human Kinetics for their contributions. I am indebted to Martin Barnard, Acquisitions Editor, for his advice and suggestions, which resulted in a more logical text. Of equal importance are the contributions of Syd Slobodnik, Developmental Editor, and Cynthia McEntire, Managing Editor, who have spared no effort to help guide me through the wearying world of publishing. Human Kinetics, you are the best!

I would also like to thank two of my colleagues, Dave Chambers, PhD, and Thomas Duck, PhD, who have been very supportive of my publishing endeavours over the years.

Finally, I would like to thank Tamara, my wife of many years, for her patience and understanding of the many hours I hid in my office to scribble about things that fascinate me.

PART I

Foundations of Strength Training

Strength, Muscular Endurance, and Power in Sports

Almost all physical activities incorporate elements of force, quickness, duration, and range of motion. Exercises to overcome resistance are strength exercises. Speed exercises maximize quickness and high frequency. Exercises of long distance or duration, or many repetitions are endurance exercises. Maximum range of motion results in a flexibility movement. Exercises with complex movements are known as coordination exercises.

Athletes vary in their talent to perform certain exercises. Talent is mostly genetic. Inherited strength, speed, and endurance play an important role in reaching high levels of performance and are called *dominant motor* or *biomotor* abilities. *Motor* refers to movement; the prefix *bio-* illustrates the biological importance of these abilities.

Main Theories Influencing Strength Training for Sports

Five theories influence strength training for sports: bodybuilding, high-intensity training (HIT), Olympic weight lifting, power training throughout the year, and Periodization of Strength.

Bodybuilding

Bodybuilders are chiefly concerned with increased muscle size. They perform sets of 6 to 12 repetitions to exhaustion. With few exceptions—possibly football and some throwing events in track and field—increased muscle size is rarely beneficial to athletic performance. Since most athletic movements are explosive, the slow speed of contraction in bodybuilding has limited positive transfer to sports. Athletic skills, at 100 to 180 milliseconds, are performed quickly, but leg extensions in bodybuilding are three times slower, at 600 milliseconds (table 1.1).

High-Intensity Training (HIT)

High-intensity training (HIT) requires high training loads through the year with all working sets performed to at least positive failure. Firm believers in HIT claim that strength can be achieved in 20 to 30 minutes and stand against high-volume strength training, so important in events of long, continuous duration (mid- and long-distance swimming, rowing, canoeing, and cross-country skiing). HIT programs are not organized according to the competition schedule. For sports, strength is *periodized* according to the physiological needs of the sport in a given phase and the date for reaching peak performance.

Olympic Weight Lifting

Olympic weight lifting was an important influence in the early days of strength training. Even now, many coaches and trainers still use traditional Olympic weight-lifting moves such as the clean and jerk and power clean despite the fact that these moves rarely work the prime movers, the muscles primarily used in specific sport skills. Carefully assessing the needs of Olympic weight-lifting techniques is essential, especially for young athletes or athletes with no strength training background, as injuries have been reported in several such instances. Even highly trained athletes have reported injuries caused by exaggerated use of Olympic weight-lifting skills.

Power Training Throughout the Year

Some coaches and trainers, especially in track and field and certain team sports, believe that power training should be performed from day one of training through the major championship. They theorize that if power is the dominant ability, it has to be trained throughout the year except during the transition phase (off-season). They use exercises such as bounding and implements such as medicine balls and the shot. Certainly, athletic fitness does improve through the year. The key element, however, is the athlete's *rate* of improvement throughout the year, especially from year to year, not just *whether* the athlete improves. Strength training has been shown to lead to

Table 1.1 Duration of Contact Phase (in Milliseconds) of Some Sporting Events and Contraction Time of Leg Extension

Event	Duration in milliseconds
100-meter dash (contact phase)	100-200
Long jump (takeoff)	150-180
High jump (takeoff)	150-180
Vaulting in gymnastics (takeoff)	100-120
Leg extension (bodybuilding)	600

With additional clarifications from Schmidtbleicher, 1984.

far better results than power training, especially when Periodization of Strength is used. Power is a function of maximum strength. To improve power, one must improve maximum strength. Under these conditions, power improvement is faster and reaches higher levels.

Periodization of Strength

Strength training for sports must be based on the specific physiological requirements of the sport and must result in the development of either *power* or *muscle endurance*. Furthermore, strength training must revolve around the needs of planning-periodization for that sport and employ training methods specific to a given training phase, with the goal of reaching peak performance at the time of major competitions.

Strength, Speed, and Endurance

Strength, speed, and endurance are the important abilities for successful performance. The *dominant* ability is the one from which the sport requires a higher contribution (for instance, endurance is the dominant ability in long-distance running). Most sports require peak performance in at least two abilities. The relationships among strength, speed, and endurance create crucial physical athletic qualities. A better understanding of these relationships will help you understand power and muscular endurance and help you plan sport-specific strength training.

Combining strength and endurance creates *muscular endurance*, the ability to perform many repetitions against a given resistance for a prolonged period (figure 1.1). *Power*, the ability to perform an explosive movement in the shortest time possible, results from the integration of maximum strength and speed. The combination of endurance and speed is called *speed-endurance*. *Agility* is the product of a complex combination of speed, coordination, flexibility, and power as demonstrated in gymnastics, wrestling, football, soccer, volleyball, baseball, boxing, diving, and figure skating. When agility and flexibility combine, the result is *mobility*, the ability to cover a playing area quickly with good timing and coordination.

A relationship of high methodical importance exists among strength, speed, and endurance. A solid foundation for specialized training is built during the

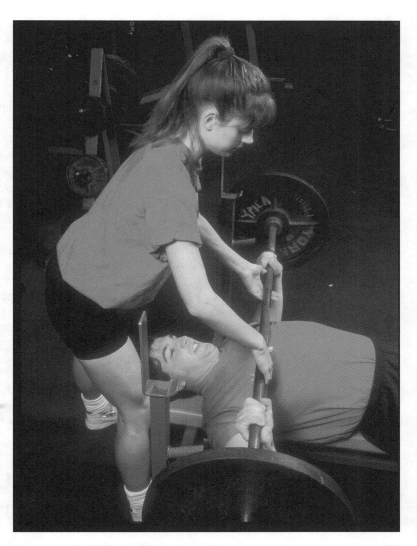

Assess weight-lifting techniques to make sure they fit in your sport-specific program.

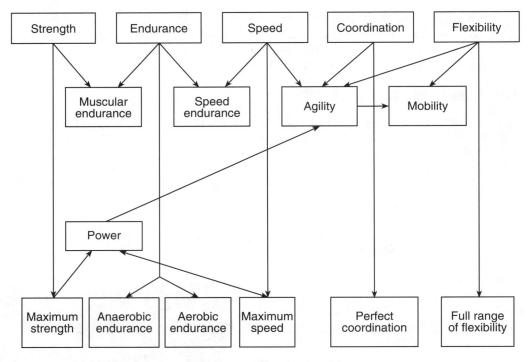

Figure 1.1 Interdependence among the biomotor abilities.

initial years of training. This sport-specific phase is a requirement for all national-level and elite athletes who aim for precise training effects. As a result of specific exercises, the adaptation process occurs in accordance with an athlete's specialization. For elite athletes, the relationship among strength, speed, and endurance is dependent on the sport and the athlete's needs.

Figure 1.2 illustrates three examples where *strength or force (F), speed (S), or endurance (E)* is dominant. In each case, when one biomotor ability dominates, the other two do not participate to a similar extent. This example, however, is pure theory, and applies to few sports. In the vast majority of sports, each ability has a given input. Figure 1.3 shows the dominant composition of strength, speed, and endurance in several sports.

Using figure 1.3 as a model, try to define the combinations among the dominant biomotor abilities for your sport. In figure 1.4 on page 8, place a circle in the location you feel is most ideal. Try to evaluate your own dominant abilities or those of your athletes and place another circle in the appropriate location inside the triangle. The second circle tells you what areas to train to match the dominant combinations of biomotor abilities for that sport.

Effect of Strength Training on Other Biomotor Abilities

Specific development of a biomotor ability must be methodical. A developed dominant ability directly or indirectly affects the other abilities. To what extent depends strictly on the resemblance between the methods employed

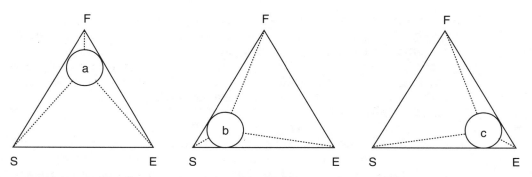

Figure 1.2 Relationships among the main biomotor abilities, where strength *(a)*, speed *(b)*, and endurance *(c)* are dominant.

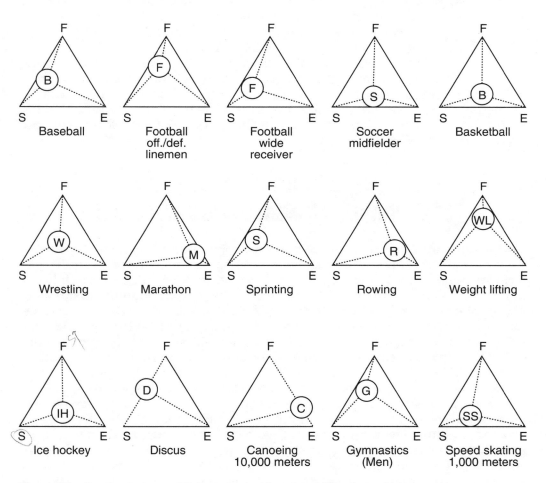

Figure 1.3 Dominant composition among the biomotor abilities for various sports.

and the specifics of the sport. So, development of a dominant biomotor ability may have a positive or, rarely, a negative transfer. When an athlete develops strength, he may experience a positive transfer to speed and endurance. On the other hand, a strength training program designed only to develop maximum strength may negatively affect the development of aerobic endurance. Similarly, a training program aimed exclusively at developing

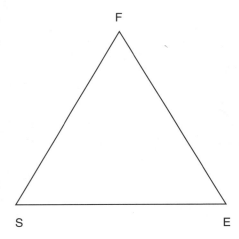

Figure 1.4 Use this triangle for the suggested exercise.

aerobic endurance may have a negative transfer to strength and speed. Since strength is a crucial athletic ability, it always has to be trained with the other abilities.

Misleading, unfounded theories have suggested that strength training slows down athletes and affects the development of endurance and flexibility. Recent research discredits such theories (Atha, 1984; Dudley & Fleck, 1987; Hickson et al., 1988; MacDougall et al., 1987; Micheli, 1988; Nelson et al., 1990; Sale et al., 1990). Combined strength and endurance training does not affect improvement (i.e., no negative transfer) of aerobic power or muscular strength. Similarly, strength programs pose no risk to flexibility. Thus, for endurance sports such as rowing, cross-country skiing, canoeing, and swimming, concurrent work can be performed safely on strength and endurance. The same is true for sports requiring strength and flexibility.

For speed sports, power represents a great source of speed improvement. A fast sprinter is also strong. High acceleration, fast limb movement, and high frequency are possible when strong muscles contract quickly and powerfully. In extreme situations, however, maximum loads may momentarily affect speed. Velocity will be affected if speed training is scheduled after an exhausting training session with maximum loads. Speed training should always be performed before strength training (see chapter 5).

Sport-Specific Combinations of Strength, Speed, and Endurance

Most actions and movements are more complex than previously discussed. Thus, strength in sports should be viewed as the mechanism required to perform skills and athletic actions. The reason for developing strength is not just for the sake of being strong. The goal of strength development is to meet the specific needs of a given sport, to develop specific strength or combinations of strength to increase athletic performance to the highest possible level.

Combining strength (F) and endurance (E) results in *muscular endurance* (M-E). Sports may require M-E of long or short duration, a distinction that must be made because of the drastic differences between them. This distinction determines the type of strength to train for each sport.

Before discussing this topic, a brief clarification of the terms *cyclic* and *acyclic* is necessary. *Cyclic* movements are repeated continuously, such as running, walking, swimming, rowing, skating, cross-country skiing, cycling, and canoeing. As soon as one cycle of the motor act is learned, the others can be repeated with the same succession. *Acyclic* movements, on the other hand, constantly change and are dissimilar to most others, such as in throwing events, gymnastics, wrestling, fencing, and many technical elements in team sports.

With the exception of sprinting, cyclic sports are endurance sports. Endurance is either dominant or makes an important contribution to performance. Acyclic sports are often speed-power sports. Many sports, however, are more complex and require speed, power, and endurance (for example, basketball, volleyball, soccer, ice hockey, wrestling, and boxing). Therefore, the following analysis may refer to certain skills of a given sport and not the sport as a whole.

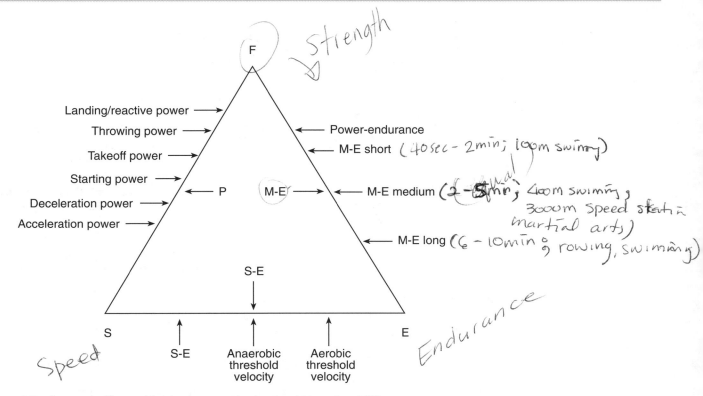

Figure 1.5 Sport-specific combinations among the dominant biomotor abilities.

Figure 1.5 analyzes various combinations of strength. The elements will be discussed in a clockwise direction starting with the F-E (strength-endurance) axis. Each strength combination has an arrow pointing to a certain part of the axis between two biomotor abilities. An arrow placed closer to F indicates that strength plays a dominant role in the sport or skill. An arrow placed closer to the midpoint of the axis indicates an equal or almost equal contribution of both biomotor abilities. The farther the arrow is from F, the less importance it has, suggesting that the other ability becomes more dominant. However, strength still plays a role in that sport.

The F-E axis refers to sports where M-E (*muscular endurance*) is the dominant strength combination (the inner arrow). Not all sports require equal parts strength and endurance. For example, swimming events range from 50 to 1,500 meters. The 50-meter event is speed-power dominant; M-E becomes more important as the distance increases.

Power-endurance is on top of the F-E axis because of the importance of strength for activities such as rebounding in basketball, spiking in volleyball, jumping to catch the ball in Australian football and rugby, or jumping to head the ball in soccer. All these actions are power-dominant movements. The same is true for some skills in tennis, boxing, wrestling, and martial arts. More than power has to be trained to perform such actions successfully throughout a game or match since these actions are performed 100 to 200 or more times per game or match. Although it is important to jump high to rebound a ball, it is equally important to duplicate such a jump 200 times per game. Consequently, both power and power-endurance have to be trained.

M-E of short duration refers the M-E necessary for events of short duration (40 seconds to 2 minutes). In the 100-meter swimming event, the start is a power action as are the first 20 strokes. From the midpoint of the race to the end, M-E becomes at least equally important to power. In the last 30 to

40 meters, the crucial element is the ability to duplicate the force of the arms' pull so that velocity is maintained and then increased at the finish. For events such as 100 meters in swimming, 400 meters in running, 500 to 1,000 meters in speed skating, and 500 meters in canoeing, M-E strongly contributes to the final result.

M-E of medium duration is typical of cyclic sports 2 to 5 minutes long, such as 200- and 400-meter swimming, 3,000-meter speed skating, track and field mid-distance running, 1,000-meter canoeing, wrestling, martial arts, figure skating, synchronized swimming, and cycling pursuit.

M-E of long duration (over 6 to 10 minutes) requires the ability to apply force against a standard resistance for a longer period as in rowing, cross-country skiing, road cycling, long-distance running, swimming, speed skating, and canoeing.

Speed-endurance (S-E) refers to the ability to maintain or repeat a high-velocity action several times per game, as in football, baseball, basketball, rugby, soccer, and power skating in ice hockey. Players in these sports need to train to develop a speed-endurance capacity.

The remaining two types of speed-endurance alter in combination and proportion of speed and endurance as distance increases. In the first case, sports require training velocity around the *anaerobic threshold* (4 millimoles [mmol] of lactate or a heart rate of approximately 170 beats per minute). In the second case, training velocity must be around the *aerobic threshold* (2 to 3 mmol of lactate or a heart rate of 125 to 140 beats per minute).

The F-S (*strength-speed*) axis refers mainly to strength-speed sports where power is dominant.

Landing and reactive power is a major component of several sports, like figure skating, gymnastics, and several team sports. Proper training can prevent injuries. Many athletes train only the takeoff part of a jump, with no concern for a controlled and balanced landing. The physical/power element plays an important role in proper landing technique, particularly for advanced athletes. Athletes must train eccentrically to be able to "stick" a landing, absorb the shock, and maintain good balance to continue the routine or perform another move immediately.

The power required to control a landing depends on the height of the jump, the athlete's body weight, and whether the landing is performed by absorbing the shock or with the joints flexed but stiff. Testing has revealed that for a shock-absorbing landing, athletes use a resistance force three to four times their body weight. Landing performed with stiff leg joints requires a force of six to eight times body weight. An athlete weighing 60 kilograms (132 pounds) requires 180 to 240 kilograms (396 to 528 pounds) to absorb the shock of landing. The same athlete requires 360 to 480 kilograms (792 to 1,056 pounds) to land with the leg joints stiff. When an athlete lands on one leg, as in figure skating, the force at the instant of landing is three to four times body weight for a shock-absorbing landing and five to seven times for landing with stiff leg joints.

Strength training can train landing power better, faster, and with much more consistency than specific skill training. Specific power training for landing can generate much higher tension in the muscles of the legs than performing an exercise with only body weight. Higher tension means improvements in landing power. In addition, through specific power training for landing, especially eccentric training, athletes can build a "power reserve" that is a force greater than the power required for a correct and controlled landing. The higher the power reserve, the easier it is for the athlete to control the landing, and the safer the landing.

Reactive power is the ability to generate the force of jumping immediately following a landing (hence "reactive"). This kind of power is necessary in the martial arts, wrestling, and boxing and for quick changes in direction, as in football, soccer, basketball, lacrosse, and tennis. The force needed for a reactive jump depends on the height of the jump and the athlete's body weight and leg power. Reactive jumps require a force equal to 6 to 8 times body weight. Reactive jumps from a platform of 1 meter (3.3 feet) require a reactive force of 8 to 10 times body weight.

Pitchers rely on throwing power to overcome the inertia of the baseball.

Throwing power refers to force applied against an implement, such as throwing a football, pitching a baseball, or throwing the javelin. The release speed is determined by the amount of muscular force exerted at the instant of release. First, athletes have to defeat the inertia of the implement, which is proportional to its mass (important only in throwing events). Then they must continuously accelerate through the range of motion so that maximum acceleration is achieved at the instant of release. The force and acceleration of release depend directly on the force and speed of contraction applied against the implement.

Takeoff power is crucial in events in which athletes attempt to project the body to the highest point, either to jump over a bar as in high jump or to reach the best height to catch a ball or spike it. The height of a jump depends directly on the vertical force applied against the ground to defeat the pull of gravity. In most cases, the vertical force performed at takeoff is at least twice the athlete's weight. The higher the jump, the more powerful the legs should be. Leg power is developed through periodized strength training as explained in chapters 6 and 10.

Starting power is necessary for sports that require high speed to cover a given distance in the shortest time possible. Athletes must be able to generate maximum force at the beginning of a muscular contraction to create a high initial speed. A fast start, either from a low position as in sprinting or from a tackling position in football, depends on the reaction time and power the athlete can exert at that instant.

Accelerating power refers to the capacity to achieve high acceleration. Sprinting speed or acceleration depends on the power and quickness of muscle contraction to drive the arms and legs to the highest stride frequency, the shortest contact phase when the leg reaches the ground, and the highest

Table 1.2 Sport-Specific Strength Development Required for Sports/Events

Sport/event	Types of strength required	Sport/event	Types of strength required
Athletics		**Gymnastics**	Reactive power, takeoff power, landing power
Sprinting	Reactive power, starting power, acceleration power, power-endurance	**Handball (European)**	Throwing power, acceleration power, deceleration power
Middle-distance running	Acceleration power, M-E medium	**Ice hockey**	Acceleration power, deceleration power, power-endurance
Distance running	M-E long	**Martial arts**	Starting power, reactive power, power-endurance
Long jump	Acceleration power, takeoff power, reactive power	**Rhythmic sportive gymnastics**	Reactive power, takeoff power, M-E short
Triple jump	Acceleration power, reactive power, takeoff power	**Rowing**	M-E medium/long, starting power
High jump	Takeoff power, reactive power	**Rugby**	Acceleration power, starting power, M-E medium
Throws	Throwing power, reactive power		
Baseball	Throwing power, acceleration power	**Sailing**	M-E long, power-endurance
Basketball	Takeoff power, power-endurance, acceleration power, deceleration power	**Shooting**	M-E long, power-endurance
Biathlon	M-E long	**Skiing**	
		Alpine	Reactive power, M-E short
Boxing	Power-endurance, reactive power, M-E medium/long	Nordic	M-E long, power-endurance
Canoeing/kayaking		**Soccer**	
500 meters	M-E short, acceleration power, starting power	Sweepers, fullbacks	Reactive power, acceleration power, deceleration power
1,000 meters	M-E medium, acceleration power, starting power	Midfielders	Acceleration power, deceleration power, M-E medium
10,000 meters	M-E long	Forwards	Acceleration power, deceleration power, reactive power
Cricket	Throwing power, acceleration power		
Cycling		**Speed skating**	
Track, 200 meters	Acceleration power, reactive power	Sprinting	Starting power, acceleration power, M-E short
4,000-meter pursuit	M-E medium, acceleration power	Mid distance	M-E medium, power-endurance
Road racing	M-E long	Long distance	M-E long
Diving	Takeoff power, reactive power	**Squash/handball**	Reactive power, power-endurance
Equestrian	M-E medium	**Swimming**	
Fencing	Reactive power, power-endurance	Sprinting	Starting power, acceleration power, M-E short
Figure skating	Takeoff power, landing power, power-endurance	Mid distance	M-E medium, power-endurance
		Long distance	M-E long
Field hockey	Acceleration power, deceleration power, M-E medium	**Synchronized swimming**	M-E medium, power-endurance
Football (American)		**Tennis**	Power-endurance, reactive power, acceleration power, deceleration power
Linemen	Starting power, reactive power		
Linebackers, quarterbacks, running backs, inside receivers	Starting power, acceleration power, reactive power	**Volleyball**	Reactive power, power-endurance, throwing power
Wide receivers, defensive backs, tailbacks	Acceleration power, reactive power, starting power	**Water polo**	M-E medium, acceleration power, throwing power
Football (Australian)	Acceleration power, takeoff power, landing power, M-E short/medium	**Wrestling**	Power-endurance, reactive power, M-E medium

propulsion when the leg pushes against the ground for a powerful forward drive. The capacity of athletes to accelerate depends on both arm and leg force. Specific strength training for high acceleration will benefit most team sport athletes from wide receivers in football to wingers in rugby or strikers in soccer (see table 1.2).

Decelerating power is important in sports such as soccer, basketball, football, and ice and field hockey. Athletes run fast and constantly change direction quickly. Such athletes are exploders and accelerators as well as decelerators. The dynamics of these games change abruptly: players running fast in one direction suddenly have to change direction with the least loss of speed, then accelerate quickly in another direction.

Acceleration and deceleration both require a great deal of leg and shoulder power. The same muscles used for acceleration (quadriceps, hamstrings, and calves) are used for deceleration, except they *contract eccentrically*. To enhance the ability to decelerate fast and quickly move in another direction, decelerating power must be trained.

Role of Strength for Water Sports

For sports performed in or on water, such as swimming, synchronized swimming, water polo, rowing, and kayaking/canoeing, the body or the boat moves forward as a result of force. As force is performed against the water, the water exerts an equal and opposite force, known as drag, on the body or boat. As the boat or the swimmer moves through the water, the drag slows the forward motion or glide. To overcome drag, athletes must produce equal force to maintain speed and superior force to increase speed. The magnitude of the drag acting on a body moving through the water can be computed using the following equation (Hay, 1993):

$$F_D = C_D P A \frac{V^2}{2}$$

where F_D = drag force, C_D = coefficient of drag, P = fluid density, A = frontal area exposed to the flow, and V = body velocity relative to the water.

The coefficients of drag refer to the nature and shape of the body, including its orientation relative to the water flow. Long and slender vessels such as canoes, kayaks, or racing shells have a smaller C_D if the long axis of the boat is exactly parallel to the water flow.

A simplified version of the above equation is presented below. This equation is not only easier to understand, but also easier to apply:

$$D \sim V^2$$

meaning that drag is proportional to the square of velocity.

In water sports, velocity increases when athletes apply force against the water. As force increases, the body moves faster. However, as velocity increases, drag increases proportionally to the square of velocity. The following example will better demonstrate this assertion. Assume that an athlete swims or rows at 2 meters per second. In this case:

$$D \sim V^2 = 2^2 = 4 \text{ kilograms}$$

In other words, the athlete pulls with a force of 4 kilograms per stroke. To be more competitive, the athlete has to swim or row at 3 meters per second. As such:

$$D \sim V^2 = 9 \text{ kilograms}$$

For an even higher velocity of 4 meters per second, drag will equal 16 kilograms. Obviously, to be able to pull with increased force, MxS must be increased. A body will not be able to generate increased velocity without increasing the force per stroke unit.

The training implications are obvious. Not only must maximum strength (MxS) be increased, but the coach must ensure that athletes display the same force for all strokes throughout the duration of the race, since all water sports have a strong endurance component. This means that a MxS phase and an adequate M-E phase must be incorporated in training, as suggested in chapter 11.

A Brief History of Periodization of Strength

The concept of Periodization of Strength for sports has evolved from two basic needs: (1) the need to model strength training around the annual plan and its training phases, and (2) the need to increase the rate of power development from year to year. The first athletic experiment using Periodization of Strength was done with Mihaela Penes, a gold medalist in javelin throw at the 1964 Tokyo Olympic Games. The results were presented in 1965 in Bucharest and Moscow (Bompa, 1965a, 1965b). The original Periodization of Strength model has been altered to suit the needs of endurance-related sports that require muscular endurance (Bompa, 1977). Both models of Periodization of Strength are discussed in this book, including training methods. The basic Periodization of Strength model has also been presented in *Periodization: Theory and Methodology of Training* (Bompa, 1999).

In 1984, Stone and O'Bryant presented a theoretical model of strength training in which Periodization of Strength included four phases: Hypertrophy, Basic Strength, Strength and Power, and Peaking and Maintenance. A comprehensive book on periodization, *Periodization of Strength: The New Wave in Strength Training* (Bompa, 1993a), was followed by *Periodization Breakthrough* (Fleck & Kraemer, 1996), which again demonstrated that to achieve high athletic benefits from strength training, Periodization of Strength is the way to go! Most recently, *Serious Strength Training* (Bompa & Cornacchia, 1998) was published by Human Kinetics.

How Muscles Respond to Strength Training

Many athletes and coaches avoid reading academic physiology texts or books filled with scientific terminology. Therefore, this book explains the scientific basis of strength training clearly and simply. The better you understand the science of training and how it is applied, the faster strength and performance will improve. Once you understand muscle contraction and the sliding filament theory, you will realize why the speed of contraction is load related and why you have more force at the beginning of a contraction than at the end. Learning about muscle fiber types and that they are inherited will help you see why some athletes are better than others at certain types of sporting activities (i.e., speed-power versus endurance).

Understanding muscle adaptation and its dependence on load and training method(s) makes it easier to grasp why I suggest a certain type of load, exercises, or training methods for some sports and not for others. It is important to know what contractions are available and which are best for your sport, because strength training success relies on your knowledge of the types of strength that exist and how to develop them. This knowledge will help you understand the concept of planning-periodization faster and easier, and improvement will soon follow.

Structure of the Body

The human body is constructed around a bone skeleton. The junction of two or more bones forms a joint held together by tough bands of connective tissue called ligaments. The skeletal frame is covered with 656 muscles, approximately 40 percent of total body weight. Dense connective tissue called tendons attach both ends of the muscle to the bone. The tension in a muscle is directed to the bone through the tendon. The greater the tension, the stronger the pull on the tendons and bone and, consequently, the more powerfully the limb moves.

An injury to the tendons or ligaments supporting a muscle can cause the joint to collapse.

Key Words

Agonistic muscle: A muscle directly engaged in a muscular contraction and working in opposition to the action of other muscles.

Antagonistic muscle: A muscle that has an opposite effect on a mover, or agonistic muscle, by opposing its contraction.

Cardiorespiratory endurance: The ability of the lungs and heart to take in and transport adequate amounts of oxygen to the working muscles, allowing activities that involve large muscle masses (e.g., running, swimming, bicycling) to be performed over long periods.

Prime movers: The muscles primarily responsible for performance of a technical movement.

Nerve Supply to Muscles

Muscles are supplied with *motor nerves* and *sensory nerves*. Motor nerves relate to movement. Each motor nerve sends impulses from the central nervous system (CNS) to the termination point on a muscle fiber, called the *motor end plate*, resulting in a muscle contraction. Sensory nerves relay information about pain and body orientation to the CNS.

Structure of the Muscle Cell

A muscle consists of special fibers of a few inches long to more than 3 feet that extend the entire length of the muscle. These fibers are grouped in bundles called *fasciculi*, held together by a sheath called the *perimysium*. Each fiber contains many threadlike protein strands called *myofibrils*, which hold the contractile units, the *sarcomeres*. Each sarcomere contains a specific arrangement of the contractile protein's *myosin* (thick filaments) and *actin* (thin filaments), whose actions are important in muscle contraction. The ability of a muscle to contract and exert force is determined by its design, the cross-sectional area, the fiber length, and the number of fibers within the muscle. The number of fibers is genetically determined and is not affected by training; however, the other variables can be. Dedicated training increases the thickness of muscle filaments, increasing both muscle size and force of contraction.

Mechanism of Muscular Contraction: The Sliding Filament Theory

Muscular contraction involves the actin and myosin in a mechanical series of events called the *sliding filament theory of contraction.* Six actin filaments surround each myosin filament. The myosin filaments contain cross bridges, tiny extensions that reach toward the actin filaments. Impulses from the motor nerve stimulate the entire fiber, creating chemical changes that allow the actin filaments to join with the myosin cross bridges. Binding myosin to actin by way of cross bridges releases energy, causing the cross bridges to swivel, pulling or sliding the myosin filament over the actin filament. This sliding motion causes the muscle to shorten (contract), producing force. Once the stimulation ends, the actin and myosin filaments separate, lengthening the muscle to its resting length, and the contraction ends. Cross bridge activity explains why the muscular force generated depends on the initial length of the muscle prior to contraction. The optimal length for muscular contraction is resting length (or slightly greater), because all the cross bridges can connect with the actin filaments, allowing maximum tension (figure 2.1).

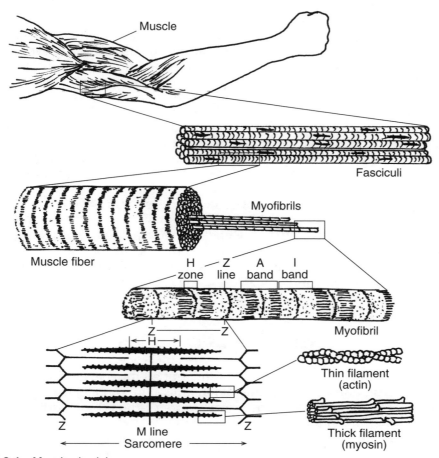

Figure 2.1 Muscle physiology.

Reprinted, by permission, from Bompa, T. and L. Cornacchia, 1998. *Serious Strength Training,* (Champaign, IL: Human Kinetics), 4

When muscle length prior to contraction is significantly shorter than resting length (i.e., already partially contracted), the contractile force decreases. In an already shortened muscle, the actin and myosin filaments overlap, leaving few cross bridges open to "pull" on the actin filaments. The fewer cross bridges available, the less tension and force produced (figure 2.1). When the muscle is lengthened beyond resting length, force potential is also small because the actin filaments are too far from the cross bridges to join and shorten the muscle. Contractile force diminishes when muscle length is either shorter or longer than resting length. The highest force output occurs when contraction begins at a joint angle of approximately 110 to 120 degrees.

The Motor Unit

Every motor nerve entering a muscle can innervate one to several thousand muscle fibers. All muscle fibers activated by an individual motor nerve contract and relax in unison. Thus, a single motor nerve together with the muscle fibers it activates is called a *motor unit.*

When a motor nerve is stimulated, the impulse sent to the muscle fibers within the motor unit either spreads completely or does not spread at all, the "all-or-none law." A weak impulse creates the same tension within the motor unit as a strong impulse.

The all-or-none law does not apply to the muscle as a whole. Although all the muscle fibers respond to the stimulation of the motor nerve within a single motor unit, not all motor units are activated during a muscle contraction. The number of motor units involved in a contraction depends on the load imposed on the muscle and directly affects the force produced. For example, a light load recruits only a small number of motor units and the strength of contraction is low. Extremely heavy loads recruit all or almost all the motor units, resulting in maximal force output (McDonagh & Davies, 1984). Since motor units are recruited in sequence, the only way to train the entire muscle is to use maximum loads, when every motor unit is used.

Muscle force depends on the number of motor units recruited during a contraction and on the number of muscle fibers within a motor unit, from 20 to 500 (average being around 200). The more fibers per motor unit, which varies the higher the force output. Genetics determines the number of fibers which is why some people can increase the size and strength of their muscles easily and others have to fight for every small gain. A motor unit stimulated by a nerve impulse responds by giving a *twitch,* or a very quick contraction, followed by relaxation.

Muscle Fiber Types

Although all motor units behave the same, not all muscle fibers do. Since all muscle fibers do not have the same biochemical (metabolic) functions, some are physiologically better suited to work under anaerobic conditions while others work better under aerobic conditions.

Fibers that rely on and use oxygen to produce energy are called aerobic, Type I, red, or *slow-twitch (ST) fibers.* Fibers that do not require oxygen are called anaerobic, Type II, white, or *fast-twitch (FT) fibers.* ST and FT fibers exist in relatively equal proportions within the body, and strength training is not thought to affect this 50-50 relationship to a great extent. Strength train-

Table 2.1 Comparison of FT and ST Characteristics

Fast twitch (FT)	Slow twitch (ST)
White, Type II, anaerobic	*Red, Type I, aerobic*
• Fast fatiguing	• Slow fatiguing
• Large nerve cell—innervates from 300 to more than 500 muscle fibers	• Smaller nerve cell—innervates from 10 to 180 muscle fibers only
• Develops short, forceful contractions	• Develops long, continuous contractions
• Speed and power	• Endurance
• Recruited only during high-intensity work	• Recruited during low- and high-intensity work

ing, however, does affect fiber size. Table 2.1 compares ST and FT fiber characteristics.

The innervation of muscle fibers determines whether they are FT or ST, depending on how many muscle fibers are connected to each motor nerve. A FT motor unit has a larger nerve cell and innervates 300 to over 500 fibers. A ST motor unit normally has a smaller nerve cell and connects 10 to 180 fibers. The FT motor unit's contraction is faster and more powerful. Successful athletes in speed-power sports are genetically equipped with a higher proportion of FT fibers, but they also fatigue faster. Individuals with more ST fibers are more successful in endurance sports as they are able to perform work of lower intensity for a longer time.

Although FT fibers are used in shorter, faster activities, it is not the speed of contraction but rather the force of the muscle that causes the motor nerves to recruit the FT fibers (Wilmore & Costill, 1988). This explains why athletes in speed-related sports (e.g., sprinters, football and baseball players) have to increase power. The high-power movements performed by these athletes activate the FT fibers, making them capable of performing explosive and fast actions.

Recruitment of muscle fibers depends on load. Moderate and low-intensity activity recruits ST fibers as workhorses. As the load increases, more FT fibers are activated during a contraction.

Distribution of fiber types can vary, both within the same muscle and between different muscles. Generally, the arms have a higher percentage of FT fibers than the legs: the biceps have 55 percent FT and the triceps have 60 percent FT; the soleus (calf muscle) has just 24 percent FT (Fox et al., 1989).

Fiber type composition (i.e., the proportion of FT fibers within a muscle) plays an important role in strength sports. Muscles containing a high percentage of FT fibers are capable of quicker, more powerful contractions. Changing the

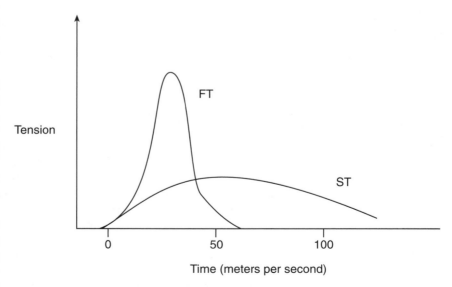

Figure 2.2 Twitch response of FT and ST fibers to the same intensity of stimulus. (Based on data from Costill, 1976; Komi and Bosco, 1978; Gollnick et al., 1972)

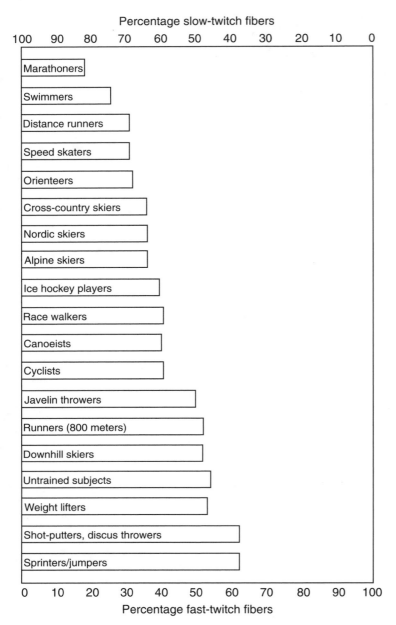

Percentage slow-twitch fibers

| 100 | 90 | 80 | 70 | 60 | 50 | 40 | 30 | 20 | 10 | 0 |

Marathoners
Swimmers
Distance runners
Speed skaters
Orienteers
Cross-country skiers
Nordic skiers
Alpine skiers
Ice hockey players
Race walkers
Canoeists
Cyclists
Javelin throwers
Runners (800 meters)
Downhill skiers
Untrained subjects
Weight lifters
Shot-putters, discus throwers
Sprinters/jumpers

| 0 | 10 | 20 | 30 | 40 | 50 | 60 | 70 | 80 | 90 | 100 |

Percentage fast-twitch fibers

Figure 2.3 Fiber type distribution for male athletes. Note the dominance in ST fibers for athletes from aerobic-dominant sports and in FT fibers for athletes from speed-power-dominant sports. (Based on data from Costill, 1976; Gollnick et al., 1972.)

proportion of FT and ST fibers within a muscle by training is critical for strength gains, yet the possibility remains controversial. Recent studies suggest, however, that a shift in fiber type from ST to FT may be possible as a result of prolonged, high-intensity training. This means that the proportion of FT fibers increases at the expense of ST fibers (see figure 2.2) (Abernethy et al., 1990; Jacobs et al., 1987).

Differences in muscle fiber type distribution are visible among athletes involved in various sports. Figures 2.3 and 2.4 illustrate a general profile of FT fiber percentages for some sports. Note the drastic differences between sprinters and marathon runners, which clearly suggest that success in some sports is at least partially determined by muscle fiber composition.

Although sprinters and jumpers are expected to have the highest percentage of FT fibers (61 percent), it is surprising that untrained subjects are very close (56 percent). Yet if the trained and untrained groups are tested in both power and maximum strength, the difference is very great. This leads to the conclusion that *training can significantly increase the ability to display power and maximum strength* (Costill et al., 1976; Gollnick et al., 1972; Komi et al., 1977).

The peak power generated by athletes is also related to fiber type distribution. The higher the distribution of FT fibers, the greater the power generated by the athlete. Similarly, the percentage of distribution of FT fibers in the muscles is also velocity related. The greater the velocity displayed by an athlete, the higher the percentage distribution of FT fibers. Such individuals make great sprinters and jumpers, and with this natural talent, they should be channeled into speed-power-dominant sports. Attempting to make them distance runners would be a waste of talent. In such events, they would be only moderately successful, when they could be excellent sprinters or baseball or football players, to mention just a few speed-power-related sports.

There are no clear differences in muscle fiber distribution between female and male athletes. Thus, although the percentage of fiber type is determined genetically irrespective of sex, what is inherited can mean a good start in the race to high performance compared to other athletes. This genetic quality alone, however, should not be used as the basis for predicting future athletic success. Such risky predictions should be based on other variables besides genetic profile.

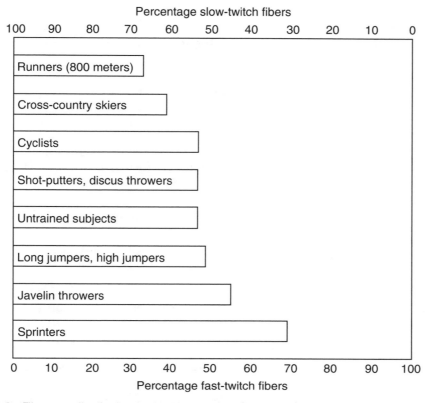

Figure 2.4   Fiber type distribution for female athletes. (See note for figure 2.3.)

Muscle Contraction: How Muscles Work

The musculoskeletal frame of the body is an arrangement of bones attached to one another by ligaments at the joints. The muscles crossing these joints provide the force for body movements. Skeletal muscles do not contract independently of one another. Rather, the movements performed about a joint are produced by several muscles, each with a different role.

Agonists or *synergists* are muscles that cooperate to perform a movement. *Antagonists* act in opposition to the agonists during movement. In most cases, especially in skilled and experienced athletes, the antagonists relax, allowing easy motion. Since athletic movements are directly influenced by the interaction between agonist and antagonist muscle groups, a jerky motion, or one rigidly performed, might result from an improper interaction between the two groups. The smoothness of a muscular contraction can be improved by focusing on relaxing the antagonists.

Prime movers are muscles primarily responsible for producing a comprehensive strength movement or technical skill. During a biceps curl, for example, the prime mover is the biceps muscle; the triceps acts as an antagonist and should be relaxed to facilitate smoother flexion.

Stabilizers or *fixators* are usually smaller muscles that contract isometrically to anchor a bone so the prime movers have a firm base from which to pull. The muscles of other limbs may come into play as well, acting as stabilizers so that the prime movers can perform their motion. For instance, during a "preacher curl," the shoulders, upper arms, and abdominal muscles contract isometrically to stabilize the shoulders, giving the biceps a stable base from which to pull.

The *line of pull* is an imaginary line that crosses the muscle longitudinally, between its two extreme heads. A muscle contraction achieves the highest physiological and mechanical efficiency when performed along the line of pull. For example, in elbow flexion, when the palm is up, the direct line of pull creates the highest efficiency. When the palm is down, contraction efficiency decreases because the tendon of the biceps muscle wraps around the bone radius. In this case, the line of pull is indirect and a large portion of the contractile force is wasted. A similar situation occurs with the squat. If the feet are shoulder-width apart with the toes pointing forward, the quadriceps have a better line of pull. The opposite is true when the feet are far apart with the toes pointing diagonally forward. For maximum strength gains and optimal muscle efficiency, strength exercises must be performed along the line of pull.

Types of Muscular Contraction

Skeletal muscles are responsible for both contraction and relaxation. Muscles contract when they are stimulated, and when the contractions are discontinued, the muscles relax. There are three types of contractions: *isotonic, isometric,* and *isokinetic.*

Isotonic (dynamic), from the Greek *isos* (equal) and *tonikos* (tension), is the most familiar type of muscle contraction. During an isotonic contraction, the tension should be the same throughout the entire range of motion. The two types of isotonic contractions are *concentric* and *eccentric.* Concentric, from the Latin *com-* + *centrum,* "having a common center," refers to contractions in which the muscle length shortens. Concentric contractions are possible only when the resistance (weight load) starts below the athlete's maximum potential. Examples of concentric contractions include the curling action of a biceps curl or the extending motion of a leg extension. Eccentric, or "negative," contractions reverse the process of a concentric action. Put more simply, an eccentric contraction returns the muscles to their original starting point. During a biceps curl, the eccentric component occurs when the arm extends to the starting point after the curl. During a leg extension, eccentric work is done when the legs bend at the knee toward the starting position. During an eccentric contraction, the muscles yield either to the force of gravity (as in free weights) or to the pull of a machine. Under such conditions, the muscle lengthens as the joint angle increases, releasing a controlled tension.

Isometric (static), from the Greek *isos* (equal) and *meter* (unit of measure), implies that during this type of contraction, the application of force against an immovable object causes the muscle to develop high tension without altering its length. In fact, the tension developed from this type of contraction is often higher than that developed during an isotonic contraction.

Isokinetic, from the Greek *isos* (equal) and *kinetic* (motion), is a contraction of constant velocity over the full range of motion. Isokinetic work requires special equipment designed to allow a constant velocity of contraction, regardless of load. During the movement, both concentric and eccentric contractions are performed while the machine provides resistance equal to the force generated by the athlete. This training allows the muscle to work maximally through the entire movement, eliminating the "sticking point," or weak spot, present in every exercise motion.

Types of Strength
and Their Significance in Training

Strength training involves various types of strength, each having a certain significance for some sports and athletes.

General strength is the foundation of the entire strength training program. It must be the sole focus of the early training phase (anatomical adaptation), as well as during the first few years of an entry-level athlete's strength training plan. A low level of general strength may limit the overall progress of an athlete. It leaves the body susceptible to injury and potentially even asymmetrical shape or a decreased ability to build muscle strength.

Specific strength is the strength of only those muscles (mainly the prime movers) that are particular to the movements of a selected sport. As the term suggests, this type of strength is specific to each sport. Thus, any comparison between the strength level of athletes involved in different sports is invalid. Specific strength to be developed to the maximum should be progressively incorporated toward the end of the preparatory phase for all advanced athletes.

Maximum strength refers to the highest force that can be performed by the neuromuscular system during a maximum contraction. It is reflected by the heaviest load an athlete can lift in one attempt and is expressed as 100 percent of maximum or *one repetition maximum (1RM)*. It is crucial for training purposes to know one's maximum strength for each exercise, since it is the basis for calculating loads for every strength phase.

Power is the product of two abilities, strength and speed, and is considered to be the ability to apply maximum force in the shortest time.

Muscular endurance is defined as a muscle's ability to sustain work for a prolonged period. It is used largely in endurance-related sports, where training for muscular endurance also has a positive transfer to cardiorespiratory endurance.

Absolute strength (AS) refers to an athlete's ability to exert maximum force regardless of body weight (BW). Absolute strength is required to reach very high levels in some sports (shot put, heaviest weight categories in weight lifting and wrestling). Since an athlete follows a systematic training program, increases in absolute strength parallel gains in body weight.

Relative strength (RS) represents the ratio between absolute strength and body weight. Relative strength is important in sports like gymnastics or those where athletes are divided into weight categories (wrestling, boxing). For instance, a gymnast may not be able to perform the iron cross on the rings unless the relative strength of the muscles involved is at least 1:1. This means that the absolute strength must be at least sufficient to offset the athlete's body weight. Gains in body weight change this proportion—as body weight increases, relative strength decreases.

Strength reserve is the difference between absolute strength and the amount of strength required to perform a skill under competitive conditions. Strength gauge techniques used to measure rowers' maximum strength per stroke unit revealed values up to 106 kilograms; the mean strength per race was 56 kilograms (Bompa et al., 1978). The same subjects were found to have absolute strength in power clean lifts of 90 kilograms. Subtracting the mean strength per race (56 kilograms) from absolute strength (90 kilograms) results in a strength reserve of 34 kilograms. The ratio of mean strength to absolute strength is 1:1.6. Similarly, other subjects were found to have a higher strength reserve with a ratio of 1:1.85. Needless to say, the latter subjects performed better in rowing races, leading to the conclusion that an athlete with a higher strength reserve is capable of reaching higher performance levels. Although the concept of strength reserve may not be meaningful to all sports, it is believed to be significant in sports such as swimming, canoeing, rowing, as well as in jumping and throwing events.

Strength Training and Muscular Adaptation

Systematic strength training results in certain structural and physiological changes, or adaptations, in the body. The level of adaptation is evidenced by the size and definition of the body's muscles. The magnitude of these adaptations is directly proportional to the demands placed on the body by the volume (quantity), frequency, and intensity (load) of training. Training benefits an athlete only as long as it forces the body to adapt to the stress of physical work. In other words, if the body is presented with a demand greater than it is accustomed to, it adapts to the stressor by becoming stronger. When the load does not challenge the body's *adaptation threshold*, the training effect will be nil or at best minimal, and no adaptation will occur.

Types of Adaptation

Different types of adaptation can occur. The following paragraphs describe the types of adaptation resulting from training.

Hypertrophy

One of the most visible signs of adaptation to strength training is the enlargement of muscle size, known as *hypertrophy*. This phenomenon is due to an increase in the cross-sectional area of individual muscle fibers. (Conversely, a reduction in size resulting from inactivity is referred to as *atrophy*.) Hypertrophy, as a physiological adaptation to training, takes two forms:

1. *Short-term hypertrophy,* as the name implies, lasts only a few hours and is the result of the "pump" effect typical of bodybuilding. This pump is largely the result of fluid accumulation (edema) in the muscle. Heavy lifting increases the amount of water being held in the intracellular spaces of the muscle, making it look even larger. The water is returned to the blood a few hours after training, and the pump disappears. This is one reason why, although bodybuilders may look big and strong, their strength is not always proportional to their muscle size.

2. *Chronic* or *constant hypertrophy* results from structural changes at the muscle level. Since it is caused by an increase in either the number or size of the muscle filaments, its effects are more enduring than those of short-term hypertrophy. This form of hypertrophy is desired for athletes using strength training to improve their athletic performance.

Individuals with a greater number of fibers tend to be stronger and bigger than those with fewer fibers. This genetically determined number was thought to remain constant throughout one's life, but a controversial theory now suggests that the heavy loads used in strength training may provoke "muscle splitting," or *hyperplasia*. If this is the case, hypertrophy may be partly induced by an increase in the number of muscle fibers. This theory is based on animal research, and the results have not yet been duplicated in research involving human subjects.

Strong evidence suggests that individual fiber hypertrophy accounts for most gains in muscle size. Increases in muscle fiber size and number of filaments (especially the myosin filaments) have been demonstrated by many researchers (Costill et al., 1979; Dons et al., 1979; Fox et al., 1989; Goldberg et al., 1975; Gordon, 1967; Gregory, 1981; MacDougall et al., 1976, 1977, 1979). In myosin filaments, heavy loads increase the number of cross bridges, leading to an increase in cross-sectional area of the fiber and to visible gains in maximum contraction force.

Not all factors responsible for hypertrophy are fully understood. Growth in muscle size is widely believed to be stimulated by a disturbance in the equilibrium between the consumption and remanufacturing of adenosine triphosphate (ATP), the "ATP deficiency theory" (Hartmann & Tünnemann, 1988). During and immediately following a heavy-load training session, ATP stores are depleted and the protein content in the working muscles is very low, if not exhausted. As the athlete recovers between training sessions, the body replenishes the protein in the muscles. During this process, the protein content in the muscle exceeds the initial level, resulting in an increase in muscle fiber size. This effect is especially pronounced in those who follow a protein-rich diet.

Another theory on hypertrophy suggests that testosterone (serum androgen, a substance that has masculinizing properties) plays a role in muscle growth. The idea is that, although there are no physiological differences between the muscles of women and men, male athletes usually have larger and stronger muscles. This difference is attributed to testosterone, which is approximately 10 times greater in men than in women. Although testosterone seems to promote muscle growth, there is no scientific proof that it is the sole determinant of muscle size.

Muscle hypertrophy may also be attributable to a conversion of ST fibers to FT fibers. Although mostly speculative at this point, some research indicates that the percentage of ST fibers decreases as a result of strength training (Abernethy et al., 1990). One reason why studies centering on this theory have been largely inconclusive may be that such research is typically conducted on subjects who are not serious athletes. The findings might be different if a study were to follow athletes from the entry to the professional level, as opposed to observing changes that occur in individuals of varying fitness levels during just 8 weeks of training.

Anatomical Adaptation

Research into anatomical adaptation suggests that training with constant, high-intensity loads may decrease the material strength of the bones (Matsuda et al, 1986). Thus, if the load does not vary from low to maximum from time to time, the resulting decrease in material bone strength may lead to bone injuries. The mechanical properties of bones are also affected by the mechanical demands of training. In other words, an athlete may be injury prone due to training that exposes the bones to an intense mechanical stress without a progressive period of adaptation. At an early age, or at the entry level, low-intensity loads may have a positive, stimulating effect on the length and girth of the long bones, whereas high-intensity, heavy-load training may permanently restrict bone growth in beginners (Matsuda et al, 1986).

These facts should be carefully considered by young and entry-level athletes, as well as trainers and coaches. The most appropriate approach for these athletes is a long-term plan in which the load is progressively increased over several years. The purpose of training is to stress the body in a way that results in adaptation, not aggravation. A well-monitored load increment also has a positive effect for mature athletes, as it results in increased bone density, which in turn allows the bones to better cope with the mechanical stresses of training.

Tendon adaptation is of equal concern for strength training. Remember, muscles do not attach to bones directly, but rather through tendons. The ability of a muscle to pull forcefully against a bone and perform a movement depends on the strength of the muscle's tendons. The adaptation of tendons is a long-term proposition. Tendons take longer to adapt to powerful contractions than do muscles; therefore, muscle strength should not exceed the rate of tendon adaptation.

Nervous System Adaptation

Gains in muscle strength can also be explained by changes in the pattern of motor unit recruitment and in the synchronization of the motor units to act in unison.

Motor units are controlled by nerve cells, called *neurons*, which can produce both *excitatory* (stimulating) and *inhibitory* impulses. Excitation initiates the contraction of a motor unit. On the other hand, inhibition prevents the muscles from exerting more force than can be tolerated by the connective tissue (tendons) and bones. These two nervous system processes perform a sort of balancing act to ensure the safety of muscular contraction. The force outcome of a contraction depends on how many motor units will contract and how many will remain in a state of relaxation. If the number of excitatory impulses exceeds the number of inhibitory impulses, a given motor unit will be stimulated and will participate in the overall contraction and production of force. If the opposite occurs, that particular motor unit will stay relaxed.

Based on the theory that as a result of training, inhibitory impulses can be counteracted, enabling the muscle to contract more powerfully, it is fair to say that gains in strength are largely the result of an increased ability to recruit more motor units to participate in the overall force of contraction. Such an adaptive response is facilitated only by heavy and maximum loads and is safe only after the tendons have adapted to high-intensity training.

Adaptation of Neuromuscular Coordination

Neuromuscular coordination for strength movement patterns takes time to develop and is a function of learning. The ability to coordinate specific sequences in which various muscles are involved in performing a lift requires precision that can only be acquired over a long period of continuous repetition. In other words, practice makes perfect. An efficient lift can be achieved only when the athlete learns to relax the antagonistic muscles so that unnecessary contractions do not affect the force of the prime movers. A highly coordinated group of muscles consumes less energy during contraction, and this translates into superior performance.

Young or beginning athletes often lack strength-related motor skills and muscle coordination. Thus, hypertrophy cannot be expected immediately. Young athletes exposed to strength training will see visible strength improvements without a corresponding increase in muscle size within 4 to 6 weeks.

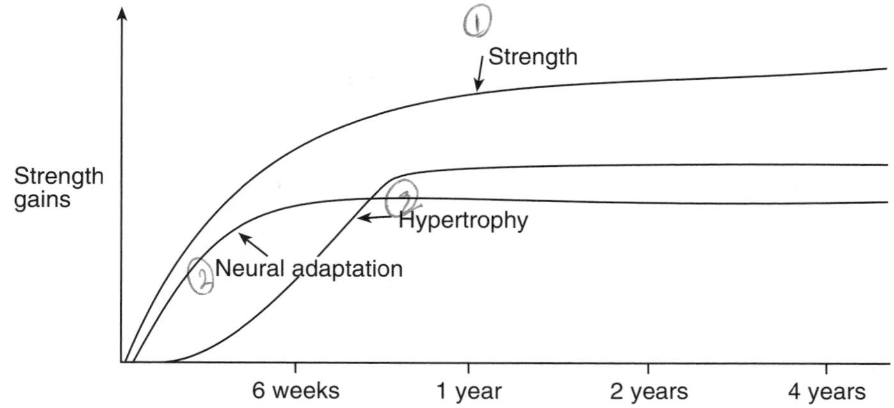

The reason for strength gain without muscle hypertrophy is *neural adaptation*, an increase in the nervous coordination of the muscles involved. As a result of training, these entry-level athletes have learned to use their muscles effectively and economically. This motor learning effect is of major importance in the early stages of strength training, and it is important for athletes to realize that this is part of a necessary progression.

Neural adaptation to strength training is evidenced by the increased ability to activate the prime movers—the chain of muscles involved in lifting—and by improved coordination of the agonists and antagonists. The normal outcome is increased strength of the intended movement.

Figure 2.5 Gains in strength as a result of neural adaptation and hypertrophy.

Power training for explosive, instantaneous muscle actions increases the neural contribution of the nervous system, or its synchronization of motor unit firing patterns, with little hypertrophy. Figure 2.5 illustrates neural and muscular adaptation in strength training. Although strength gains occur steadily over time, early improvements result from neural adaptation. The benefits of hypertrophy are visible after several months. From this point on, gains in strength relate to both hypertrophy and neural adaptation depending on the load and training method employed.

chapter 3

Periodization Principles for Strength

Training guidelines fulfill a given training goal. Proper application ensures superior organization with the fewest errors. The principle of progressive increase of load in training leads to better adaptation and improved strength gains.

The Five Basic Laws of Strength Training

Any strength training program should apply the five basic laws of training to ensure adaptation, keeping athletes free of injury. This is especially important for young athletes.

Law Number One: Develop Joint Flexibility

Most strength training exercises use the entire range of motion of major joints, especially the knees, ankles, and hips. Good joint flexibility prevents strain and pain around the knees, elbows, and other joints. Ankle flexibility (plantar flexion, or bringing the toes toward the calf) should be a major concern for all athletes, especially beginners. Good flexibility prevents stress injuries. Athletes must start developing ankle flexibility during prepubescence and pubescence so that in the latter stages of athletic development it need only be maintained.

Law Number Two: Develop Tendon Strength

Muscle strength improves faster than tendon and ligament strength. Misuse and faulty utilization of the principle of specificity, or lack of a long-term vision, causes many training specialists and coaches to overlook overall strengthening of ligaments. Tendons and ligaments grow strong through anatomical adaptation. Without proper anatomical adaptation, vigorous strength training can injure the tendons and ligaments. Training tendons

Faster muscle ≠ tendon, ligament

Key Words

Amortization phase: The eccentric or yielding phase of an activity; also called the "shock-absorbing phase."

Hormone: A discrete chemical substance secreted into body fluids by an endocrine gland that has a specific effect on the activities of other cells, tissues, and organs.

Innervate: To stimulate the transmission of nervous energy to a muscle.

Testosterone: The male sex hormone; it possesses masculinizing properties.

and ligaments causes them to enlarge in diameter, increasing their ability to withstand tension and tearing.

Law Number Three: Develop Core Strength

The arms and legs are only as strong as the trunk. A poorly developed trunk is a weak support for hard-working limbs. Strength training programs should first strengthen the core muscles before focusing on the arms and legs. The core muscles act as shock absorbers for jumps, rebounds, or plyometric exercises; stabilize the body; and represent a link, or transmitter, between the legs and arms. Weak core muscles fail in these essential roles, limiting the athlete's ability to perform. Most of these muscles seem to be dominated by ST fibers because of their supporting role to the arms and legs. They contract constantly, but not necessarily dynamically, to create a solid base of support for the actions of other muscle groups of the body.

Many people complain of low back problems yet do little to correct them. The best protection against low back problems is well-developed back and abdominal muscles. Coaches and athletes must pay more attention to this area of the body.

Abdominal Muscles.   The abdominal and back muscles surround the core area of the body with a tight and powerful support structure of muscle bundles running in different directions. Since many athletes have weak abdominal muscles in relation to their backs, general and specific abdominal muscle training is recommended. The rectus abdominis runs vertically and pulls the trunk forward when the legs are fixed, as in sit-ups, maintaining good posture. If the abdominal muscles are poorly developed, the hips tilt forward and lordosis or a swayback develops at the lumbar area of the spine because the low back muscles are much stronger.

The internal and external obliques help the rectus abdominis bend the trunk forward and perform all twisting, lateral bending, and trunk-rotating motions. They help an athlete recover from a fall in many sports and perform many actions in boxing, wrestling, and the martial arts. The anterior and lateral abdominal muscles perform delicate, precise trunk movements. These large muscles run vertically, diagonally, and horizontally.

Isolating the abdominal muscles requires an exercise that bends the spine but not the hips. Exercises that flex the hips are performed by the iliopsoas (a powerful hip flexor) and to a lesser extent by the abdominals. Sit-ups are the most popular abdominal exercise. The best sit-up position is lying on the back with the calves resting on a chair or bench. This position isolates the abdominals since the hips are already bent.

Back Muscles.   The back muscles, including the deep back muscles of the vertebral column, are responsible for many movements such as back extension and extending and rotating the trunk. The trunk acts as the transmitter and supporter of most arm and leg actions. The vertebral column also plays an essential role as a shock absorber for landing and takeoff actions.

Excessive, uneven stress on the spine or sudden movement while in an unfavorable position may lead to back problems. For athletes, back complaints may be due to wear and tear caused by improper positioning or forward tilting of the body. Disc pressure varies according to body position relative to external stress. Stress on the spine increases during lifting in standing or seated positions or when the upper body swings, such as in upright rowing or elbow flexion. Sitting produces greater disc pressure than standing; the least stress occurs when the body is prone (such as in bench presses or pulls). In many exercises that use the back muscles, abdominal muscles contract isometrically, stabilizing the body.

The Iliopsoas. The iliopsoas is an essential muscle for hip flexion and running. Though not large, it is the most powerful hip flexor, responsible for swinging the legs forward during running and jumping. Sports performed on the ground require a well-developed iliopsoas. Exercises such as leg and knee lifts against resistance are key to training this important muscle.

Law Number Four: Develop the Stabilizers

Prime movers work more efficiently with strong stabilizer or fixator muscles. Stabilizers contract, primarily isometrically, to immobilize a limb so that another part of the body can act. For example, the shoulders are immobilized during elbow flexion, and the abdominals serve as fixators when the arms throw a ball. In rowing, when the trunk muscles act as stabilizers, the trunk transmits leg power to the arms, which then drive the blade through the water. A weak stabilizer inhibits the contracting capacity of the prime movers.

Improperly developed stabilizers may hamper the activity of major muscles. When under chronic stress, the stabilizers spasm, restraining the prime movers and lessening athletic effectiveness. At the *shoulders,* supra- and infraspinatus muscles rotate the arm. The simplest, most effective exercise to strengthen these two muscles is to rotate the arm with a partner tightly holding the fist. The resistance provided by the partner stimulates the two muscles stabilizing the shoulder. At the *hips,* the piriformis muscle performs outward rotation. To strengthen this muscle, the athlete should stand with knees locked. While a partner provides resistance by holding one foot in place with both hands, the athlete performs inward-outward leg rotations. At the *knees,* the popliteus muscle rotates the calf. A simple exercise is for the athlete to sit on a table or desk with the knees flexed. A partner provides resistance by holding the foot as the athlete performs inward-outward rotations of the calf.

Stabilizers also contract isometrically, immobilizing one part of the limb and allowing the other to move. Stabilizers can also monitor the state of the long bones' interactions in joints and sense potential injury resulting from improper technique, inappropriate strength, or spasms produced by poor stress management. If one of these three conditions occurs, the stabilizers restrain the activity of the prime movers, avoiding strain and injuries.

Unfortunately, few coaches take the time to strengthen the stabilizers. Time should be set aside during the transition and preparatory periods, especially the anatomical adaptation phase for stabilizer training. The core muscles, rotators, and stabilizers should be developed using long-term progression (figure 3.1). A casual approach would be a disservice to the serious athlete.

Law Number Five: Train Movements, Not Individual Muscles

Athletes should resist training muscles in isolation as in bodybuilding. The purpose of strength training in sports is to simulate sport skills. Athletic skills are multijoint movements occurring in a certain order, called a *kinetic chain* (movement chain). For instance, a takeoff to catch a ball has the following kinetic chain: hip extensions, then knee extensions, and finally ankle extensions, in which the feet apply force against the ground to lift the body.

Stages of development	Prepuberty (initiation)	Puberty (athletic formation)	Postpuberty (specialization)	High performance
Forms of training	• Simple exercises • Games/play	• AA • Relays • Games	• AA • Specific strength	• Specific
Training methods	• Informal • CT	• CT	• CT • Power training	• Hypertrophy • MxS • Power • M–E
Volume	• Low	• Low to medium	• Medium	• Medium • High
Intensity	• Very low	• Low	• Low • Medium	• Medium • High • Maximum
Means of training	• Own body weight • Partners • Light medicine balls	• Medicine balls • Light free weights • Tubing	• Medicine balls • Machines (light) • Tubing	• Free weights • Others

Figure 3.1 Suggested long-term periodization for strength training. CT = (circuit training)

According to the principle of specificity, body position and limb angles should resemble those for the specific skills. When athletes train a movement, the muscles are integrated and strengthened to perform the action with more power. Therefore, athletes should not resort to weight training alone, but should broaden their training routines, incorporating medicine balls, rubber cords, shots, and plyometric equipment. Exercises performed with these instruments allow athletes to initiate skills more easily. Chapters 10 and 11 provide further examples of how these training instruments are used for better specific improvement.

Principle of Progressive Increase of Load in Training

According to Greek mythology, the first person to apply the principle of progressive increase of load was Milo of Croton. To become the world's strongest man, Milo started to lift and carry a calf every day. As the calf grew heavier, Milo grew stronger. By the time the calf was a full-grown bull, Milo was the world's strongest man thanks to long-term progression.

Improved performance is a direct result of quality training. From the initiation stage to the elite performance stage, workload in training must increase gradually according to each athlete's physiological and psychological abilities. Physiologically, training gradually increases the body's functional efficiency, increasing its work capacity. Any dramatic increase in performance requires a long period of training and adaptation (Astrand & Rodahl, 1985). The body reacts physiologically and psychologically to the increased training load. Similarly, nervous reaction and functions, neuromuscular coordination, and psychological capacity to cope with stress also occur gradually. The entire process requires time and competent technical leadership.

Several sports have a consistent training load throughout the year, called a *standard load*. Most team sports maintain 6 to 12 hours of training per week for the entire year. Standard loading results in early improvements, followed by a plateau and then detraining during the competitive phase (figure 3.2). This may cause decreased performance during the late competitive phase, since the physiological basis of performance has decreased and prevent annual improvements. Only steady training load increments will produce superior adaptation and performance.

The *overload* principle is another traditional strength training approach. Early proponents of this principle claimed strength and hypertrophy will increase only if muscles work at their maximum strength capacity against workloads greater than those normally encountered (Lange, 1919; Hellebrand & Houtz, 1956). Contemporary advocates suggest that the load in strength training should be increased throughout the program (Fox et al., 1989). As such, the curve of load increment constantly rises (figure 3.3).

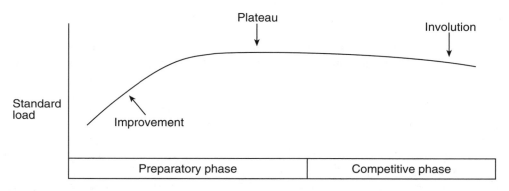

Figure 3.2   A standard load results in improvements only in the early part of the annual plan.

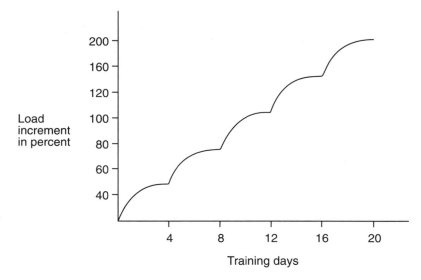

Figure 3.3   Load increments according to the overloading principle. (Based on data from Fox et al., 1989; Hellebrand & Houtz, 1956.)

Proponents of overloading suggest two ways to increase strength: (1) brief maximum contractions resulting in high muscle activation; and (2) submaximum contractions to exhaustion, inducing hypertrophy. The latter approach is popular among bodybuilders; however, it is categorically impractical in athletics. Athletes cannot be expected to lift to exhaustion every day. Such physiological and psychological strain leads to fatigue, exhaustion, and overtraining. To be effective, a strength training program must follow the concept of Periodization of Strength, with specific goals for each phase leading up to the major competitions of the year.

The *step-type approach* is more effective than overloading. The athlete's ability to tolerate heavy loads improves as the result of adaptation to stressors applied in strength training (Councilman, 1968; Harre, 1982). The step-type method requires a training load increase followed by an unloading phase during which the body adapts, regenerates, and prepares for a new increase. The frequency of the increase in training load must be determined by each individual's needs, rate of adaptation, and competitive calendar. An abrupt increase in training load may go beyond the athlete's capacity to adapt, affecting the physiological balance. The rate of the athlete's performance improvement determines training load increase. The faster the rate of performance improvement, the greater the training loads required for the athlete to keep up.

The step-type approach (figure 3.4) does not mean steadily increasing the load in each training session through the arithmetic addition of equal quantities of work. A single training session is insufficient to cause visible body change. To achieve such adaptation, the same type of training loads must be repeated several times. Often training sessions of the same type are planned for an entire week, followed by an increase in the training load.

In figure 3.4, let's say the horizontal line represents a week, or a *microcycle*, of training and that the load is increased on Monday. This increase fatigues the body since it is not accustomed to such stress. The body adjusts by Wednesday, adapts to the load over the next 2 days, and by Friday, the athlete feels stronger and capable of lifting heavier loads. Fatigue is followed by adaptation, then a physiological rebound or improvement. This new level is called a new *ceiling of adaptation*. By Monday, the athlete is physiologically and psychologically comfortable. The previous adaptation has been challenged so that constant improvements occur from step to step.

The third step in figure 3.4 is followed by a lower step, or *unloading phase*. A reduction in overall demand allows the body to regenerate. During regeneration, the athlete partially recovers from the fatigue accumulated in the

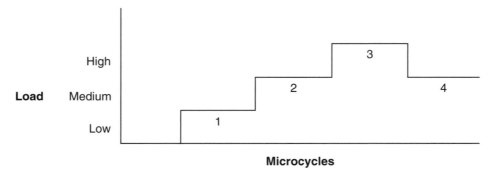

Figure 3.4   Illustration of a *macrocycle*. Each vertical line represents an increase in load, whereas the horizontal line represents the adaptation phase required by the new demand.

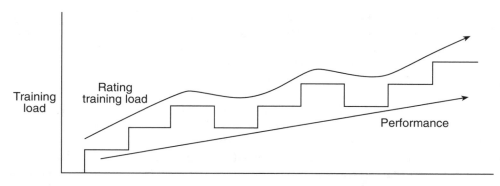

Figure 3.5   Curve of rating the training load appears to be undulatory (wavy arrow), whereas performance improves continuously (straight arrow).

first three steps, replenishes energy stores, and psychologically relaxes. The body accumulates new reserves in anticipation of further increases in training load. Training performance usually improves following the regeneration phase.

The unloading phase represents the new lowest step for the next macrocycle. Since the body has adjusted to the previous loads, this new low step is of greater magnitude than the previous low, but is nearly equal to the medium one.

The shorter the adaptation phase, the lower the height, or the amount of increase, in training load. A longer adaptation phase may permit a higher increase. Although training load increases in steps, the load curve for a training plan of longer duration has a wavy shape that represents the continuous increases and decreases in the training components (figure 3.5).

Variations of Step Loading

Although the step-loading method is applicable to every sport and athlete, two variations are possible but must be applied carefully and with discretion.

In *reverse step loading* (figure 3.6), the load decreases rather than increases from step to step. Some Eastern European weight lifters maintain that it is more specific to their physiological needs in that the highest loads are planned immediately following a cycle of low-intensity training. Reverse step loading has been used in weight lifting since the late 1960s but has not been accepted in any other sport. The reason is simple: The goal of strength

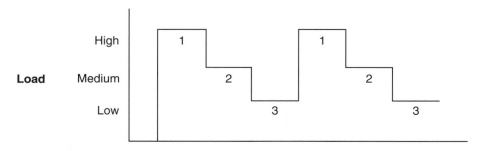

Figure 3.6   Reverse step loading.

training for sports is progressive adaptation—gradually increasing the athlete's training capabilities. Performance improvements are possible only when training capabilities have increased. Reverse loading should only be used during the peaking cycle prior to competition (see chapter 12). Endurance improvements are much better achieved by step loading.

The *flat step loading* pattern (figure 3.7), is appropriate for advanced athletes with strong strength training backgrounds. High-demand training is performed at the same level for three cycles, followed by a low-load, recovery week. The load is then increased to medium during the third and other macrocycles as the athlete adapts. The high-demand cycles must be applied in concert with other types of training. As such, the three cycles have to be of high demand for all elements—technical, tactical, speed, and endurance training. When planning a lower intensity cycle, all other elements must be of lower demand as well to facilitate relaxation and recovery.

The dynamics of the loading pattern for a well-trained athlete are a function of the training phase and type of strength training sought. During the early part of the preparatory phase, the step loading pattern prevails, ensuring a better progression. The same loading pattern is suggested for athletes with 1 to 2 years' experience in strength training. For endurance sports, where the development of muscle endurance is the focus of specific strength training, and for athletes competing at or beyond the national level, the flat loading pattern is suggested (figure 3.8).

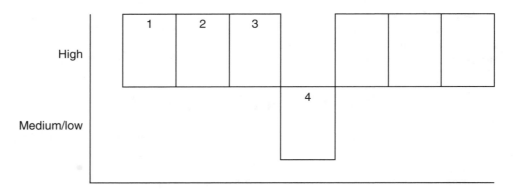

Figure 3.7 Flat loading pattern.

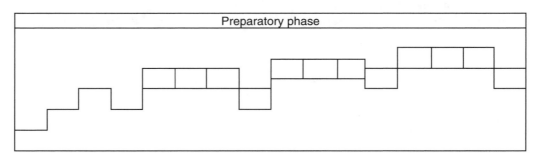

Figure 3.8 Suggested combination of step and flat loading patterns for the preparatory phase. Note that step loading is used at the beginning of the program since the load is progressively increased. After the first 5 weeks of progressive adaptation, flat loading is used to ensure that training is very demanding and results in the specific adaptation necessary for performance improvement.

Principle of Variety

Contemporary training requires many hours of work from the athlete. The volume and intensity of training are continuously increasing, and exercises are repeated numerous times. To reach high performance, the volume of training must surpass a threshold of 1,000 hours per year. Any athlete serious about training must dedicate 4 to 6 hours to strength training each week, in addition to technical, tactical, and other elements of general and specific conditioning.

Under these conditions, boredom and monotony can become obstacles to motivation and improvement. The best way to overcome these obstacles is to incorporate as much variety as possible into training routines. Instructors and coaches have to be well versed in the area of strength training and know as many exercises as possible to ensure such variety. In addition to improving training response, variety has a positive effect on the psychological well-being of athletes. The following suggestions will help enrich your strength training program:

- Alternate exercises designed for the prime movers as often as possible, especially prior to and during the competitive phase; or increase the number of sets per prime mover.
- Vary the loading system using the principle of progressive increase of load in training.
- Vary the type of muscle contraction, especially between concentric and eccentric.
- Vary the speed of contraction (slow, medium, and fast), especially during the preparatory phase. Slow to medium contractions may not be possible during later phases, as Periodization requires mostly heavy loads with high application of force and explosive actions.
- Vary the equipment (if possible) from free weights to heavy implements, isokinetics, etc.
- Vary between training phases (see the planning sections in part II).

Principle of Individualization

Contemporary training requires individualization. Each athlete must be treated according to individual ability, potential, and strength training background. Often coaches follow the training programs of successful athletes, disregarding their athlete's needs, experience, and abilities. Even worse, such programs are sometimes inserted into the training schedules of junior athletes. Young athletes are not ready, physiologically or psychologically, for such programs.

Before designing a training program, analyze the athlete's training potential. Athletes equal in performance do not necessarily have the same work capacity. Individual work abilities are determined by several biological and psychological factors and must be considered in specifying the amount of work, the load, and the type of strength training. Training background also determines work capacity. Work demand should be based on experience. Even when athletes exhibit great improvement, coaches must still be cautious in estimating training load. When assigning athletes of different backgrounds and experiences to the same training group, coaches should not ignore individual characteristics and potential.

Coaches should not introduce junior athletes to strength training until they are physically and psychologically ready.

Another factor is the athlete's rate of recovery. When planning and evaluating the content and stress of training, assess demanding factors apart from training. Be aware of the athlete's lifestyle and emotional involvements. School work or other activities can affect rate of recovery.

Gender differences also require consideration. The total body strength of women is 63.5 percent that of men. Upper body strength in women is an average 55.8 percent that of men. Lower body difference is much less, averaging 71.9 percent (Laubach, 1976). Women tend to have lower hypertrophy levels than men, mostly because their testosterone level is 10 times lower (Wright, 1980). Female athletes can follow the same training programs as male athletes without worrying about excessive bulky muscles. Women can apply the same loading pattern, the same training methods, and follow similar planning without concern. Strength training is as beneficial for women as for men. In fact, strength gains for women occur at the same or an even greater rate (Wilmore et al., 1978). Strength training for women should be rigorously continuous, without long interruptions. Plyometric training should progress carefully over a longer period. Since women generally tend to be physically weaker than men, visible gains in future performance will come from improved and increased strength training.

Principle of Specificity

To be effective and achieve greater adaptation, training must be designed to develop sport-specific strength. A strength training program and the selected training method(s) should consider the dominant energy system of the sport and the prime movers involved. Training specificity is also the most important mechanism for sport-specific neural adaptation.

The *dominant energy system* in the sport should be carefully considered. For instance, muscle-endurance training is most appropriate for endurance sports like rowing, long-distance swimming, canoeing, or speed skating (see chapters 6 and 11). Also consider the *specific muscle groups* involved (prime movers) and the movement patterns characteristic of the sport. Exercises should mimic the sport's key movement patterns or dominant skills. They must also improve the power of the prime movers. Normally, gains in power transfer to skill improvement.

Specificity vs. a Methodical Approach

The principle of specificity sprang from the idea that the optimal strength training program must be specific. Mathews and Fox (1976) developed this theory into a principle of training. According to this principle, an exercise or type of training that is specific to the skills of a sport results in faster adaptation and yields faster performance improvement. Specificity should be applied only to advanced athletes during the competitive phase. Athletes perfect only the dominant strength in their selected sport.

Misuse of specificity results in asymmetrical and inharmonious body development and neglects the antagonistic and stabilizer muscles. Misuse can also hamper the development of the prime movers and result in injuries. Overemphasizing specificity can result in narrow development of the muscles and one-sided, specialized muscle function. Compensation strength exercises should always be used in training, especially during the preparatory phase of the annual plan. These exercises balance the force of agonistic and antagonistic muscles.

Although specificity is an important principle, its long-term application can result in stressful, boring programs, leading to overtraining, overuse injury, and sometimes burnout. Specificity is best applied at appropriate times in a program based on a methodical, long-term approach. Such a program should have three main phases (see figure 3.9).

During *general and multilateral strength training*, all muscle groups, ligaments, and tendons are developed in anticipation of future heavy loads and

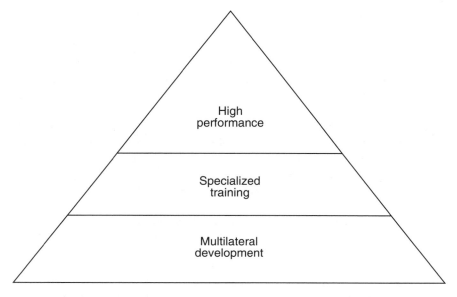

Figure 3.9 Suggested long-term approach to specificity of strength training.

specific training. Such an approach would likely lead to an injury-free career. This phase may last 2 to 4 years depending on the athlete's age and abilities. Throughout this phase, the coach needs to be patient. Overall multilateral development is a basic requirement for reaching a highly specialized level of training.

After laying the foundation, the athlete begins the *specialized training specific phase* which will continue throughout his career. This is not a strength training program that addresses the specific needs of the sport through all phases of an annual training plan. Rather, this program includes Periodization of Strength, which always starts with a buildup or anatomical adaptation phase (see Periodization of Strength in chapter 6). Depending on the age of the athlete, this phase can last 2 to 3 years.

The high-performance phase applies to athletes at the national and international level. During this stage, specificity prevails from the latter part of the preparatory phase through the competitive phase of the annual plan. This phase ends when the athlete stops competing.

Specificity of Exercises for Strength Training

It is difficult to mimic the technical skill of a given sport in strength training, so coaches must try to imitate the *dynamic structure* of the skill as well as the *spatial orientation*, or the position of the body compared to the surrounding environment. Coaches should select exercises that align the body and limbs with the positions used to perform a skill.

The *angle* between body parts or limbs influences how and which parts of a given muscle contract. Effective training of the prime movers requires familiarity with this aspect. For example, sit-ups are popular abdominal exercises; however, body position changes the difficulty as well as the segment of the muscle (rectus abdominis) contracted maximally. Horizontal sit-ups involve mostly the upper part of the muscle. Inclined sit-ups primarily benefit the central section of the muscle, since the movement is performed with an almost full range of motion. If the trunk is fixed and the legs are lifted, the role of the abdominals decreases and the action is performed mostly by the hip flexors (iliopsoas muscle). The best position for activating the abdominals is one that immobilizes the hips so the trunk moves by contracting the rectus abdominis muscle (inclined position, or with the legs resting on a chair, bench, or against a wall).

Similar concerns apply to the bench press. If the bench press is performed on a flat bench, the central parts of the pectorals, the triceps, and parts of the deltoid muscle benefit. If the same exercise is performed on an inclined bench, the upper parts of the pectorals fully contract. To stress the lower pectorals, athletes should place their heads at the lower end of an incline bench. The grip used for the bench press also affects the muscles involved. A wide grip mainly stresses the exterior part of the pectorals. A shoulder-width grip develops the inner part of the pectorals. A narrow grip activates mostly the deeper part of the pectorals and the triceps muscle.

To achieve maximum training specificity, an exercise has to imitate the angle of the skill performed. For instance, the arm extensions used by shot putters and football linemen use the triceps muscles. A bodybuilder exercise to develop the triceps is elbow extensions either bent-over or in an erect position with the elbow above the shoulder. Such exercises isolate the triceps from the other muscles involved in shot putting or tackling (analytic method) and consequently are not very effective for these athletes. Incline bench presses at an angle of 30 to 35 degress would be better, since the angle is similar to that used in these sports. This exercise also works the other active muscles such as the pectorals and deltoids.

Specificity of Strength Exercises and the Need for Specific Adaptation

In many cases, athletes and coaches rate the success of a strength training program based on the amount of muscle the athlete builds (hypertrophy). With the exception of football linemen, shot putters, and heavyweight boxers and wrestlers, constant increase in muscle size is not a desirable effect for most athletes. Power and speed sports, or sports with quick, explosive action (baseball, football, hockey, most track-and-field events, volleyball, etc.) rely on *nervous system training* that includes many power exercises and maximum loads (greater than 80 percent of 1RM) that result in *neural adaptation* (Enoka, 1996; Sale, 1986; Schmidtbleicher, 1992). Neural adaptation in strength training for most sports means increasing power and the speed of contraction without increasing muscle mass.

To achieve higher neural adaptation, carefully select training methods and exercises. Researchers and international-class coaches share similar views about what represents the specificity of strength training. These views are summarized below.

• Strength training methods must be specific to the speed of contraction used in sports (Coyle et al., 1991; Kanehisa & Miyashita, 1983). This means that from the second half of the preparatory phase through the competitive phase, coaches should select methods that specifically increase the speed of contraction and, therefore, the level of power.

• Training methods and exercises must increase the contraction force in the intended direction of movement. This means selecting exercises according to the muscles used to perform the technical skill of a given sport (prime movers). Olympic weight lifting and bodybuilding exercises, especially during the second part of the preparatory and competitive phases, waste time.

• Training methods must increase the activation and excitation of the prime movers. Selected exercises must be sport-specific and activate the prime movers.

• Training methods must increase the discharge rate of motor neurons (Hortobagyi et al., 1996) or stimulate the muscles to perform an athletic action with power and high speed. Motor neurons innervate, stimulate, and arouse the muscles. The more specific the training method and exercises, the better a muscle is trained to perform quick and powerful athletic movements.

• Motor unit recruitment and firing rate increase with higher loads and faster contractions (De Luca et al., 1982). Training methods that enhance maximum strength and power are the only ones that increase the firing rate of motor units and FT muscle fiber recruitment.

• Exercise action must be performed along the neural pathway (Häkkinen, 1989). Exercises have to be selected so that contractions are performed in the same direction as nerve stimulation. If an exercise does not realistically simulate or is not specific to a technical skill, the muscle contraction is not along the neural pathway, resulting in a lower exercise efficiency in training.

• The sequence in which muscles are contracted during an exercise is crucial to the specifics of adaptation. Exercises, especially *multijoint exercises* (i.e., squats involving three joints), must simulate the sequence in which muscles contract while performing a specific technical skill.

• Neural adaptation resulting from specificity of strength training increases the number of active motor units. Well-selected training methods, such as maximum-strength methods and power training, activate more motor units. As a result, an athlete has the ability to perform an exercise with higher speed of contraction and more power.

chapter 4

Program Design

This chapter will help you design your own programs using your understanding of properly calculated rest intervals and sport-specific strength training.

Training Volume

Volume, the quantity of work performed, incorporates the duration of training hours; the number of kilograms, pounds, or tonnes/short tons lifted per training session or phase of training; the number of exercises per training session; and the number of sets and repetitions per exercise or training session. Instructors, coaches, and athletes should keep records of the total kilograms/pounds lifted per session or training phase to help plan future training volumes.

Training volume varies based on classification, strength training background, and type of strength training performed. A high volume of training is planned for athletes attempting to develop muscular endurance or maximum strength because of the many repetitions performed and the high load. A medium volume is typical for training different elements of power, because the load is low to medium and the rest interval is relatively long.

Overall training volume becomes more important as athletes approach high-performance. There are no shortcuts. Athletic performance improves only by constant physiological adaptation through training volume increments. As athletes adapt to higher volumes of training, they experience better recovery between sets and training sessions. This, in turn, results in more work per training session and per week, making possible further increases in training volume.

Increments in strength training volume depend on the athlete's biological makeup, the specifics of the sport, and the importance of strength in that sport. Mature athletes with strong strength training backgrounds can tolerate higher volumes.

A dramatic or abrupt increase in volume can be detrimental, irrespective of the athlete's sport or ability, resulting in fatigue, uneconomical muscular work, and possible injury. A progressive plan with an appropriate method of monitoring load increments will avoid these detriments.

Key Words

Adenosine triphosphate (ATP): A complex chemical compound formed with the energy released from food and stored in all cells, particularly the muscles.

Electromyography (EMG): Measurement of the electrical activity of the muscle stimulated by a given load.

Fatigue: Discomfort and decreased efficiency resulting from prolonged or excessive exertion.

Volume: A quantitative element of training. In strength training, it measures the total work for a given exercise or training phase (sets × repetitions × load).

The *total volume* depends on several factors, the determinant being the importance of strength to the sport. For instance, international-class weight lifters often plan 30 tonnes (33 short tons) per training session and approximately 40,000 tonnes (44,000 short tons) per year. For other sports, the volume differs drastically (table 4.1). Power and speed sports require a much higher volume than boxing; in sports where muscular endurance is dominant, such as rowing or canoeing, the volume of strength per year can be three to six times higher than indicated in table 4.1.

Table 4.1   Suggested Guideline for Volume (in Tonnes) of Strength Training per Year

Sport/event	Volume/microcycle in training phases			Volume/year	
	Preparatory	**Competitive**	**Transition**	**Minimum**	**Maximum**
Shot put	24-40	8-12	4-6	900	1450
Football	30-40	10-12	6	900	1400
Baseball/cricket	20-30	8-10	2-4	850	1250
Jumps	20-30	8-10	2	800	1200
Rowing	30-40	10-12	4	900	1200
Kayaking/canoeing	20-40	10-12	4	900	1200
Wrestling	20-30	10	4	800	1200
Swimming	20	8-10	2-4	700	1200
Downhill skiing	18-36	6-10	2-4	700	1250
High jump	16-28	8-10	2-4	620	1000
Cycling	16-22	8-10	2-4	600	950
Triathlon	16-20	8-10	2-4	600	1000
Ice hockey	15-25	6-8	2-4	600	950
Speed skating	14-26	4-6	2-4	500	930
Lacrosse	14-22	4-8	2-4	500	900
Basketball	12-24	4-6	2	450	850
Javelin	12-24	4	2	450	800
Volleyball	12-20	4	2	450	600
Sprinting	10-18	4	2	400	600
Gymnastics	10-16	4	4	380	600
Rugby	10-20	4-6	4	320	600
Squash	8-12	4	4	350	550
Figure skating	8-12	2-4	2	350	550
Tennis	8-12	2-4	2	350	550
Boxing/martial arts	8-14	3	1	380	500
Golf	4-6	2	1	250	300

Intensity (Load) of Training

In strength training, intensity is expressed as a percentage of load or one repetition maximum (1RM). Intensity, a function of the strength of the nervous stimuli employed in training, is determined by muscular effort and CNS energy expended. Stimulus strength depends on the load, speed of movement, and variation of rest intervals between repetitions. Training load, expressed as intensity, refers to the mass or weight lifted. In isokinetic training, load is expressed as the force the athlete generates against the resistance provided by the machine. Strength training employs the following loads (table 4.2).

A *supermaximum* load exceeds one's maximum strength. In most cases, loads between 100 and 125 percent can be used by applying the eccentric method (yielding to the force of gravity). When using supermaximum loads, have two spotters, one at each end of the barbell, to prevent accidents. Only athletes with a strong strength training background should use supermaximum loads. Most other athletes should be restricted to loads of no more than 100 percent.

Maximum load is 90 to 100 percent of maximum. *Heavy* is 80 to 90 percent of 1RM, *medium* is 50 to 80 percent of 1RM, and *low* is 30 to 50 percent of 1RM. Load should relate to the type of strength being developed and, more important, to the sport-specific combination resulting from the blending of strength with speed and strength with endurance. Details on training these sport-specific combinations are presented in the section on power training in chapter 10. Figure 4.1 gives general guidelines for the load to be used in developing each of these combinations. The load will not be the same through all training phases. On the contrary, Periodization will alter the load according to the goals of each training phase. Note that the load ranges from 20 percent to more than 105 percent of 1RM, and the corresponding intensities are shown in the next row. Below that are the sport-specific combinations and the suggested load for each.

Number of Exercises

The key to an effective program is adequate exercise selection. It is often difficult to establish an optimum number of exercises and some coaches, desiring to develop more muscle groups, select too many. The resulting

Table 4.2 Intensity Values and Load Used in Strength Training

Intensity value	Load	Percent of 1RM	Type of contraction
1	Supermaximum	>105	Eccentric/isometric
2	Maximum	90-100	Concentric
3	Heavy	80-90	Concentric
4	Medium	50-80	Concentric
5	Low	30-50	Concentric

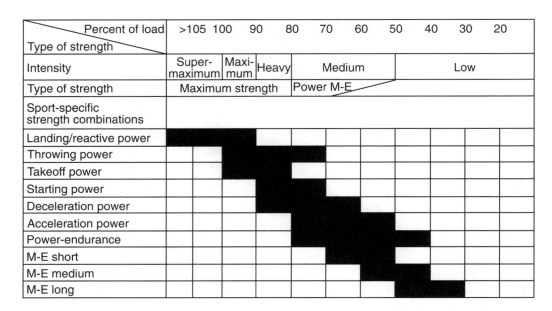

Figure 4.1 Relationship between the load and different types and combinations of strength.

program is overloaded and fatiguing. The number and type of exercises must be selected according to to following factors.

Age and Performance Level

One of the main objectives of a training program for juniors or beginners is development of a solid anatomical and physiological foundation. For strength training, the coach should select many exercises (9 to 12) that address the primary muscle groups. Such a program may last 2 to 3 years, depending on present age and the expected age for achieving high performance.

The main training objective of advanced athletes is to reach the highest possible level of performance. Therefore, their strength programs, especially during the competitive phase, must be specific, with only a few exercises (3 to 6) directed at the prime movers.

Needs of the Sport

Strength training exercises, particularly for elite athletes, should meet the specific needs of the sport. For example, an elite high jumper may perform only three to four exercises to adequately strengthen all prime movers; a football player or wrestler may have to perform six to nine exercises to accomplish the same goal.

Phase of Training

A general strength training program is desirable early in the preparatory phase. After the transition phase, a new annual plan should start building the foundation for future training. For such a program to involve most muscle groups, the number of exercises has to be high (9 to 12), regardless of the specifics of the sport. As a program progresses, the number of exercises reduces, culminating in the competitive phase when only specific, essential exercises are performed (3 to 5). For instance, a football, hockey, basketball, or volleyball player will perform some 9 to 10 exercises during the preparatory phase and only 3 to 5 during the league season.

Order of Exercises

Exercises should alternate between limbs and muscle groups to ensure better recovery. If all parts of the body are exercised, the following order is suggested: legs, arms, abdomen; legs, arms, back; and so on. When selecting the number of exercises, consider their involvement in performing the skills of the sport.

Strength training books and articles propose a different order: large muscle groups first, then small muscle groups. However, this fatigues the small muscle groups, and athletes will be unable to train the large muscles. This is typical of the undue influence bodybuilding and weight lifting have on strength training for other sports.

Select sport strength training exercises to mimic the skills of the particular sport to maximize strengthening the prime movers and, in some cases, produce "motor memory," consolidating the technical skills involved. Strength exercises that resemble the technical pattern repeat similar motions, giving the exercises a learning component. Imitation of technical skills also involves the chain of muscles in a pattern similar to their involvement in the sport. For instance, it makes sense for a volleyball player to perform half squats and toe raises together because spiking and blocking require the same moves. The chain of muscles involved is acting in the same sequence as in jumping. Thus, a volleyball player is not concerned with whether the small or large muscle groups are involved first, only with mimicking the motion and involving the chain of muscles in the same way as in spiking and blocking.

The athlete has two options for the order in which to perform the exercises prescribed by the coach. First the athlete may follow the order of exercises in sequence from the top down (a "vertical" sequence), as listed on the daily program sheet. This method leads to better recovery for the muscle groups involved. By the time exercise number one is performed again, the muscles have recovered. Second, the athlete may perform all the sets for exercise one then move to the next exercise (a "horizontal" sequence). This sequence may cause local fatigue so great that by the time all the sets are performed for one exercise hypertrophy may result instead of power or maximum strength. Therefore, the vertical sequence is more beneficial because it allows a longer rest interval between sets and better regeneration.

Number of Repetitions and Speed of Lifting

Both the number of repetitions and the speed of execution are functions of load. The higher the load, the fewer the repetitions and the more slowly they are performed. For development of maximum strength (85 to 105 percent), the number of repetitions is very low (1 to 7) (figure 4.2). For exercises to develop power (50 to 80 percent of maximum), the number of repetitions is moderate (5 to 10, performed dynamically). For M-E of short duration, 10 to 30 repetitions will work. M-E of medium duration requires around 30 to 60 repetitions nonstop. M-E of long duration requires a high number of repetitions, sometimes up to one's limit, or more than 100 to 150.

Figure 4.2 shows the relationship between load and repetition. Instructors who regard 20 repetitions appropriate for M-E will find the number of repetitions suggested shocking. However, 20 repetitions make an insignificant contribution to overall performance of M-E medium or M-E long sports,

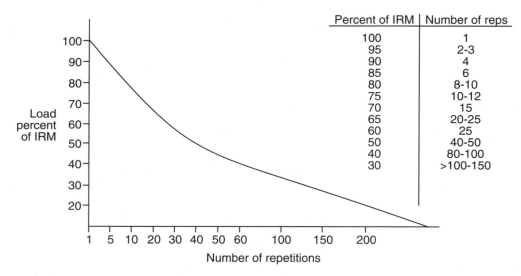

Figure 4.2 Curve of load vs. number of repetitions.

such as rowing, kayaking/canoeing, long-distance swimming/speed skating, and cross-country skiing.

Speed is critical in strength training. For the best training effects, the speed of execution must be fast and explosive for some types of work; for others, it should be slow to medium. The key to proper execution speed is the way in which athletes apply force against resistance. For instance, when a football player, a thrower, or a sprinter lifts a heavy load of 90 percent of 1RM, the motion may look slow, but the force against the resistance is applied as fast as possible. Otherwise the athlete will not recruit and synchronize all the motor units necessary to defeat resistance. The FT muscle fibers are trained and recruited for the action only when the application of force is fast and vigorous.

Number of Sets

A set is the number of repetitions per exercise followed by a rest interval. The number of sets depends on the number of exercises and the strength combination. The number of sets decreases as the number of exercises increases since athletes do not have the energy and work potential to perform many repetitions with a high number of sets. The strength combination being trained also influences the number of sets. For a rower, canoeist, or cross-country skier attempting to develop M-E of long duration, the key element is the number of repetitions per set. Since the number of repetitions is high, it is difficult to perform more than three to four sets.

The number of sets also depends on the athlete's abilities and training potential, the number of muscle groups to be trained, and the training phase. A high jumper or diver in a specialized training program may use three to five exercises in six to eight sets per session. A higher number of exercises would require fewer sets, with obvious disadvantages. Consider a hypothetical high jumper who is using eight exercises involving several muscle groups of the legs, upper body, and arms. For each exercise or muscle group, the athlete performs work of 400 kilograms (880 pounds). Since the athlete can perform only four sets, the total amount of work per muscle group is 1,600 kilograms (3,520 pounds). When the number of exercises is reduced to four, the athlete can now perform, say, eight sets. The outcome (8 × 400 kilograms (880 pounds)) is 3,200 kilograms (7,040 pounds). The athlete can double, even triple the total work per muscle group by decreasing the number of exercises and increasing the number of sets.

The training phase also dictates the number of sets per training session. During the preparatory (preseason) phase, when most muscle groups are used, a higher number of exercises is performed with fewer sets (see chapters 6 and 7). As the competitive phase approaches, training becomes more specific and the number of exercises decreases while the number of sets increases. Finally, during the competitive phase (season), when training is to maintain a certain level of strength or a given strength combina-

Rest intervals are critical to any successful training program.

tion, everything is reduced, including the number of sets, so that the athlete's energy is spent mostly for technical/tactical work.

A well-trained athlete can perform 3, 8, 10, even 12 sets. Certainly, it makes sense to perform a higher number of sets. The more sets per muscle group, the more work the athlete can perform, ultimately leading to higher strength gains and improved performance.

Rest Interval

Energy is necessary for strength training. During training, an athlete uses the fuel of a given energy system according to the load employed and the duration of activity. During high-intensity strength training, energy stores can be taxed to a great extent and sometimes even completely exhausted. To complete the work, say four to six sets, athletes must take a rest interval (RI) so that the depleted fuel can be replenished before another set is performed.

Coaches and athletes must recognize that the RI between sets or training sessions is as important as the training itself. The amount of time allowed between sets determines, to a great extent, how much energy can be recovered before the following set. Careful planning of the RI is critical in avoiding needless physiological and psychological stress during training.

The duration of the RI depends on several factors, including the combination of strength being developed, the load employed, the speed of performance, the number of muscles involved, and the level of conditioning. In calculating the RI, total weight must also be considered, since heavy athletes with larger muscles tend to regenerate at a slower rate than lighter athletes. RI calculations should include the rest taken between sets and between days of strength training.

Rest Interval Between Sets

The rest interval (RI) is a function of the load employed in training, the type of strength being developed, and the rate or explosiveness of performing the task (see table 4.3).

During a rest interval, a high-energy compound of adenosine triphosphate (ATP) and creatine phosphate (CP) to be used as an energy source is replenished proportionate to the duration of the RI. When the RI is calculated properly, lactic acid (LA) accumulates more slowly, enabling the athlete to maintain the planned training program. If the RI is shorter than 1 minute, LA concentration is high; when shorter than 30 seconds, lactate levels are so high that even well-trained athletes find it difficult to tolerate. A proper RI, on the other hand, facilitates the removal of LA from the body. Some sports require athletes to tolerate LA, such as short-distance running, swimming, rowing, and canoeing events, most team sports, as well as boxing and wrestling. Plan days of strength training that result in LA buildup for these athletes while considering the following:

- A 30-second complete rest restores approximately 50 percent of depleted ATP/CP.
- A 1-minute RI for several sets of 15 to 20 reps is insufficient to restore the muscle's energy and enable performance of high muscular tension.
- An RI of 3 to 5 minutes or longer allows almost complete ATP/CP restoration.
- After working to exhaustion, a 4-minute RI is insufficient to eliminate LA from the working muscles or to replenish all the energy requirements such as glycogen.

Table 4.3 Suggested Guidelines for Rest Interval Between Sets for Various Loads and Their Applicable Circumstances

Load percent	Speed of performance	RI (minutes)	Applicability
>105 (eccentric)	Slow	4-5	Improve maximum strength and muscle tone
80–100	Slow to medium	3-5	Improve maximum strength and muscle tone
60–80	Slow to medium	2	Improve muscle hypertrophy
50–80	Fast	4-5	Improve power
30–50	Slow to medium	1-2	Improve M-E

Consequences of an Inadequate RI Between Sets

One consequence is an increased reliance on the LA system for energy. The degree to which ATP/CP replenishes between sets depends on the duration of the RI. The shorter the RI, the less ATP/CP is restored and, consequently, the less energy available for the next set. If the RI is too short, the LA system provides the energy needed for subsequent sets. Reliance on this energy system results in increased LA accumulation in the working muscles, leading to pain and fatigue and impairing the ability to train effectively. Also, during the RI, the heart pumps the highest volume of blood to the working muscles. A short RI diminishes the amount of blood sent to the working muscles. Athletes will not have the energy to complete the planned training session. To combat excessive LA accumulation, a longer RI is required.

A second consequence of an inadequate RI is local muscular and CNS fatigue. Most research findings point to the following possible causes and sites of fatigue:

• The *motor nerve,* via which the nervous system transmits nerve impulses to muscle fibers. A nerve impulse has certain degrees of force, speed, and frequency. The higher the force impulse, the stronger the muscle contraction, which gives athletes greater ability to lift heavier loads. The force of nerve impulses is greatly affected by fatigue, and as the level of fatigue increases, the force of contraction decreases. Thus, longer RIs of up to 7 minutes are necessary for CNS recovery during the maximum strength phase.

• The *neuromuscular junction,* which is the nerve attachment on the muscle fiber that relays the nerve impulses to the working muscle. This type of fatigue is largely due to an increased release of chemical transmitters from the nerve endings (Tesch, 1980). Following a set, a 2- to 3-minute RI usually returns the electrical properties of the nerve to normal levels. After powerful contractions such as those typical of maximum strength training, however, an RI of longer than 5 minutes is needed for sufficient recovery to occur.

• The *contractile mechanisms* (actin and myosin). LA accumulation decreases the peak tension, or the power of the muscle to contract maximally, and leads to a higher acidic concentration in the muscle, affecting its ability to react to the nerve impulses (Fox et al., 1989; Sahlin, 1986). Depletion of muscle glycogen stores, which occurs during prolonged exercise (more than 30 minutes), also causes fatigue of the contracting muscle (Conlee, 1987; Karlsson & Saltin, 1971; Sahlin, 1986). Other energy sources available to the muscle, including glycogen from the liver, cannot fully cover the energy demands of the working muscle.

• The *central nervous system,* which experiences local muscle fatigue. During training, chemical disturbances occur inside the muscle that affect its potential to perform work (Bigland-Ritchie et al., 1983; Hennig & Lomo, 1987). When the effects of these chemical disturbance are signaled back to the CNS, the brain sends weaker nerve impulses to the working muscle, which decreases its working capacity in an attempt to protect the body. During an adequate RI of 4 to 5 minutes, the muscles are allowed to recover almost completely. The brain then senses no danger and sends more powerful nerve impulses to the muscles, resulting in better muscular performance.

Rest Interval Between Strength Training Sessions

The rest interval between strength training sessions depends on the conditioning level and recovery ability of the individual, the training phase, and the energy source used in training. Well-conditioned athletes always recover faster, especially as training progresses toward the competitive phase, when they are supposed to reach their highest physical potential.

Consider the energy source taxed in training when determining the length and frequency of the RI between strength training sessions. Normally, strength training is planned following technical or tactical training. If athletes tax the same energy system and fuel (e.g., glycogen) during technical and strength training, the next training of this type must be planned for 2 days later since it takes 48 hours for full restoration of glycogen (Fox et al., 1989; Piehl, 1974). Even with a carbohydrate-rich diet, glycogen levels will not return to normal in less than 2 days. If athletes perform only strength training, as some do on certain days during the preparatory phase, the restoration of glycogen occurs faster: 55 percent in 5 hours and almost 100 percent in 24 hours. This means that strength training can be planned more frequently.

Activity During Rest

To facilitate faster recovery between sets, advise athletes to perform certain activities during the RI. Relaxation exercises such as shaking the legs, arms, and shoulders, or light massage, seem to speed up recovery between sets. Relaxation exercises are indicated, especially since heavy-load exercises increase the quantity of mystromin (a protein occurring within the framework of muscle tissue), which causes muscle rigidity (Baroga, 1978). The mental control of muscle relaxation is very important. Relaxation means economy of energy and facilitation of the quickness of contraction so that the antagonistic muscles are relaxed and do not oppose the contraction of the agonistic muscles.

During the RI, it is also important to perform "diversionary activities" to involve the nonfatigued muscles in some light contractions (Asmussen & Mazin, 1978). Such physical activities have been reported to facilitate faster recovery of the prime movers. Local muscle fatigue is signaled to the CNS via sensory nerves. As a result, the brain sends inhibitory signals to the fatigued muscles, decreasing their work output during the RI. Consequently, the muscles relax better, which facilitates the restoration of the energy stores.

Loading Patterns

If too many sets at a lower load are employed, the outcome will be hypertrophy training, not maximum strength (MxS). This may lead to fatigue that might impair MxS development. According to some loading patterns, even if athletes start with one to two sets of a submaximum load, it is essential to increase to maximum load relatively quickly to obtain the most favorable conditions for MxS development.

In the pyramid pattern examples that follow, each program starts from its base and works toward the peak, or from the bottom to the top. The suggested load is performed for all the exercises selected for the workout before moving to the next load.

The *pyramid* is one of the most popular loading patterns. Its structure, shown in figure 4.3, implies that the load increases progressively to maximum while the number of reps decreases proportionately. The physiological advantage of using the pyramid is that it ensures the activation or recruitment of most if not all the motor units.

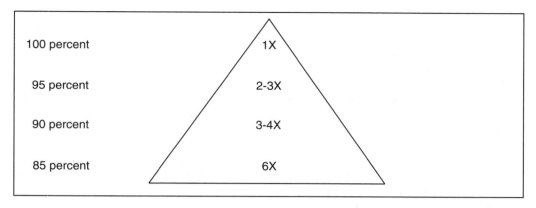

Figure 4.3 Pyramid loading pattern. The number of repetitions (inside the pyramid) refers to the number per set.

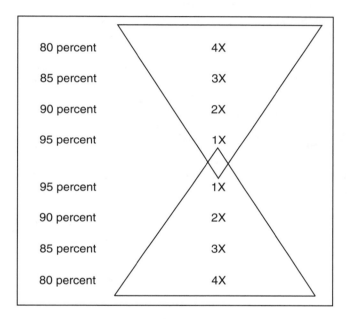

Figure 4.4 Double-pyramid loading pattern suggested by Grosser and Neumeier (1986).

The *double pyramid* consists of two pyramids, one inverted on top of the other. The number of repetitions decreases from the bottom up, then increases again in the second pyramid (figure 4.4). Though the double pyramid has its merits, some cautions are necessary. Most proponents of this pattern suggest that the last sets, with loads of 85 and 80 percent, are meant to improve power. The assumption is that since the load is lower, the force can be applied faster. By the time these final sets are performed, however, both the CNS and the muscles involved may be exhausted, in which case these sets will not produce the expected benefits. On the contrary, since the fatigue may impair fast recruitment of the FT fibers, the actual outcome of the last sets of this loading pattern will be development of muscle hypertrophy rather than power.

If the intent is to enhance FT fiber recruitment, it must be done in the early part of the session. Do not expect power enhancement at the end of a training day; fatigue may interfere. However, if both MxS and hypertrophy training are planned in the same training session, the double pyramid may be an acceptable solution.

The *skewed pyramid* (figure 4.5) is proposed as an improved variant of the double pyramid. The load is constantly increased throughout the session, except during the last set, when it is lowered (80-85-90-95-80 percent). The intent of lowering the last set is variation and motivation, since athletes will be asked to perform the lift as quickly as they can. As in the case of the double pyramid, fatigue may hamper a quick application of force, but this should not stop athletes from trying. As only one set is performed and the number of repetitions is low (4 to 6), exhaustion will not be experienced, so the single set will not trigger gains in hypertrophy.

The *flat pyramid* represents the best loading pattern for achieving maximum MxS benefits (figure 4.6). In traditional pyramids, the load often varies from 70 to 100 percent. Load variations of such magnitude cross three levels of intensity: medium, heavy, and maximum. The load necessary to produce gains in MxS is between 85 and 100 percent; therefore, a traditional pyramid that uses a load of 70 to 100 percent may result in gains in both P and MxS. Although this may be of general benefit to athletes, it does not maximize gains in MxS.

If the intent of training is to develop MxS only, I strongly recommend the flat pyramid. This type of loading pattern starts with a warm-up lift of, say, 60 percent, followed by an intermediary set at 80 percent, then stabilizing the load at 90 percent for the entire workout. If the instructor wishes to add variety at the end of training, a set of lower load may be used (figure 4.6 shows an example of 80 percent). The physiological advantage of the flat pyramid is that by using a load of only one intensity level, the best neuromuscular adaptation for MxS is achieved without "confusing" the body with several intensities. If the goal is MxS, consider the flat pyramid. Variations of the flat pyramid are certainly possible, as long

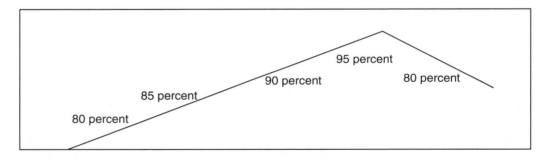

Figure 4.5 Suggested loading pattern for the "skewed pyramid" (Bompa, 1993a).

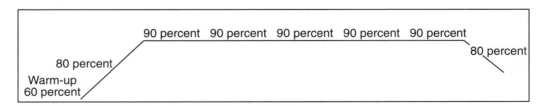

Figure 4.6 The flat pyramid represents the best loading pattern for the MxS (Bompa, 1993a).

as the load stays within the 85- to 100-percent intensity range required for gains in MxS.

Training Program Design

To design a strength training program, consider the following steps.

Select the Type of Strength

The type or sport-specific combination of strength is selected based on the concept of Periodization and is phase specific. This concept enables a coach or instructor to decide the percentage of 1RM to be used and the number of repetitions and sets. Details on training methods and progression are provided in chapters 7 through 11.

Select the Exercises to Be Used in Training

Select training exercises according to the specifics of the sport, the athletes' needs, and the phase of training. Each athletic skill is performed by prime movers, which can differ from sport to sport, depending on the specific skill requirements. Therefore, the instructor must first identify the prime movers and then select the strength exercises that best involve these muscles. At the same time, consider the athletes' needs. These may depend on their backgrounds and individual strengths and weaknesses. Since the weakest link in a chain always breaks first, compensation exercises should be selected to strengthen the weakest muscles.

The selection of exercises is also phase specific, as illustrated in chapter 6. Normally, during the anatomical adaptation phase, most muscle groups are employed to build a better and more multilateral foundation. As the competitive phase approaches, training becomes more specific and exercises are selected specifically to involve the prime movers.

Test Maximum Strength

Maximum strength is the highest load an athlete can lift in one attempt and is used by coaches to calculate their athletes' 1RM. A coach should know each athlete's maximum strength in at least the dominant exercises of the training program. Often the load and number of repetitions are chosen randomly, or by following the programs of other athletes, instead of using the objective data from each athlete. This data is valid only for a certain cycle of training, usually a macrocycle, because each athlete's degree of training and potential changes continuously.

Some coaches and instructors believe that testing for 1RM is dangerous, that lifting 100 percent can result in injury. It is not dangerous for trained athletes to lift 100 percent once every 4 weeks, or at the beginning of each macrocycle. Most injuries occur during training and competitions, not during testing. If we avoid challenging muscles to 100 percent, they can hardly adapt to apply their maximum potential in competition. It is important to remember, however, that a test for 1RM must follow a thorough, progressive warm-up. If there is still reluctance to test 100 percent, see appendix B for estimating 1RM by testing for 3RM, 4RM, or 5RM.

Develop the Actual Training Program

Use the information gathered in the previous steps to determine the number of exercises, the percentage of 1RM to be used, the number of reps, and the number of sets based on the athlete's ability to tolerate work. All of this information will be used to design the training program for a macrocycle. The program cannot be the same for each macrocycle. Training demand must increase progressively so the athlete will adapt to a larger workload, which will be translated into an increase in strength. The training demand may be increased by increasing the load, decreasing the RI, increasing the number of repetitions, or increasing the number of sets.

Before suggesting the headings for a simple chart that can be used as a training program, the notation used to express the load, number of reps, and number of sets should be explained. Many books and articles on this subject go so far as to actually suggest the load an athlete should use in pounds/kilograms! This certainly leads one to question on what basis someone can actually suggest the poundage athletes should use without knowing anything about them. Instead, the load must be suggested as a percentage of 1RM, and athlete's must be tested, especially during the preparatory phase at the beginning of each new macrocycle. By knowing the 1RM, the percentage to be used in training can be selected according to the training goals of each phase.

The notation of load, number of reps, and number of sets can be expressed as follows:

$$\frac{Load}{no.\ of\ reps}\ sets$$

$$\frac{80}{10}4$$

The numerator (80%) refers to the load to be used, the denominator (10) represents the number of repetitions, and the multiplier (4) indicates the number of sets.

The advantage of suggesting the load in percent of 1RM is that when working with a larger group of athletes, such as a football team, the coach does not have to calculate the poundage for each player. By suggesting the load in percentage, the program is valid for each athlete. Individualization is therefore built in with this method. Each athlete uses their personal 1RM as the basis for calculating poundage, which may vary from player to player.

Any strength training program should be written on a sheet of paper or in the training journal. Table 4.4 illustrates an example format for a strength training program. The first column lists the number of the exercise to be performed in a given strength training session, from 1 to X. The second column shows the exercises. The third column specifies the load, number of reps, and sets. The last column indicates the RI to be taken following each set.

Test to Recalculate 1RM

This test is required before beginning a new macrocycle to ensure that progress in maximum strength is achieved and the new load is related to the gains made in strength.

Exercise Prescription

All athletic skills and actions are performed by muscles as a result of contraction. There are 656 muscles distributed throughout the human body, which are capable of performing a high variety of movements. If athletes

Table 4.4   Chart Used to Design a Strength Training Program

Exercise no.	Exercise	Load, no. of reps, no. of sets	RI (minutes)
1	Leg presses	$\frac{80}{6}4$	3
2	Bench presses	$\frac{75}{8}4$	3
3	Leg curls	$\frac{60}{10}3$	2
4	Half squats	$\frac{80}{8}4$	3
5	Abdominal curls	15×4	2
6	Dead lifts	$\frac{60}{8}3$	2

A training chart can be posted in the gym for athletes to see.

wish to improve a skill or a physical performance, they must concentrate on training the muscles that perform the athletic action, or the prime movers.

To design a good strength program, select carefully the necessary training methods and exercises. The process of prescribing exercises for a given muscle group (or groups) must be based on phase-specific considerations. During the anatomical adaptation phase, exercises must be selected that develop most muscle groups, both agonistic and antagonistic, to build a stronger base for the training phases to follow. As the competitive phase approaches, these exercises become very specialized, prescribed specifically for the prime movers.

For an adequate exercise prescription, consider the following steps:

1. Analyze how the skill is performed (direction, angle, and limb position).
2. Determine the prime movers responsible for the skill performance.
3. Select exercises that involve the prime movers based on their similarity to the direction and angle of contraction for the selected skill(s).

Exercise prescription should be based on an understanding of how the muscles are producing a movement, not on exercises borrowed from weight lifting or bodybuilding. Almost every athlete does bench presses and "cleans" irrespective of whether they are suited to the needs of a given sport. The theory that these exercises are good for every sport is a fallacy! An exercise is good for a sport only if it follows the principle of specificity. It must involve the prime movers and the synergistic muscles used in performing the skills of the particular sport or event.

Coaches often turn to bodybuilding for exercise ideas without understanding the differences between sports and bodybuilding. One difference is in the type of method—analytic or composite—used to determine how an exercise achieves a specific training goal. Bodybuilders use the analytic method for high muscle definition. They analyze each muscle's individual action and movement, then train each muscle in isolation to achieve the best size development.

In athletics, however, the composite method should be used because it involves all the muscles of a joint (or joints) necessary to produce an athletic skill, rather than an individual muscle. Exercises should involve the muscles and joints in a sequence similar to the performance of a skill. For instance, to train the muscles involved in starting in sprinting, use reverse leg presses rather than knee extensions. Using a paddle for the leg press, turn the athlete's back toward the paddle, place the toes on the paddle, a hand on the support, and press the leg backward.

There is another important difference between the analytic and composite methods. The analytic method results in only local adaptation with no cardiorespiratory benefits. In the composite method, however, by using large muscle groups of one to three joints, as in the reverse leg press, there is a cardiorespiratory gain as well, which is an important training goal for sports.

Suggested Exercises

In chapter 3, under "Principle of Specificity," I showed that to achieve sport-specific adaptation, exercises must be carefully selected. I also cautioned readers against being overly influenced by bodybuilding and weight lifting, since the exercises and methods used in these two disciplines are specific to their goals but are far from conducive to the specific adaptation essential for athletic success in sports. The following example demonstrates the negative influence bodybuilding and Olympic weight lifting still have on some strength coaches.

While evaluating a strength training program a gym instructor proposed for a master downhill skier, I was stunned to find that it had 34 exercises! For areas such as the chest, abdominals, and deltoid muscles, the program listed 5 different exercises per muscle group. In my opinion, this makes no sense, as the chest and deltoid muscles are not the prime movers involved in skiing. On the other hand, the instructor had prescribed 3 exercises for the ankles and just 1 for the knees, despite the fact that the knee extensors are the prime movers in skiing. I suggested 9 exercises for the preparatory phase and 4 for the competitive phase, repeated in several sets, for the best adaptation to the needs of Alpine skiing.

One argument making the rounds is that because Olympic weight lifters are competitive in standing long jump, a standard test for power, everyone seeking to develop strength should perform Olympic weight-lifting exercises. What the Olympic weight-lifting enthusiasts miss, however, is that the reason for their proficiency in standing long jump is not the exercises they perform, but rather the training load they use (over 80 percent of 1RM). There is nothing miraculous about performing Olympic weight-lifting exercises. On the contrary, few of them involve the prime movers used in most sports. Why then should one use power lifts or snatches, when squats have equal or even better training effects on the knee and hip extensors? As for the benefits of heavy loads (see chapter 9), it can be clearly demonstrated that they recruit to action most of the FT muscle fibers that are so essential in maximizing strength and power abilities.

The prime movers used in a particular sport can serve as a fundamental guideline for selecting exercises for strength training. Table 4.5 shows which exercises are most beneficial for certain sports. It was compiled using the above guidelines to suggest exercises based on the prime movers used predominantly in each sport. Beginning on page 60 "Muscles Involved in Various Exercises" illustrates many of these exercises and lists the primary muscles developed by

Table 4.5 Suggested Exercises for Various Sports

Sports Events	Neck Flexion/Extension	Shoulder Shrugs	Incline/Bench Press	Military Press	Parallel Bar Dips	Front Lat Pull-Downs	Seated Rows/Upright Rows	Wrist Flexion/Extension	Back Extension/Hyperextension	Good Morning (bent knees)	Dead Lifts/Power Cleans	Power Lifts to Chest Level	Abdominal Curls	V-Sits/Weighted Sit-ups	Knee Lifts	Leg Curls	Squats	Jump Half Squats	Leg Extensions	Leg Presses	Reverse Leg Press	Toe Raises	Low Impact Plyometrics	High Impact Plyometrics	Drop Jumps	Bounding Exercises	Reactive Jumps	Medicine Ball Throws	Shot/Heavy Ball Throws	Combined Weights/Plyometrics Tubing
Athletics																														
Sprinting	×				×		×		×		×	×	×	×	×		×		×	×	×	×	×		×	×	×		×	
Mid/Distance	×				×		×		×			×	×	×			×		×	×	×	×		×					×	
Long/Triple Jump	×				×				×		×	×	×				×		×	×	×	×	×	×	×	×	×		×	×
High Jump			×			×	×		×		×	×	×		×		×			×	×	×	×	×	×	×	×		×	
Pole Vault				×		×	×		×		×	×	×		×		×		×	×	×	×	×	×	×		×		×	
Shot Put		×				×	×		×	×	×	×		×	×		×		×	×	×	×	×	×	×		×	×	×	
Discus/Hammer		×				×	×		×	×	×	×					×		×	×	×	×	×	×	×	×	×	×	×	×
Javelin						×	×		×	×	×	×	×	×	×		×		×	×	×	×	×	×	×	×	×		×	
Boxing	×																													
Baseball					×	×	×	×	×	×	×	×	×	×			×			×	×	×	×		×		×		×	
Basketball					×		×		×	×	×	×	×	×			×			×	×	×	×		×		×		×	×
Canoeing/Kayaking	×		×		×	×	×										×													
Cycling					×				×		×	×					×		×	×	×	×		×						
Field Hockey					×	×	×		×		×	×	×	×			×		×	×	×	×	×	×	×		×	×	×	
Figure Skating		×							×	×	×	×	×				×	×	×	×	×	×	×	×	×		×	×	×	
Football	×				×	×	×		×	×	×	×	×	×	×		×		×	×	×	×	×	×	×		×		×	
Ice Hockey	×	×			×	×	×	×	×	×	×	×	×	×			×	×	×	×	×	×	×	×	×		×		×	×
Martial Arts	×			×	×	×	×		×		×	×	×	×	×		×	×	×	×	×	×	×	×	×		×	×	×	×
Rowing	×	×			×	×	×		×		×	×		×			×		×	×	×	×		×			×		×	
Rugby	×				×		×				×	×	×				×		×	×	×	×	×	×	×	×	×	×	×	×
Skiing	×	×		×			×																							
Alpine		×			×		×		×		×	×	×	×	×		×		×	×	×	×	×	×	×	×	×		×	×
Nordic		×					×		×		×	×		×			×			×	×	×								
Soccer					×		×		×		×	×					×		×	×	×	×	×	×	×		×		×	×
Speed Skating						×	×		×		×	×					×	×	×	×	×	×	×	×	×	×	×		×	×
Swimming						×	×		×		×	×	×	×			×	×	×	×	×	×	×	×	×	×	×		×	
Freestyle						×	×																							
Breaststroke							×																							
Butterfly							×																							
Tennis	×	×	×	×	×	×	×		×	×	×	×	×	×	×		×		×	×	×	×	×	×	×	×	×	×	×	×
Volleyball	×			×	×	×	×		×	×	×	×	×	×			×		×	×	×	×	×	×	×	×	×	×	×	×
Water polo	×		×			×	×		×		×	×					×			×	×	×	×		×		×		×	
Wrestling	×		×	×	×	×	×		×		×	×	×	×			×	×	×	×	×	×	×	×	×	×	×	×	×	×

59

Muscles Involved in Various Exercises

Neck Flexion/Extension

Region: neck

Primary muscles: prevertebral muscles; sternocleidomastoids; deep posterior muscles; cervical region; trapezius

Shoulder Shrugs

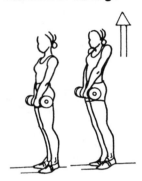

Region: shoulders

Primary muscles: trapezius

Incline/Bench Presses

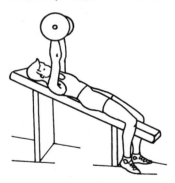

Region: chest; upper arms

Primary muscles: pectoralis major; anterior deltoids; triceps

Military Presses

Region: shoulders; upper arms

Primary muscles: triceps; deltoids; upper pectoralis major

Parallel Bar Dips

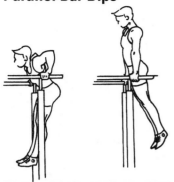

Region: shoulders; upper and lower arms

Primary muscles: triceps; deltoids; pectoralis major

Front Lat Pull-Downs

Region: shoulder girdle

Primary muscles: latissimus dorsi; upper pectoralis major; trapezius

Seated Rows/Upright Rows

Region: shoulders

Primary muscles: latissimus dorsi; trapezius; biceps; deltoids; brachialis; brachioradialis

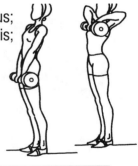

Wrist Flexion/Extension

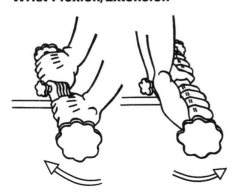

Region: wrist

Primary muscles: flexor carpi radialis; flexor carpi ulnaris; extensor carpi ulnaris

Back Extension/Hyperextension

Region: lower back

Primary muscles: erector spinae; gluteus maximus

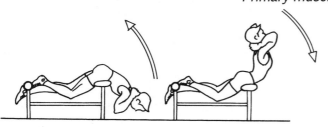

Good Morning (bent knee)

Region: lower back

Primary muscles: erector spinae; gluteus maximus

Dead Lifts

Region: trunk

Primary muscles: erector spinae; hamstrings; gluteus maximus

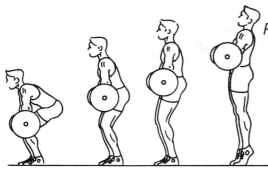

Power Lifts to Chest Level

Region: trunk, lower back, shoulders

Primary muscles: quadriceps; gluteus maximus; erector spinae; hamstrings; trapezius; deltoids

Abdominal Curls/V-Sits/Weighted Sit-Ups

Region: trunk

Primary muscles: rectus abdominis; external obliques/internus abdominis

Knee Lifts

Region: hips

Primary muscles: iliopsoas

Leg Curls

Region: upper legs, hips

Primary muscles: hamstrings; gluteus maximus

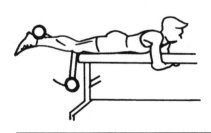 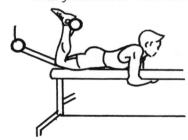

Squats

Region: upper and lower legs

Primary muscles: gluteus maximus; quadriceps; erector spinae; abdominals

Jump Half Squats

Region: upper and lower legs

Primary muscles: gluteus maximus; quadriceps; erector spinae; abdominals; soleus; gastrocnemius; vastus lateralis and medialis

---

Leg Extensions

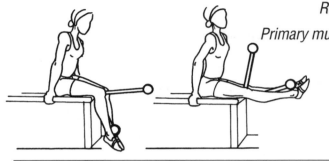

Region: upper legs

Primary muscles: quadriceps; rectus femoris; vastus medialis and lateralis

---

Leg Presses

Region: upper legs

Primary muscles: quadriceps; rectus femoris; vastus medialis and lateralis; tibialis anterior

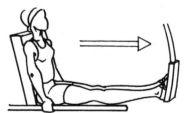

Reverse Leg Presses

Region: upper legs, hips

Primary muscles: quadriceps; gastrocnemius

Toe Raises

Region: lower legs

Primary muscles: gastrocnemius; soleus

each. Some plyometric exercises are also suggested for increasing power. For further information on plyometric training and exercises, see chapter 10.

You may notice that for some sports, especially those using many muscle groups, numerous exercises are available. In choosing exercises, carefully consider another element—the training phase. As will be explained in chapter 6, the number of exercises selected in training is directly related to the specifics of a training phase. The closer the athlete gets to the competitive phase, the lower the number of exercises. A lower number of exercises is essential if the intent is to increase the number of sets. The direct benefit of this is more specific adaptation to the needs of the sport and performance improvement during the competitive phase.

Maximum Muscle Efficiency in Relation to Limb Position

Strength training for sports is influenced by various theories, many of which are affecting the training methods chosen as well as the selection of exercises. For example, it is theorized that a given grip is more effective than another in stimulating certain muscle groups, and that certain foot positions for squats are better than others, and so on.

To evaluate the maximum effectiveness of muscle contractions as related to limb position, a research study was conducted by Cornacchia and LaFramboise, 1998. Most studies on the effectiveness of muscle contraction use electromyography (EMG), which measures the electrical activity or excitability level of the muscles involved. The higher the electrical activity, the more effective the muscle contraction. In EMG studies, researchers can use the peak of the electrical activity (peak force) or, even better, calculate or integrate the full force under the curve. This improved method is called integrated electromyography, or iEMG, and was used in the Cornacchia and LaFramboise study to evaluate muscle efficiency as affected by limb position.

The load used for the iEMG study was 80 percent of 1RM, which means MxS. Data were analyzed employing two one-way repeated-measures analyses of variance to determine which exercise yields the greatest percentage of iEMG for each muscle. Table 4.6 shows which exercises produced the greatest amount of stimulation within each target muscle group. The findings are presented in percentage of maximum. Obviously, the exercise showing the highest percentage must be considered the best for the particular muscle group(s).

Table 4.6　iEMG Maximum Motor Unit Activation

Exercise	Percent iEMG	Exercise	Percent iEMG
Rectus Femoris (Quadriceps)		**Latissimus Dorsi** *(continued)*	
Safety squats (90-degree angle, shoulder-width stance)	88	Lat pull-downs to the front	86
Seated leg extensions (toes straight)	86	Seated pulley rows	83
Half squats (90-degree angle, shoulder- width stance)	78	**Biceps Brachii (Long Head)**	
Leg presses (110-degree angle)	76	Biceps preacher curls (Olympic bar)	90
Smith machine squats (90-degree angle, shoulder-width stance)	60	Incline seated dumbbell curls (alternate)	88
Biceps Femoris (Hamstrings)		Standing biceps curls (Olympic bar/narrow grip)	86
Standing leg curls	82	Standing dumbbell curls (alternate)	84
Lying leg curls	71	Concentration dumbbell curls	80
Seated leg curls	58	Standing biceps curls (Olympic bar/wide grip)	63
Modified hamstring dead lifts	56	Standing E-Z biceps curls (wide grip)	61
Semitendinosus (Hamstrings)		**Anterior Deltoids**	
Seated leg curls	88	Seated front dumbbell presses	79
Standing leg curls	79	Standing front dumbbell raises	73
Lying leg curls	70	Seated front barbell presses	61
Modified hamstring dead lifts	63	**Medial Deltoids**	
Gastrocnemius (Calf Muscle)		Standing dumbbell side laterals	57
Donkey calf raises	80	Seated dumbbell side laterals	53
Standing one-legged calf raises	79	Cable side laterals	49
Standing two-legged calf raises	68	**Posterior Deltoids**	
Seated calf raises	61	Standing dumbbell bent laterals	85
Triceps Brachii (Outer Head)		Seated dumbbell bent laterals	83
Decline triceps extension (Olympic bar)	92	Standing cable bent laterals	77
Triceps pressdowns (angled bar)	90	**Pectoralis Major**	
Triceps dips between benches	87	Decline dumbbell bench presses	93
One-arm cable triceps extensions (reverse grip)	85	Decline bench presses (Olympic bar)	90
Overhead rope triceps extensions	84	Push-ups between benches	88
Seated one-arm dumbbell triceps extensions (neutral grip)	82	Flat dumbbell bench presses	87
Narrow-grip bench presses (Olympic bar)	72	Flat bench presses (Olympic bar)	85
Latissimus Dorsi		Flat dumbbell flys	84
Bent-over barbell rows	93	**Pectoralis Minor**	
One-arm dumbbell rows (alternate)	91	Incline dumbbell bench presses	91
T-bar rows	89	Incline bench presses (Olympic bar)	85
		Incline dumbbell flys	83
		Incline bench presses (Smith machine)	81

chapter 5

Short-Term Planning: Microcycles

A successful strength training program is part of a long-term plan. Strength training should not be performed just for the sake of it or because it improves performance. Though strength training does improve performance, strength training is a required training component. Such a program must have a purpose, normally phase specific. Strength training must meet the objectives of the training phase and coincide with the overall plan.

Since a training plan is a methodical, scientific strategy for improving performance, planning is the most important tool in attempting to design a well-organized training program. An effective training program is well designed, based on scientific knowledge, and incorporates the principles of Periodization of Strength throughout the year.

The plan, whether short or long term, also reflects the coach's methodological knowledge and takes into account the athlete's background and physical potential. A good training plan is simple, objective, and flexible, as it may have to be modified to match the athlete's physiological adaptation and performance improvements. Planning theory is very complex, and this book only discusses planning as it pertains to strength training. Further information can be found in *Periodization: Theory and Methodology of Training* (Bompa, 1999). Information on the training session plan, the microcycle, the annual plan, and the long-term plan for junior athletes will be discussed here. Refer to the "Periodization" sections of chapter 6 for more specific information.

Before You Begin

The following methodological guidelines will ensure that each person's strength training needs are met safely and efficiently.

Check the Equipment

Equipment varies, so often athletes must adjust to new equipment and free weights from gym to gym. Before using any equipment, be sure it is checked for maximum safety; although many private clubs check equipment regularly, some do not. Strength training equipment must be maintained properly so that wear and rust do not endanger users. Constantly check for loose belts and cracks, and periodically lubricate cables, chains, and rods to ensure smooth operation.

Among the most popular equipment used for strength training are free weights and circuit machines such as those built by Universal Gym Machine. Secure the collars before using free weights and, in the case of power racks, check to make sure the barbells are properly placed on the supports and the pins are secure. When using circuit machines, seats and other movable parts should be properly adjusted and secured. Make sure that the weight key used for stacks is locked in place by inserting and twisting it or by pressing it to the end.

Question whether equipment other than free weights and circuit machines can duplicate the skills performed by the prime movers and permit constant acceleration through the range of motion. The first criterion pertains to training specificity, an important requirement during all training phases. The second criterion is crucial for speed-power sports, especially from the conversion phase through the competitive phase. If constant acceleration cannot be reproduced, there is no positive transfer from strength training to the sport's skills and performance.

Know and Use Spotting Techniques

Advanced strength trainers prefer free weights. Training partners act as spotters, especially when maximum loads or the eccentric method are used. The eccentric method with free weights is impossible to perform and dangerous without spotters. Young and inexperienced athletes especially should be assisted by trained instructors and use power/squat racks.

Even experienced athletes should use spotters for high-risk movements (employing heavy loads) such as squats, military presses, cleans, and bench presses. Spotters can offer feedback on the technical accuracy of the lifts performed. To avoid problems, including injuries, spotters should observe the following suggestions. Before spotting, spotters should know the exercise, spotting technique, and the number of repetitions to be performed. They should check the equipment and, in the case of free weights, make sure that the weights are evenly distributed and the collars are properly secured. Assuming a ready position, feet shoulder-width apart, the spotter should check the performer's grip on the barbell and, if necessary, help the performer lift the barbell from the rack.

During the performance, the spotter is ready to give a "lift-off" at the beginning of the lift, especially for maximum loads. They are attentive throughout the lift and stand close enough to provide help if necessary. They count the number of repetitions to ensure a coordinated effort. When necessary, spotters give motivation and feedback regarding performance. Technical feedback is crucial in avoiding injuries (e.g., during the bench press, if one arm is higher, the weights might fall off the lower end of the barbell). If the lift is performed incorrectly, the spotter should stop the exercise. If the attempt fails, the spotter secures the barbell and helps the lifter place it on the rack or supports.

Use Correct Form and Body Position

Proper lifting technique is an important factor in performance improvement and prevention of injury, especially for free weight exercises. The form or technique of lifting must be constantly stressed, especially during the early years of involvement in strength training.

Keep a straight upper body and a flat back for all exercises, especially those involving lifting and carrying. Avoid an overarched, hollow back or rounded back in all circumstances. Pay particular attention with heavier loads. In both positions, the spine, particularly the intervertebral discs, are under excessive strain. An athlete lifting a 50-kilogram (110-pound) weight with a rounded back yields an intervertebral stress some 65 percent higher than with a straight back (Hartmann & Tünnemann, 1988).

Head postion determines back posture. Improper head position may cause undesirable muscle tension. An exaggerated, vigorous head extension (backward drop) increases tension in the back extensor muscles, causing a hollow back. A forward bend of the head causes a rounded back, stretching the back muscles and "shooting" the hips. The head follows rather than leads the hips. Pay close attention to head position! The best position for half squats is with the upper body erect, the back straight, and the head upright, with the eyes looking forward or slightly upward.

The intervertebral discs of the spine can be cushioned by contracting the abdominals, creating pressure against the training belt and compensating the back. In many lifting moves, the hips and abdominals act as stabilizers, supporting the working muscles of the arms and legs.

Proper Breathing

Breathing technique is an important concern for anyone strength training, especially beginners. Young athletes should be instructed on proper breathing. Some breath holding is normal during strength training, especially during heavy lifts. However, if the breath is held for the entire lift, blood pressure, intrathoracic pressure, and intra-abdominal pressure will increase due to the Valsalva maneuver, forced expiration against a closed glottis (the space between the vocal cords). This may restrict the return of blood, causing veins to swell and the face to redden (MacDougall et al., 1985). The Valsalva maneuver, although seemingly hazardous, has a beneficial function. The intrathoracic and intra-abdominal pressure solidifies the trunk, which stabilizes the vertebral column and creates a strong support for the muscles to pull against.

The Valsalva maneuver is a reflex reaction to lifting heavy loads and should not be perceived negatively unless the breath is held for a long time, which can result in fainting. Since athletes rarely hold their breath for longer than 2 to 3 seconds in strength training, fainting almost never occurs. Nevertheless, coaches should take every precaution necessary to prevent the Valsalva maneuver, especially for beginners, by teaching athletes to breathe correctly and by encouraging young athletes to breathe naturally during strength training.

The natural pattern for breathing in strength training is to inhale just before and during the lowering or eccentric phase of the lift and exhale during the lifting or concentric phase. The exhalation is preceded by a very short Valsalva, releasing most of the air from the lungs at the very end of the lift. In any case, athletes should be instructed not to hold their breath for too long, especially during an MxS training session.

The same is true for athletes performing isometric contractions. While in contraction, hold your breath for only a very short time or not at all. When your muscles contract, the natural tendency is to hold your breath, but you should concentrate on breathing throughout the contraction. For jumping and throwing exercises, inhale before the action and exhale while performing it.

Strength Training Accessories

Belts, training gloves, and shoes are common strength training accessories. Strength training belts counteract weak abdominal muscles for all lower body exercises and support the low-back and abdominal muscles as a lift is performed, creating an approximate balance between the low-back and abdominal muscles. A belt should not be used as a substitute for strengthening these muscles. On the contrary, during the AA phase, and even during other phases of training, athletes should dedicate time to fortifying the back and abdominal muscles. Muscle weaknesses can also be addressed through compensation work during the transition phase.

Although popular with fitness fans, gloves, which protect the palms from blisters, are rarely worn by dedicated athletes, who are content to let their functional calluses protect their palms.

Shoes for strength training have higher heels than normal athletic shoes. They provide good arch support and keep the feet and ankles tight. Elevated heels also have a mechanical advantage. For instance, to overcome the weight of a barbell as it is lifted, athletes tend to lean backward, and a slight slip or fall onto the back at this time might be dangerous. Shoes with higher heels counteract this tendency by bringing the vertical projection of the center of gravity slightly forward. This prevents athletes from leaning backward as the barbell is lifted and balances the weight of the barbell with the force and mass of the body.

Another advantage of strength training shoes is that they compensate for lack of ankle flexibility during certain exercises. For better balance, half squats (and even deep squats) should be performed flat-footed; however, because many athletes lack good ankle flexibility, they tend to stay on the balls of their feet or toes as the position is taken. The higher heels on strength training shoes allow athletes to take a flat-footed and balanced position for these exercises.

Wrapping or taping joints is often used to provide additional support for athletes with weak or vulnerable joints and for beginners. If a joint is wrapped (wrist, elbow, ankles, or knees), make sure that the wrapping is not so tight as to affect blood circulation. If possible, loosen the wrap during the rest interval for comfort and to increase circulation.

Medical Clearance

Anyone desiring to participate in sports, especially those involving strength training, must obtain medical clearance, especially young athletes and beginners who may have undiagnosed heart conditions or cardiovascular disease. The strenuous nature of many sports and strength training activities may aggravate such health conditions. Strength training with heavy loads involves the Valsalva maneuver, which increases blood, chest, and abdominal pressure, and can unduly stress an already weak heart and cardiovascular system. In addition, these increased pressures may limit or even restrict blood flow to and from the heart (Compton et al., 1973).

Some children may experience other health problems such as growth plate or orthopedic abnormalities like degenerating arthritis. In these cases, strength training may result in increased skeletal and joint stress. For their protection, individuals with such problems should be restricted from strenuous training in general, and strength training in particular, by a physician. Thus, every concerned coach should require medical clearance for every athlete.

The Training Session Plan

The training session is the main tool for organizing the daily program. To achieve better management and organization, the training session can be structured into four main segments.

Introduction

The *introduction* represents the organizational component of a training session when the coach or instructor shares with the athletes the training objectives for the day and how they are to be achieved. This is also the time when the coach organizes the athletes into groups and gives them necessary advice regarding the daily program.

Warm-Up

The specific purpose of the *warm-up* is to prepare athletes for the program to follow. During the warm-up, body temperature is raised, which appears to be one of the main factors in facilitating performance. The warm-up stimulates the activity of the CNS, which coordinates all the systems of the body, speeds up motor reactions through faster transmission of nerve impulses, and improves coordination. Also, by elevating the body temperature, muscles, tendons, ligaments, and other tissues are warmed up and stretched, which prevents or reduces ligament sprains and tendon and muscle strains.

For strength training, the warm-up has two parts: *general warm-up* and *specific warm-up*. General warm-up (10 to 20 minutes) involves light jogging, cycling, or step-ups, followed by calisthenics and stretching exercises to increase blood flow, which raises the body temperature. This prepares the muscles and tendons for the planned program. During the warm-up, athletes should also prepare mentally for the main part of the training session by visualizing the exercises to be performed and motivating themselves for the eventual strain of training.

Specific warm-up (3 to 5 minutes) is a short transition to the working part of the session. By performing a few repetitions on the equipment to be used and employing much lighter loads than are planned for the day, athletes will be better prepared for a successful workout.

Main Part

The *main part* of the training session is dedicated to the actual training program, including strength training. In most sports, technical and tactical work are the main objectives of training, with strength development being a secondary priority. First-priority activities are thus performed immediately after the warm-up, followed by a certain type of strength training.

The succession of the types of training to be performed in a given day depends on the phase of training as well as its objectives. Table 5.1 on page 73 illustrates suggested options, where T stands for technical training, TA for tactical, MxS for maximum strength, P for power, SP for speed, END for endurance, and M-E for muscular endurance.

The combinations among the above options must be based on scientific principles, with the dominant energy systems in a given sport representing the fundamental guideline. Before discussing certain combinations for both the training session and the microcycle, however, it is important to remember the following:

Sprints are explosive power events of short duration.

• In short-duration (less than 10 to 15 seconds), explosive types of sports, power tends to be the important element of strength. These sports include sprinting, jumping, and throwing events in track and field; sprinting in cycling; tennis; ski jumping; free-style skiing; diving; pitching; batting; throwing in football; any take-off and quick changes of direction in team sports; and quick limb actions in boxing, wrestling, and the martial arts.

• Speed-endurance (15 to 40 seconds) of fast actions interspersed with quick changes of direction and jumps tend to rely on power-endurance. These include 50 to 100 meters in swimming; 200 to 400 meters in track and field; 500 meters in speed skating; tennis; figure skating; and many game elements in team sports.

• Prolonged activities performed against any type of resistance (ground, water, snow, ice, etc.) depend heavily on muscle endurance. These include team sports; rowing; swimming more than 100 meters; kayaking/canoeing; and Nordic skiing.

These types of activities and the types of strength required to be competitive illustrate the complexity of team sports and the necessity for exposing these athletes to P, P-E, and M-E.

Other important elements in planning the training session and microcycle include the complexities of training in many sports that require technical and tactical training, maximum speed, speed-endurance, and aerobic endurance, all of which tax different energy systems.

How can these components of training be combined without producing a high degree of fatigue, or without the adaptation of one element interfering with the needs of improving the others? There is only one answer, but with two parts:

1. Combine these training components so athletes tax only one energy system per day.

2. Alternate the energy systems in each microcycle so athletes train according to the prevailing energy system(s) in the particular sport.

The options proposed in table 5.1 are based on these principles. The alternations of different types of strength and energy systems are discussed under "The Microcycle" on page 74.

Training options	1	2	3	4
Sequence of types of training	Warm-up	Warm-up	Warm-up	Warm-up
	*T	*TA	*TA	*END
	*SP	*P-E	*M-E	*M-E
	*MxS/P	*M-E		

Table 5.1 Suggested Options for Training Sessions

In option 1 of table 5.1, the training elements in the given sport that are taxing the energy produced under the anaerobic alactic energy system are planned in the same workouts:

$$T + SP + MxS/P$$

Activities that require more nervous system concentration, mental focus, and thus a fresh mind have to be trained first (i.e., T and/or speed). Maximum speed should be trained before MxS because gains in MxS/P have been found to be more effective when preceded by a few short but maximum-velocity sprints (Baroga, 1978; Ozolin, 1971). Fox et al. (1989) also suggest that changes in the CNS act as stimuli for gains in strength. Display of the muscles' maximum potential is often limited by the inhibiting influence of proprioceptors such as the Golgi tendon organs. The CNS itself also seems to inhibit the activation of all the motor units available in a muscle or muscle group. To partially overcome this, the coach should plan work of maximum intensity in some workouts, which would have stimulating effects on training MxS and P.

Although table 5.1 is not exhaustive, it would hardly be advisable to perform power training such as plyometrics following END or M-E. An exhausted body is not able to perform quick and powerful muscle contractions. That is why the types of strength training (MxS and P) that require a high recruitment of FT muscle fibers are performed before endurance.

The duration of a strength training session depends on the importance of strength in the sport and on the training phase. During the preparatory phase, a strength training session can last 1 to 2 hours; in the competitive phase it is much shorter (30 to 45 minutes). The work is dedicated primarily to the maintenance of strength gained during the preparatory phase. Exceptions to this basic rule are made for throwers in track and field, linemen in football, and wrestlers in the heavyweight category, who require more time for strength training (1 to 1.5 hours).

The training proposed in option 1 (table 5.1) is applicable for sports such as football, baseball, sprinting, jumping and throwing events in track and field, diving, tennis, as well as other sports where anaerobic alactic can be planned on a given day of the week.

Option 2 is suggested for any sports where certain types of training that tax elements of endurance are important. Thus, TA, especially prolonged drills, can be followed by a combination of strength where a certain degree of endurance is used, either P-E or M-E. You will certainly notice the difference in physiological requirements between the first and second options. This difference is even more striking between the first option and the third and fourth options. In the case of option 3, TA of longer duration is combined with M-E, both of which tax anaerobic lactic and aerobic endurance.

Finally, the last example considers a sport where aerobic endurance is dominant. In such a case, M-E, which is of secondary importance to aerobic endurance, is trained at the end of the session.

Cool-Down

Whereas the warm-up serves as a transition from the normal biological state of daily activities to high-intensity training, the cool-down is a transition with the opposite effect of bringing the body back to its normal functions. During a cool-down of 10 to 20 minutes, athletes can perform certain activities that facilitate faster recovery and regeneration from the strains of training. With this purpose in mind, it would be inappropriate for athletes to leave for the showers immediately after the last exercise.

As a result of training, especially following intensive work, athletes build high amounts of lactic acid and their muscles are exhausted, tense, and rigid. To overcome this fatigue and speed up the recovery process, relaxation exercises should be performed (see chapter 13). The removal of lactic acid from the blood and muscles is also necessary if the effects of fatigue are to be eliminated quickly. This is best achieved by performing 15 to 20 minutes of light, continuous aerobic activity that causes the body to continue perspiring. This will remove about half of the lactic acid from the system, which helps athletes recover faster before the next training session.

The Microcycle

A microcycle is a weekly training program. It is probably the most important planning tool. Throughout the annual plan, the nature and dynamics of microcycles change according to the phase of training, the training objectives, and the physiological and psychological demands.

Load Increments per Macrocycle

The work in each macrocycle follows a step-type progression (figure 5.1). From an intensity standpoint, microcycles follow the principle of progressive increase of load in training.

As illustrated in figure 5.1, during the first three cycles, the load is progressively increased, followed by a regeneration cycle in which the load is decreased to facilitate recuperation and replenishment of energy before another macrocycle begins. Based on this model, a practical example has been produced (table 5.2) in which increments in load are suggested using the notation given in chapter 4.

By examining figure 5.1, you will see that the work, or the total load in training, is increased in steps, with the highest increase occurring in step 3. To increase the work from step to step, the instructor or coach has two options: increase the load or increase the number of sets from five in step 1 to seven in step 3 (as in table 5.2).

In table 5.2, both options were used at the same time. This approach can be changed to suit the needs of different classifications of athletes. The sample approach can be used for athletes with a good strength training background; young athletes will have difficulty tolerating a high number of sets. Young athletes should have a high number of exercises that will develop the entire muscular system and adapt the muscle attachments on the bones (tendons) to strength training. However, a high number of sets and exercises at the same time would be difficult to tolerate, so it is advisable to opt for a high number of exercises at the expense of the number of sets.

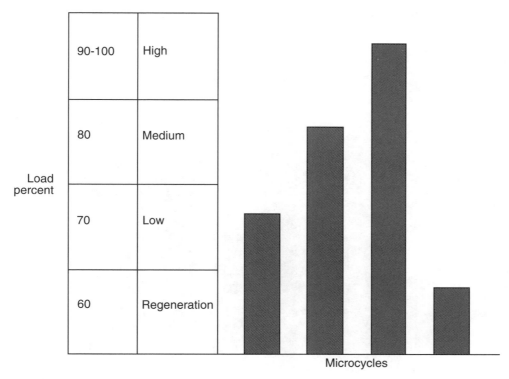

Figure 5.1 Dynamics of increasing the training load over four microcycles.

Table 5.2	Practical Example of Load Increments in Training (a Macrocycle)			
Training load	$\frac{70}{10}2\frac{80}{8}2\frac{85}{5}1$	$\frac{80}{9}2\frac{85}{5}2\frac{90}{3}2$	$\frac{85}{7}2\frac{90}{3}3\frac{95}{2}2$	$\frac{70}{10}4$
Step no.	1	2	3	4

Step 4 represents a regeneration cycle in which both the load and the number of sets are lowered to facilitate the removal of fatigue acquired during the firsts three steps, to replenish the energy stores, and to allow psychological relaxation. It is essential to mention that the load suggested in each microcycle refers to the work per day, which can be repeated two to four times per week depending on the training goals.

Load Increments per Microcycle

The work, or the total load per microcycle, is increased mainly by increasing the number of days of strength training per week. Remember that in athletics, strength training is subordinate to technical and tactical training. Consequently, the load of strength training per week should be calculated keeping in mind the overall volume and intensity of training.

Before discussing strength training options per microcycle, it is important to mention that the total work per week is also planned according to the

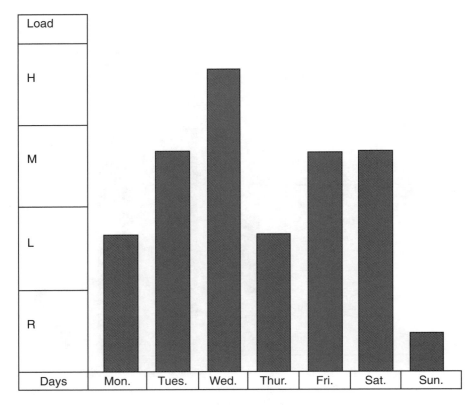

Figure 5.2   A low-intensity microcycle (first level in figure 3.4, page 34) with one high-intensity training day (H) and several medium- (M) and low- (L) intensity days. Sunday is a rest day (R).

principle of progressive increase of load in training. Figures 5.2 through 5.4 illustrate three microcycles, each of which is suggested for each of the conventional steps referred to above.

In most cases, strength training is planned on the same days as other activities such as technical or tactical work. Similarly, in the training session, a coach may plan to work on the development of certain physical qualities such as speed, strength, or endurance. So what is the best approach to consider in planning strength training per microcycle?

Microcycle Planning: Types of Strength and Restoration of Energy Systems

Some proponents suggest that strength training should be planned on "easy days." This makes some sense; however, from a physiological standpoint, this issue demands a more complex analysis.

To some extent, the majority of sports require training of most, if not all, the motor abilities of speed, strength, and endurance. Each ability uses and is dependent on a particular energy system, and the rate of recovery and restoration of the fuel used differs for each system. The restoration of glycogen, the main fuel for strength training, takes between 24 and 48 hours. Glycogen restoration after continuous intensive work is achieved in approximately 48 hours, whereas after intermittent activity such as strength train-

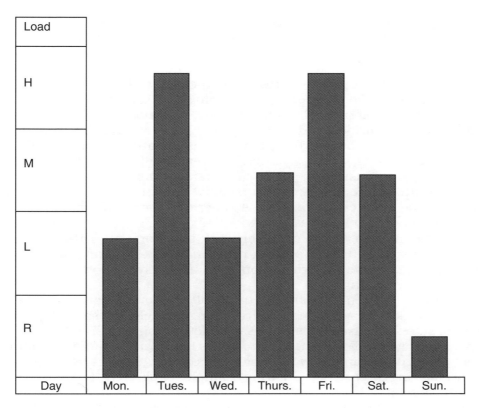

Figure 5.3 A medium-intensity microcycle (second level in figure 3.4, page 34).

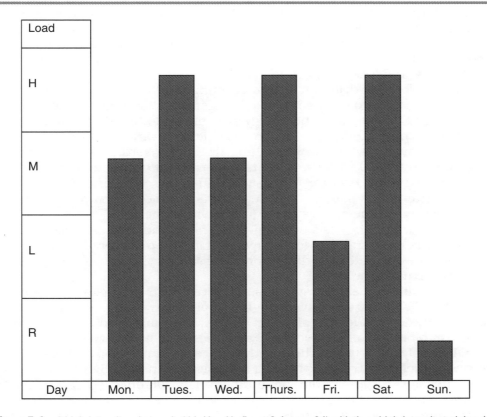

Figure 5.4 A high-intensity microcycle (third level in figure 3.4, page 34) with three high-intensity training days.

ing, it requires about 24 hours (Brooks et al., 1973; Fox et al., 1989). Following maximum-intensity training where the CNS is also taxed, it often takes up to 48 hours for complete restoration. The rate of regeneration from aerobic activities is much faster, approximately 8 hours. A quick restoration of energy stores also occurs as a result of so-called technical work, which is often of lower intensity. These types of training days can be considered "easy."

Let's assume that a coach plans intensive training sessions on Monday, Wednesday, and Friday and easy days on Tuesday and Thursday. Since there are 48 hours between the intensive days, and especially since this time includes an easy day, glycogen can reach full restoration before another planned intensive day. This can change drastically, however, if the coach schedules intensive strength training sessions on the easy days. In that case, the athletes are taxing the anaerobic energy system on the easy days as well as the intensive days, which taxes the glycogen every day, and the strength training represents an obstacle to restoration. This complicates the energy expenditure-restoration ratio and can also bring athletes to a state of fatigue and even exhaustion. And it is only a short step from exhaustion to overtraining.

Consequently, strength training must be planned on the same days as technical and tactical or speed and power training, namely, the same days as the glycogen stores are taxed. This results in athletes depleting all of their glycogen stores, but the overall training program does not interfere with its restoration before the next high-intensity training is scheduled 48 hours later.

The following three tables illustrate examples of planning types of strength training as related to other athletic activities and the dominant energy systems. Table 5.3 suggests a microcycle for speed-power sports (football, baseball, ice hockey, lacrosse, etc.) where energy systems are alternated. Note that strength training is consistently planned on days when other types of activities tax the same energy system. For instance, drills for speed training (SP), which tax the anaerobic alactic system, are followed by either power (P) or power-endurance (P-E) training. Also note that 2 days of anaerobic activities (Monday and Tuesday) are followed by a day when aerobic training is taxed in the form of drills for tempo running (400 to 600 yards at 60% of maximum speed, 4 to 6 repetitions) or longer duration tactical (TA) drills.

Table 5.4 illustrates how the energy systems and the specifics of strength could be alternated for a sport where aerobic endurance is dominant, such as rowing, kayaking/canoeing, cycling, triathlon, Nordic skiing, or swimming more than 400 meters. Each time aerobic endurance is trained, the only type of strength training proposed is muscular endurance (M-E). When anaerobic training is planned (Tuesday), it is followed by power-endurance (P-E), which taxes the same system (anaerobic lactic).

Note that two taxing days of training (Monday and Tuesday) are followed by a lighter aerobic training for compensation and to supercompensate the glycogen stores depleted the day before. The same approach is used again in the second part of the cycle.

The alternation of energy systems and strength training could follow the model of table 5.5 for sports with high-complexity training (technical, tactical, and physical), such as all team sports, the martial arts, and racquet sports. On Monday, all the proposed activities tax the anaerobic alactic system. Obviously, only two to three of the suggested training activities may be planned, which for strength training may mean either MxS or P.

On Tuesday, an anaerobic lactic day can be planned (TA and specific endurance training, SP-END). To tap the same energy system, the strength training program should consist of activities aimed at developing power-

Table 5.3	Alternation of Energy Systems and Types of Strength for Sports Where Speed and Power Are the Dominant Abilities (Precompetitive/Early Competitive Phases)				
Mon.	**Tues.**	**Wed.**	**Thurs.**	**Fri.**	**Sat.**
*T	*SP	*Tempo	*T	*SP	*Tempo
*MxS	*P/P-E	*TA	*MxS	P/P-E	*TA

Table 5.4	Alternation of Energy Systems and Types of Strength for Sports Where Aerobic Endurance Is Dominant (Precompetitive and Competitive Phases)				
Mon.	**Tues.**	**Wed.**	**Thurs.**	**Fri.**	**Sat.**
*Aerobic End.	*Anaerobic End.	*Aerobic End.	*Mixed Training	*Aerobic End.	*Aerobic End.
*M-E	*P-E	*Compensation	*P-E	*M-E	*Compensation

Table 5.5	Alternation of Energy Systems and Types of Strength for Team Sports (Preparatory and Precompetitive Phases)				
Mon.	**Tues.**	**Wed.**	**Thurs.**	**Fri.**	**Sat.**
*T	*TA	*T	*T/TA	*T/TA	*T/TA
*SP	*SP-END	*TA	*Anaerobic	*SP	*Aerobic
*MxS/P	*P-E		*MxS/P	*P-E	

endurance (P-E). Wednesday is a compensation day of less demanding T and TA. For the remaining three training days, two to three types of training activities, of which strength training is a part, must be selected.

Number of Strength Training Sessions per Microcycle

The number of strength training sessions per microcycle depends on the following:

• *Athlete's classification.* Young athletes should be progressively introduced to strength training. At first, they could be exposed to two short strength training sessions following technical or tactical work. Progressively over a period of 2 to 4 years, this could be increased to three to four sessions. Athletes competing at national or international competitions could take part in three to four strength training sessions, mainly during the preparatory phase.

• *Importance of strength in the chosen sport.* Based on the type of skills, energy requirements, and dominant abilities in a given sport, strength training can have a lower or higher importance. For a sport where aerobic endurance is clearly dominant, such as marathon running, strength is less important. On the other hand, in sports where power is dominant, such as football and throwing events, strength plays a predominant role. In the first example, one to two specific strength training sessions per week may suffice, whereas in the second example, training must occur at least four times per microcycle, especially during the preparatory/preseason phase.

• *Phase of training.* The number of strength training sessions depends on the phase of training: three to five during the preparatory phase and two to three during the competitive phase.

Some sports may have four strength training sessions per week, so some are performed on consecutive days. In such circumstances, coaches who are influenced by weight-lifting or bodybuilding concepts apply the so-called split routine, or train different body parts separately each day to achieve faster recovery. It must be reiterated that such influences are unacceptable in athletics. The reason weight lifters and bodybuilders use the split routine is because they train daily, and international-class lifters often train two to three times a day. They do nothing but "pump iron." It would be very difficult for them to train the same muscle groups in each training session, often 6 to 12 times per microcycle. These conditions would make it very hard for the muscles involved to recover between training sessions, so the split routine is incorporated.

This is not true for sports, where strength training is performed in addition to technical and tactical training. For maximum effectiveness, and for the most economical use of energy, strength training exercises must be selectively chosen to stress mainly the prime movers. To increase effectiveness, reduce strength training exercises for sports to the lowest level possible. The main benefit of doing so is that the number of sets can be increased and the prime movers can contract many times. The outcome is more power development for the required muscles.

The following example will better demonstrate the above premise. A coach designs a strength training program to make a ballplayer faster and selects three exercises for leg power (knee extensors, knee flexors, and toe raises), one each for the abdominals and back, and two for the arms and shoulders—seven exercises total. As anyone who understands physiology knows, you cannot be a fast runner without having strong knee extensors and flexors. Let's assume that this is the preparatory phase, and that the coach plans to have four strength training sessions per week, four sets, 8 repetitions, with a load of 100 kilograms (224 pounds) for 1 hour and 15 minutes. If the coach uses the split routine, the knee extensors and flexors will be trained as follows:

2 sessions per week × 4 sets × 8 repetitions × 100 kilograms (224 pounds) = 6,400 kilograms (14,336 pounds)

If, on the other hand, the coach decides that the split routine is not applicable to the athlete's needs, the result will be:

4 sessions per week × 4 sets × 8 repetitions × 100 kilograms (224 pounds) =
12,800 kilograms (28,672 pounds)

The difference between these two options is 6,400 kilograms (14,336 pounds)! The conclusion should be obvious—the split routine is impractical and inapplicable in strength training for sports.

chapter 6

The Yearly Training Plan: Periodization of Strength

The yearly training plan is as important a tool for achieving long-range athletic goals as the microcycle is for short-term planning. It must be based on the concept of Periodization of Strength and employ its training principles as guiding precepts. An organized and well-planned annual training program is a requirement for maximizing strength improvements.

A primary objective of training is for the athlete to reach peak performance at a specific time, usually for the main competition of the year. To achieve this high level of performance, the entire training program must be properly periodized and planned so that the development of skills and motor abilities proceeds logically and methodically throughout the year.

Periodization

Periodization comprises two basic components. The first component, periodization of the annual plan, pertains to how the year is divided into various training phases. The second component is the Periodization of Strength, or how to structure strength training to maximize its effectiveness in meeting the needs of the specific sport.

Periodization of the Annual Plan

The first component of periodization consists of breaking down the annual plan into shorter, more manageable training phases. Such division enhances the organization of training and allows the coach to conduct the program systematically. In most sports, the annual training cycle is divided into three main phases of training: preparatory (preseason), competitive (season), and transition (off-season). Each training phase is further subdivided into cycles, the most important being the microcycle. The duration of each training phase

Key Words

Atrophy: Gradual shrinking of muscle tissue from lack of strength training.

Conversion: Transformation of gains in maximum strength (MxS) into either power (P) or muscle-endurance (M-E).

Detraining: Reversal of adaptation to exercise. Its effects occur more rapidly than training gains, with significant reduction of strength (and work) capacity apparent within 2 weeks of cessation of training.

Power: Performance of work expressed per unit of time; a power exercise is fast, explosive.

The Annual Plan						
Phases of training	Preparatory			Competitive		Transition
Sub-phases	General preparation	Specific preparation	Pre-competitive	Competitive		Transition
Macro-cycles						
Micro-cycles						

Figure 6.1   Periodization of the annual plan (mono-cycle).

depends heavily on the competition schedule, as well as on the time needed to improve skills and to develop the dominant biomotor abilities. During the preparatory phase, the coach's primary objective is to develop the physiological foundations of the athletes, whereas during the competitive phase, it is to strive for perfection according to the specific demands of competition.

Figure 6.1 illustrates the periodization of the annual plan into phases and cycles of training. This particular plan has only one competitive phase, so athletes have to peak only once during the year. Such a plan is called a *mono-cycle* or *single-peak* annual plan. Not all sports have only one competitive phase. For example, track and field, swimming (in some countries), and several other sports have indoor and outdoor seasons or two major competitions for which athletes must peak. Such a plan is usually called a *bi-cycle* or *double-peak* annual plan (table 6.1).

Periodization of Strength

In planning, the coach should be more concerned with deciding what kind of physiological response or training adaptation will lead to the greatest improvements than with deciding what drills or skills to work on in a given training session or phase. Once the first decision is made, it will be easy to select the appropriate type of work that will result in the desired develop-

Table 6.1   Periodization of a Bi-Cycle Is Made Up of Two Preparatory (Prep. I and II), Two Competitive (Comp. I and II), and Two Transition (T and Trans.) Phases

The Annual Plan

Prep. I	Comp. I	T	Prep. II	Comp. II	Trans.

Table 6.2	Periodization of Strength for a Mono-Cycle (C = Cessation of Strength Training)				
Preparatory			**Competitive**		**Transition**
AA	MxS	Conversion to P/M-E	Maintenance of *P *M-E	C	Compensation Training

ment. Only by considering these overriding physiological factors will the coach be able to choose an approach that will result in the best training adaptation and ultimately lead to increases in physiological capacity and improved athletic performance. Such an innovative approach is facilitated by periodization. Recall from chapter 1 that the purpose of strength training for sports is not the development of strength for its own sake. Rather, the goal is to perfect either power (P), muscular endurance (M-E), or both according to the needs of each sport. The Periodization of Strength, with its specific sequence of training phases, is the best approach for achieving that goal, as will be demonstrated in this chapter. As illustrated by table 6.2, Periodization of Strength has certain phases with specific strength training objectives.

Phase One: Anatomical Adaptation Phase

Following a transition phase, during which athletes usually do very little strength training, it is scientifically and methodologically sound to start a strength program aimed at adapting the anatomy for the future strength program. The main objectives of this phase are to involve most muscle groups and to prepare the muscles, ligaments, tendons, and joints to endure the subsequent lengthy and strenuous training phases. Strength training programs should not focus on only the legs or arms. Focus on strengthening the core area—the abdominals, lower back, and spinal column musculature. These sets of muscles work together to ensure that the trunk supports the legs and arms during all movements and also act as a shock-absorbing device for many skills and exercises, especially landing and falling.

When preparing athletes, especially young ones, for the strength training phases to follow, start from the core section of the body and work toward the extremities. In other words, before strengthening the legs and arms, concentrate on developing the supporting links between them—the spinal column and the trunk in general.

Additional objectives for anatomical adaptation (AA) are to balance strength between the flexors and extensors surrounding each joint; balance the two sides of the body, especially the shoulders and arms; perform compensation work for the antagonistic muscles; and strengthen the stabilizer muscles (see "Exercise Prescription" in chapter 4).

In many cases, athletes tend to overwork areas that are already strong by performing only exercises they know well. They avoid working on weaker areas or performing exercises at which they are not as proficient. To compound the problem, some coaches and instructors, through either misunderstanding or misapplying the principle of specificity, prescribe only exercises specific to the skills the athletes use most in the selected sport. Consequently, a balanced development between body parts or muscle groups is rarely achieved.

In some cases, balanced development between agonistic and antagonistic muscles is impossible because some agonistic muscles are larger and stronger than others. For instance, the knee extensors (quadriceps) are stronger than the knee flexors (hamstrings). The same is true for the ankle plantar flexor (gastrocnemius) and extensors (tibialis anterior). Since activities such as running and jumping are heavily involved in most sports, the knee extensors and ankle plantar flexors are exposed to more training. It is important, however, for professionals in the field to be aware of the agonistic-antagonistic ratios and attempt to maintain them through training. If they neglect to do so, and the agonists, the prime movers of given sports skills, are constantly trained, the imbalance will likely result in injuries (for example, rotator cuff injuries in baseball).

The transition and anatomical adaptation phases are ideal for balanced development of antagonistic muscles since there is no pressure due to competition. Little information exists regarding the agonistic-antagonistic ratios, especially for the high-speed limb movements typical of sports. Table 6.3 provides some information on the subject, but for low, isokinetic speeds. This information should only be used as a guideline in trying to maintain these ratios, at least for anatomical adaptation and transition.

Throughout the AA phase, the goal is to involve most, if not all, muscle groups in a multilateral-type program. Such a program should include a high number of exercises (9 to 12) performed comfortably without "pushing" the athletes. Remember, vigorous strength training always develops the strength of the muscles faster than the strength of the muscle attachments (tendons) and joints (ligaments). Consequently, such programs can often result in injuries to these tissues.

When large muscle groups are weak, the small muscles have to take over the strain of the work. As a result, the small muscle groups may injure more quickly. Other injuries occur because undertrained muscles lack the force to control landings, absorb shock, and balance the body quickly to be ready to perform another action (not because of a lack of landing skills).

Table 6.3	Agonist-Antagonist Ratios for Slow Concentric Isokinetic Movements	
Joint	**Strength training**	**Ratio**
Ankle	Plantar flexion/dorsiflexion (gastrocnemius, soleus/tibialis anterior)	3:1
Ankle	Inversion/eversion (tibialis anterior/peroneals)	1:1
Knee	Extension/flexion (quadriceps/hamstrings)	3:2
Hip	Extension/flexion (spinal erectors, gluteus maximus, hamstrings/iliopsoas, rectus abdominis, tensor fascia latae)	1:1
Shoulder	Flexion/extension (anterior deltoids/trapezius, posterior deltoids)	2:3
Shoulder	Internal rotation/external rotation (subscapularis/supraspinatus, infraspinatus, teres minor)	3:2
Elbow	Flexion/extension (biceps/triceps)	1:1
Lumbar spine	Flexion/extension (iliopsoas, abdominals/spinal erectors)	1:1

From Dan Wathen, 1994. In Baechle, T.R. (Ed.) *Essentials of Strength Training and Conditioning*. Champaign, IL: Human Kinetics.

The duration of the AA phase depends on the length of the preparatory phase, the athletes' background in strength training, and the importance of strength in the given sport. A long preparatory phase allows more time. Athletes who have a weak strength training background logically require a much longer AA. This allows progressive adaptation to training loads and, at the same time, improves the ability of muscle tissue and muscle attachments to withstand the heavier loads of the following phases. Finally, compared to sports where strength training is less important (such as marathon running), a well-planned and longer AA will influence the final performance and hopefully produce injury-free athletes. For young, inexperienced athletes, 8 to 10 weeks of AA are necessary. Mature athletes with 4 to 6 years of strength training require no more than 3 to 5 weeks of AA. For these athletes, an AA phase any longer than this will likely have no significant training effect.

Phase Two: Maximum Strength Phase

The main objective of this phase is to develop the highest level of force possible. Most sports require either power (long jump), muscular endurance (800- to 1500-meter swimming), or both (rowing, canoeing, wrestling, and team sports). Each of these types of strength is affected by the level of MxS. Without a high level of MxS, P cannot reach high levels. Since P is the product of speed and MxS, it is logical to develop MxS first, then convert it to P. During this phase, the objective is to develop MxS to the highest level of the athletes' capacity.

The duration of this phase, from 1 to 3 months, is a function of the sport or event and the athletes' needs. A shot-putter or football player may need a lengthy phase of 3 months, whereas an ice hockey player may need only 1-2 months to develop this type of strength. Since the load is normally increased in three steps, the duration of the maximum strength phase must be a multiple of 3. Based on these examples, a shot-putter or lineman may need 9, 12, or 15 weeks of MxS, but a hockey or soccer player may only need 6 to 9 weeks. The duration of this phase also depends on whether athletes follow a mono- or a bi-cycle annual plan. For obvious reasons, young athletes may have a shorter maximum strength phase, with loads below maximum.

Phase Three: Conversion Phase

The main purpose of this phase is to convert or transform gains in MxS into competitive, sport-specific combinations of strength. Depending on the characteristics of the sport or event, MxS must be converted to a type of either P or M-E, or both. By applying an adequate training method for the type of strength sought and using training methods specific to the selected sport (for example, speed training), MxS is gradually converted. Throughout this phase, depending on the needs of the sport and the athletes, a certain level of MxS must be maintained, or toward the end of the competitive phase, P may slightly decline (detraining). This is certainly the case for professional football and baseball players, because each of these sports has such a long season.

For sports where P or M-E is the dominant strength, the appropriate method must be dominant in training. When both P and M-E are required, the training time and method(s) should adequately reflect the optimal ratio between these two abilities. For instance, for a wrestler, the ratio should be almost equal; for a canoeist's 500-meter program, P should dominate; and for a rower, M-E should prevail. For team sports, the martial arts, wrestling, boxing, and most other power-dominant sports, plan exercises that lead to the development of agility and quick reaction and movement times before or during the conversion phase. Only this type of approach will prepare the athletes for the sport-specific requirements of competitions.

The duration of the conversion phase depends on which ability must be developed. For conversion to P, 4 to 5 weeks of specific power training is sufficient. On the other hand, conversion to M-E requires as many as 6 to 8 weeks because the physiological and anatomical adaptation to such demanding work takes much longer.

Phase Four: Maintenance Phase

The tradition in many sports is to eliminate strength training when the competitive season starts. However, if strength training is not maintained during the competitive phase, athletes will be exposed to a *detraining effect* with the following repercussions:

- Muscle fibers decrease to their pretraining size (Staron et al., 1981; Thorstensson, 1977).

- Some detraining effects can be observed after just 5 to 6 days. Detraining becomes more evident after 2 weeks because skills requiring strength are not performed as proficiently (Bompa, 1993a).

- Loss of power due to decreases in motor recruitment becomes more visible. The body fails to recruit the same number of motor units as it once could, so there is a net decrease in the amount of force that can be generated (Edgerton, 1976; Hainaut & Duchatteau, 1989; Houmard, 1991).

- Speed decreases followed by power, since muscle tension depends on the force and speed of stimuli and firing rate.

As the term suggests, the main objective of strength training for this phase is to maintain the standards achieved during the previous phases. Once again, the program followed during this phase is a function of the specific requirements of the sport. The ratios among MxS, P, and M-E have to reflect such requirements. For instance, a shot-putter may plan two sessions for MxS and two for P, whereas a jumper may consider one and three, respectively. Similarly, a 100-meter swimmer may plan one session for MxS, two for P, and one for M-E, whereas a 1,500-meter swimmer may dedicate the entire strength program to perfecting M-E. For team sports, ratios should be calculated according to the role of strength in the particular sport, as well as being position specific. For instance, a pitcher should perform MxS, P, and power-endurance equally, and compensation work should be considered to avoid injuries of the rotator cuff. Distinctions should be made between linemen and wide receivers in football and sweepers, midfielders, and forwards in soccer. Linemen should spend equal time on MxS and P, and wide receivers only need to perform P; soccer players have to maintain both power and power-endurance.

The number of sessions dedicated to maintenance of the required strength must be between two and four, depending on the athletes' level of performance and the role played by strength in the skill and performance. Considering the objectives of the competitive phase, the time allocated to the maintenance of strength is secondary. Therefore, the coach has to develop a very efficient and specific program. Two to a maximum of four exercises involving the prime movers may suffice to maintain previously reached strength levels. At the same time, the duration of each strength training session must be short, 30 to 60 minutes. The strength training program should end at least 5 to 7 days before the main competition of the year. The purpose of this *cessation phase (C)* is to conserve energy for the competition.

Phase Five: Transition Phase

Traditionally, the last phase of the annual plan has been inappropriately called the "off-season," but in reality it represents a transition from one annual plan to another. The main goal of this phase is to remove the fatigue acquired during the training year and replenish the exhausted energy stores by decreasing volume and especially intensity. Furthermore, during the months of training and competition, most athletes are exposed to numerous psychological and social stressors that drain their mental energies. During the transition phase, athletes have time to relax psychologically by being involved in various physical and social activities that are enjoyable.

For serious athletes, the duration of this phase should be no longer than 4 to 6 weeks, or many fitness benefits will diminish. Athletes work hard to make gains in skill, general fitness, and strength. If a longer off-season is considered, athletes will experience detraining effects resulting in the loss of most training gains and deteriorating most of the strength gains. Therefore, athletes and coaches should remember that strength "is hard to gain and easy to lose."

If athletes do not perform any strength training at all during the transition phase, muscles may decrease in size, resulting in considerable power loss (Wilmore & Costill, 1988). Since power and speed are interdependent, loss of speed will also occur. Some authors claim that the disuse of muscles also reduces the frequency of neuromuscular stimulation and the pattern of muscle fiber recruitment; thus, strength loss may be the result of not activating some muscle fibers.

Although physical activity is reduced by 60 to 70 percent during the transition phase, athletes should still find the time to work on antagonistic, stabilizer, and other muscles that may not necessarily be involved in the performance of a skill. Similarly, compensation exercises should be planned for sports where an imbalance may develop between parts or sides of the body, such as in pitching, throwing events, archery, soccer (work upper body), and cycling.

Detraining

Improvement or maintenance of a desired level of strength is possible only if an adequate load or training intensity is constantly administered. When strength training is decreased or ceased, as often happens during competitive or long transition phases, there is a disturbance in the biological state of the muscle cells and bodily organs. As a result, there is a marked decrease in athletes' physiological well-being and work output (Fry et al., 1991; Kuipers & Keizer, 1988).

Decreased or diminished training can leave athletes vulnerable to the "detraining syndrome" (Israel, 1972) or "exercise-dependency syndrome" (Kuipers & Keizer, 1988). The severity of strength loss depends on the time elapsed between training sessions. Many organic and cellular adaptation benefits may be degraded, including the increments of the protein content of myosin.

When training proceeds as planned, the body uses protein to build and repair damaged tissues. When the body is in a state of disuse, it begins to catabolize or break down protein because it is no longer needed for tissue repair (Appell, 1990; Edgerton, 1976). As this process of protein degradation continues, some of the gains made during training are reversed. Testosterone levels, which are important for strength gains, have also been shown to decrease as a result of detraining, which may diminish the amount of protein synthesis (Houmard, 1991).

A rise in psychological disturbances such as headaches, insomnia, a feeling of exhaustion, increased tension, increased mood disturbances, lack of appetite, and psychological depression are among the usual symptoms associated with total abstinence from training. Individual athletes may develop any one or a combination of these symptoms. In any case, these symptoms all have to do with lowered levels of testosterone and beta-endorphin, a neuroendocrine compound that is the main forerunner of euphoric postexercise feelings (Houmard, 1991).

These symptoms are not pathological and can be reversed if training resumes shortly. If training is discontinued for a prolonged period, however, athletes may display these symptoms for some time. This indicates the inability of the human body and its systems to adapt to the state of inactivity. The length of time needed for these symptoms to incubate varies from athlete to athlete, but they generally appear after 2 to 3 weeks of inactivity and vary in severity.

The decrease in the muscle fiber cross-sectional area is quite apparent after several weeks of inactivity. These changes are the result of protein breakdown, as well as a reduction in the recruitment pattern of the working muscle. The increased levels of some chemicals (Na^+ and Cl^-) in the muscle play a role in the breakdown of muscle fiber (Appell, 1990).

The general trend toward muscle fiber degeneration is partly due to degeneration of the motor units, in which ST fibers are usually the first to lose their ability to produce force. FT fibers are generally least affected by inactivity. This is not to say that atrophy does not occur in these fibers—it just takes a little longer than in ST fibers. For inactive athletes, the rate of strength loss per day can be roughly 3 to 4 percent in the first week (Appell, 1990). For some athletes, especially in power-speed-dominant sports, this can be a substantial loss.

Speed tends to be the first ability affected by detraining, since the breakdown of protein and the degeneration of motor units decreases the power capabilities of muscle contraction. Speed loss may also be due to the nervous system's sensitivity to detraining. Since the motor unit itself is the first thing to deteriorate, the reduction in nerve impulses in the muscle fiber make it contract and relax at very rapid rates. The strength and frequency of these impulses can also be affected by decreases in the total number of motor units recruited during a series of repeated contractions (Edgerton, 1976; Hainaut & Duchatteau, 1989; Houmard, 1991). As a result of diminished motor recruitment patterns, the loss in power becomes more pronounced. The body fails to recruit the number of motor units it once could, resulting in a net decrease in the amount of force generated.

Variations of Periodization of Strength

The Periodization of Strength example presented earlier in this chapter, as well as in table 6.1 (page 84), was helpful for illustrating the basic concept, but it cannot serve as a model for every situation or every sport. Each individual or group of athletes requires specific treatment based on training background, specific characteristics of the sports and events, as well as gender differences. Thus, it was necessary to develop the following section on variations of Periodization, with follow-up illustrations of specific Periodization models for sports and events.

Certain sports and certain positions in team sports require strength and heavy mass. For instance, it is advantageous for throwers in some track-and-field events, linemen in football, and heavyweight wrestlers or boxers to be both heavy and powerful. These athletes would follow a unique Periodization model with a phase of training planned to develop hypertrophy (see chapter 8). By developing hypertrophy first, strength potential seems to increase faster, especially if it is followed by MxS and P development phases. The latter are known to stimulate motor unit activation and to increase the recruitment of FT muscle fibers.

Table 6.4 suggests a Periodization model for heavy and powerful athletes such as throwers, linemen in football, and heavyweight wrestlers and boxers. After the traditional anatomical adaptation (AA), there is a phase of hypertrophy (Hyp.) of at least 6 weeks, followed by MxS and conversion to power (Conv. to P). To meet the needs of the above athletes, during the maintenance phase, time should be equally dedicated to preserving P and MxS. The yearly plan concludes with compensation training specific to the transition phase.

For the same types of sports, the preparatory phase can sometimes be very long (for example, U.S. and Canadian college football), and the coach may decide to build even more muscle mass. Another model can be followed for these situations (table 6.5) in which phases of hypertrophy are alternated with phases of MxS. Note that the numbers above each phase in table 6.5 and some of the following tables indicate the duration of that phase in weeks.

Although strength training patterns for female athletes are similar, during long phases of MxS, females need more individual variation, more frequent changes, and shorter phases. Table 6.6 illustrates such a periodization in which the preparatory phase is longer. This assumes either a summer sport (track,

Table 6.4 Periodization Model for Athletes Requiring Hypertrophy

Preparatory				Competitive	Transition
AA	Hyp.	MxS	Conv. to P	Maintenance: *Power *MxS	Compen.

Table 6.5 Variation of Periodization for Development of Hypertrophy and MxS

Preparatory									Competitive	Transition
3 AA	7 Hyp.	6 MxS	3 H	3 MxS	3 H	3 MxS	3 Conv. to P	Maintenance: P/MxS		Compen.

Table 6.6	Hypothetical Periodization for Athletes Who Might Require More Frequent Alternations of Training Phases								
Preparatory								**Competitive**	**Transition**
7 AA	6 MxS	3 P	3 MxS	3 P	3 MxS	4 Conv. to P		16 Maintenance: P	6 Compen.

rugby, field hockey, some positions in football) or a sport played during winter and early spring (volleyball), accounting for the long preparatory phase.

For power-dominated sports, similar variations of P and MxS phases are necessary since gains in power are faster if muscles are trained at various speeds of contraction (Bührle, 1985; Bührle & Schmidtbleicher, 1981). In addition, both P and MxS train the FT fibers, resulting in more effective recruitment of these fibers that are determinant in the production and display of MxS and P. This type of periodization is superior to the traditional "work to exhaustion" method proposed by coaches influenced by bodybuilding. Lots of pain does *not* result in power gain because it does not train the nervous system to improve synchronization and quick recruitment of FT fibers. The outcome is large increments in MxS and P.

The alternation of MxS and P phases also changes the pattern of motor recruitment, which results in higher CNS stimulation, especially during the P phase or when the load for MxS is greater than 85 percent. For the development of MxS, maximum loads used with eccentric contraction and explosive power exercises, such as high-impact plyometrics, result in recruitment of more FT fibers, which is the greatest benefit to the athletes.

A CNS stimulus occurs only in the early stages of long phases of MxS. If the same methods and loading pattern are maintained for longer than 2 months, especially for athletes with a strong strength training background, the pattern of fiber recruitment becomes standard, eventually reaching a plateau. No drastic improvements can be expected. The employment of submaximum loading will definitely not stimulate the FT muscle fibers or result in the development of MxS and P. For sports where speed and power are dominant abilities, bodybuilding methods defeat their purpose. That explains why several of the tables in this chapter propose alternations of MxS and P phases. Also, the importance of MxS phases should not be underestimated, since any deterioration in MxS would affect the ability to maintain power at the desired level throughout the competitive phase. In sports where athletes have to peak twice a year, such as swimming, track and field, and the like, a bi-cycle annual plan is followed. Table 6.7 illustrates the Periodization of Strength for a double-peak (bi-cycle) annual plan.

Similarly, some sports have three main competitions, so athletes have to peak three times a year. The annual plan for such sports is called a tri-cycle plan and is often followed by athletes in wrestling, boxing, and the martial arts. Table 6.8 offers a Periodization model for a tri-cycle plan.

For sports with a long preparatory phase, such as softball, football, and track cycling, table 6.9 shows a unique periodization option. It was developed at the request of a football coach who wanted to improve his players' MxS and P. I suggested the coach follow a periodization with two peaks: an "artificial peak" and a real peak (the football season). In testing with both the football

Table 6.7 Periodization of Strength for a Bi-Cycle

Oct.	Nov.	Dec.	Jan.	Feb.	Mar.	Apr.	May	Jun.	Jul.	Aug.	Sep.
Prep. I			Comp. I		T	Prep. II		Comp. II		T	
AA	MxS		Conv. to P	Maint.	AA	MxS		Conv. to P	Maint.	Compen.	

Table 6.8 Hypothetical Periodization of Strength for a Tri-Cycle

Sep.	Oct.	Nov.	Dec.	Jan.	Feb.	Mar.	Apr.	May	Jun.	Jul.	Aug.
Prep. I		Comp. I	T	Prep. II	Comp. II		T	Prep. III	Comp. III		T
AA	MxS	P/M-E	AA	MxS	P/M-E		AA	MxS	P/M-E		Compen.

Table 6.9 Double-Peak Periodization in Which Peak Performance Was Achieved at the End of April ("Artificial Peak") and in the Fall

Dec.	Jan.	Feb.	Mar.	Apr.	May	Jun.	Jul.	Aug.	Sep.	Oct.	Nov.
Preparatory								Competitive		Transition	
AA	MxS		Conv. to P	T	AA	MxS		Conv. to P	Maint.: P/MxS	Compen.	

players and sprinters in cycling, this double-peak periodization was very successful, with all athletes increasing their MxS and P to the highest level ever. This new approach for a typical mono-cycle sport was based on the following:

- A very long preparatory phase with training methods that used heavy loading and had little variety was considered too stressful and thus had dubious physiological incentive.
- A double-peak periodization has the advantage of planning two phases for MxS and two for P. (Linemen followed a slightly different approach with hypertrophy training incorporated into the MxS phase.) The benefits were what the coach had expected: increase in overall muscle mass, increase in maximum strength, and the highest level of power ever achieved by his players.

Periodization Models for Sports

To make this book more practical and more applicable, several sport-specific Periodization models for strength are included. To better understand their physiological implications for each sport, three factors are listed before each Periodization model is presented:

- The *dominant energy system(s)* for the sport
- *Limiting factor(s)* for performance from the strength training standpoint
- *Training objective(s)*

For training purposes, the energy systems should be linked to the limiting factors for strength. Doing so will make it relatively easy to decide the strength training objectives. For instance, for sports in which the anaerobic alactic system is dominant, the limiting factor for performance is power. On the other hand, where the lactic acid or aerobic system is dominant, such sports always require a certain component of M-E. In this way, the coach can better train the athletes physiologically and, as a result, improve performance. For example, increments in power should never be expected if bodybuilding methods are applied. The phrase "limiting factors for performance" means that the desired performance will not be achieved unless they are developed at the highest possible level. A low level of development of the sport-specific combination of strength will limit or hinder the achievement of a good performance.

The following examples cannot cover all variations possible for each sport. To develop such a model, one would have to know the exact competition schedule a coach has selected. Thus, for sports such as track and field (athletics) and swimming, the Periodization models are designed around the main competitions in winter and summer. Examples are also given for certain positions in team sports (e.g., football and soccer) without exhausting every possibility.

Athletics (track and field)

Sprinting

A sprinter requires explosive speed and long, powerful strides. Endurance is not as important a consideration as acceleration since the sprinter needs to move quickly over a short distance.

- Dominant energy systems: anaerobic alactic and lactic
- Limiting factors: reactive power, starting power, acceleration power, P-E
- Training objectives: MxS, reactive power, starting power, acceleration power, P-E

Model for Sprints (Specific P = Those Listed Above Under "Limiting Factors")

Oct.	Nov.	Dec.	Jan.	Feb.	Mar.	Apr.	May	Jun.	Jul.	Aug.	Sep.
Prep. I				Comp. I		T	Prep. II		Comp. II		Transition
5 AA	6 MxS		4 Conv. to P	10 Maintenance: improve P/ specific P		2 AA	5 MxS	4 Conv. to P	9 Maintenance: improve P/ specific P		6 Compen.

Model for Long Jumps

Oct.	Nov.	Dec.	Jan.	Feb.	Mar.	Apr.	May	Jun.	Jul.	Aug.	Sep.
Prep. I				Comp. I		T	Prep. II		Comp. II		Transition
5 AA	6 MxS		4 Conv. to P	10 Maintenance: MxS, P		2 AA	5 MxS	4 Conv. to P	9 Maintenance: P		6 Compen.

Shot Put

Training for the shot put event in track and field requires hypertrophy, maximum strength, and power phases. Dominant muscular strength in the legs, torso, and arms is required to generate maximum throwing power and acceleration of the shot.

- Dominant energy system: anaerobic alactic
- Limiting factors: throwing power, reactive power
- Training objectives: MxS, throwing power, reactive power

Model for Shot Put

Oct.	Nov.	Dec.	Jan.	Feb.	Mar.	Apr.	May	Jun.	Jul.	Aug.	Sep.
Prep. I			Comp. I			T	Prep. II	Comp. II			Transition
3 AA	5 Hyp.	6 MxS Hyp.	3 Conv. to P	8 Maint.: MxS, Hyp., improve P		2 AA	3 Hyp.	4 MxS, Hyp. / 2 Conv. to P	10 Maint.: MxS, improve P		6 Compen.

Note: Hypertrophy training follows AA and must be maintained in some places, but at a ratio of 3 MxS to 1 hypertrophy.

Baseball/Softball (elite and amateur)

The pre-competitive phase elite baseball players face restricts the amount of preparation time, and their long competition schedule can lead to fatigue or injury. Maintaining power and maximum strength will help players succeed through the season.

- Dominant energy system: anaerobic alactic
- Limiting factors: throwing power, acceleration power
- Training objectives: MxS, throwing power, acceleration power

Model for an Elite Baseball Team

Dec.	Jan.	Feb.	Mar.	Apr.	May	Jun.	Jul.	Aug.	Sep.	Oct.	Nov.
Preparatory			Precomp.	Competitive							Transition
4 AA	6 MxS		4 Conv. to P	Maintenance: P, P-E							Compen.

Since the competition phase is very long, detraining of strength may occur. Therefore, players must maintain P and, as much as possible, MxS as well.

Model for an Amateur Baseball or Softball Team

Nov.	Dec.	Jan.	Feb.	Mar.	Apr.	May	Jun.	Jul.	Aug.	Sep.	Oct.
Preparatory						Competitive				Transition	
4 AA	6 MxS	3 P	3 MxS	3 P	3 MxS	4 Conv. to P	Maintenance			Compen.	

Note: Alternation of MxS with P phases for maximum gains in power.

Basketball (elite and college)

Basketball demands that players be strong, quick, and agile. Joint and tendon injuries are very common. Proper strength training prepares a basketball player for the rigors of the season.

- Dominant energy systems: anaerobic lactic and aerobic
- Limiting factors: takeoff power, acceleration power, P-E
- Training objectives: MxS, takeoff power, acceleration power, P-E

Model for an Elite Basketball Team

Aug.	Sep.	Oct.	Nov.	Dec.	Jan.	Feb.	Mar.	Apr.	May	Jun.	Jul.
Preparatory			Competitive							Transition	
3 AA	6 MxS	3 Conv. to P	Maintenance: P, P-E							Compen.	

Model for a College Basketball Team

Jul.	Aug.	Sep.	Oct.	Nov.	Dec.	Jan.	Feb.	Mar.	Apr.	May	Jun.
Preparatory				Competitive						Transition	
6 AA		6 MxS	4 Conv. to P	Maintenance: P, P-E						Compen.	

Boxing

Boxers must be able to react quickly and powerfully to an opponent's attack. Both aerobic and anaerobic energy is used during a bout and should be trained.

- Dominant energy systems: anaerobic lactic and aerobic
- Limiting factors: P-E, reactive power, M-E medium, M-E long (professional boxers)
- Training objectives: P-E, reactive power, M-E medium and long

Model for Boxing (Spec. Prep. = Specific Preparatory for a Match, M = Match)											
Sep.	**Oct.**	**Nov.**	**Dec.**	**Jan.**	**Feb.**	**Mar.**	**Apr.**	**May**	**Jun.**	**Jul.**	**Aug.**
Prep.		Spec. prep.	M T	Prep.	Spec. prep.	M	T	Prep.	Spec. prep.	M	Transition
3 AA	3 MxS	3 Conv. to P	6 Maint.: P/M-E	2 AA	3 MxS	3 Conv. to P	7 Maint.: P/M-E	2 AA	3 MxS	3 Conv. to P / 8 Maint. P/M-E	Compen.

Note: MxS at 68 to 80 percent of 1RM.

Canoeing/Kayaking

Terry Wild Studio/© 1996 Jim Airgood

500 and 1,000 meters

Flatwater sprints are all about speed and specific endurance. The racer must be able to quickly pull the paddle against the resistance of the water to move quickly to the finish line.

- Dominant energy systems: anaerobic alactic and lactic, aerobic
- Limiting factors: starting power, MxS, P-E
- Training objectives: starting power, P-E, MxS, M-E short and medium

Model for Canoeing/Kayaking (500 and 1,000 Meters)

Oct.	Nov.	Dec.	Jan.	Feb.		Mar.	Apr.	May	Jun.	Jul.	Aug.	Sep.
Preparatory									Competitive			Transition
5 AA	6 MxS		4 P	1 T	3 MxS	3 P	3 MxS		8 Conv. to P	13 Maintenance: P		6 Compen.

Marathon

As opposed to sprints, marathon races require muscular endurance-long. In addition, the racer must have a well-developed aerobic energy system to endure the length of the race.

- Dominant energy system: aerobic
- Limiting factor: M-E long
- Training objectives: M-E long, P-E

Model for Canoeing/Kayaking (Marathon)

Nov.	Dec.	Jan.	Feb.	Mar.	Apr.	May	Jun.	Jul.	Aug.	Sep.	Oct.
Preparatory						Competitive					Transition
6 AA	6 MxS	3 P	3 MxS		Conv. to M-EL	9	Maintenance: P				Compen.

Cycling (road racing)

Road racing overwhelms the aerobic system. Cyclist must be prepared to work hard over a long distance, generating constant rotations per minute to maintain speed and power against the resistance of the pedals, environment, and terrain.

- Dominant energy system: aerobic
- Limiting factors: M-E long, acceleration power, P-E
- Training objectives: M-E long, P-E, acceleration power

Model for Road Racing											
Nov.	Dec.	Jan.	Feb.	Mar.	Apr.	May	Jun.	Jul.	Aug.	Sep.	Oct.
Preparatory						Competitive					Transition
4 AA	6 MxS		6 M-EL		3 MxS	9 Conv. to M-EL	Maintenance: P				Compen.

Figure Skating

Figure skaters must develop powerful takeoff and landing (eccentric) strength to be able to complete the required jumps. Strong anaerobic and aerobic energy systems are also required, especially for long programs.

- Dominant energy systems: anaerobic lactic and aerobic
- Limiting factors: takeoff power, landing power, P-E
- Training objectives: takeoff power, landing power, MxS

Model for Figure Skating

May	Jun.	Jul.	Aug.	Sep.	Oct.	Nov.	Dec.	Jan.	Feb.	Mar.	Apr.
Preparatory							Competitive				Transition
11 AA		3 MxS	3 P	3 MxS	4 P/P-E	3 MxS	6 Conv. to P/P-E		10 Maintenance		7 Compen.

Note: Alternation of phases for MxS with P/P-E.

Football (elite and college)

Linemen

Linemen must be able to react explosively when the ball is put into play and withstand the opponent's strength. A hypertrophy phase is included to build bulk.

- Dominant energy systems: anaerobic alactic and lactic
- Limiting factors: starting power, reactive power
- Training objectives: MxS, hypertrophy, starting power, reactive power

© 1994 Beth Schneider

Model for Linemen in Elite Football

Apr.	May	Jun.	Jul.	Aug.	Sep.	Oct.	Nov.	Dec.	Jan.	Feb.	Mar.
Preparatory				Competitive							Transition
4 AA	6 Hyp.		6 MxS	4 Conv. to P	Maintenance: MxS, P						6 Compen.

Model for Linemen in College Football

Mar.	Apr.	May	Jun.	Jul.	Aug.	Sep.	Oct.	Nov.	Dec.	Jan.	Feb.
Preparatory						Competitive					Transition
4 AA	6 Hyp.		9 MxS	4 Conv. to P		Maintenance: MxS, P					7 Compen.

Wide Receivers, Defensive Backs, Tailbacks

Unlike linemen, wide receivers, defensive backs, and tailbacks require speed and agility rather than muscular bulk.

- Dominant energy systems: anaerobic alactic and lactic
- Limiting factors: acceleration power, reactive power, starting power
- Training objectives: acceleration power, reactive power, starting power, MxS

Model for Wide Receivers, Defensive Backs, and Tailbacks in Elite Football

Apr.	May	Jun.	Jul.	Aug.	Sep.	Oct.	Nov.	Dec.	Jan.	Feb.	Mar.
Preparatory					Competitive						Transition
4 AA	3 MxS	2 P	3 MxS	2 P	3 MxS	4 Conv. to P	Maintenance: P				6 Compen.

Model for Wide Receivers, Defensive Backs, and Tailbacks in College Football

Mar.	Apr.	May	Jun.	Jul.	Aug.	Sep.	Oct.	Nov.	Dec.	Jan.	Feb.
Preparatory						Competitive					Transition
4 AA	3 MxS	3 P	3 MxS	3 P	3 MxS	4 Conv. to P	Maintenance: P				7 Compen.

Ice Hockey

Acceleration and quick changes of direction are important elements of ice hockey. Training should focus on refining skills and developing power and aerobic and anaerobic endurance.

- Dominant energy systems: anaerobic lactic and aerobic
- Limiting factors: acceleration power, deceleration power, P-E
- Training objectives: MxS, acceleration power, deceleration power, P-E

Model for Ice Hockey											
Jun.	Jul.	Aug.	Sep.	Oct.	Nov.	Dec.	Jan.	Feb.	Mar.	Apr.	May
Preparatory					Competitive						Transition
4 AA	6 MxS	3 P	3 MxS	6 Conv. to P/P-E	23 Maintenance: P, P-E, MxS						8 Compen.

Martial Arts

Both aerobic and anaerobic energy systems must be developed over the long preparatory phase. Reactive strength and agility are necessary to respond to an opponent's strategy.

- Dominant energy systems: anaerobic alactic and lactic, aerobic
- Limiting factors: starting power, P-E, reactive power, M-E
- Training objectives: starting power, reactive power, P-E, M-E

Model for the Martial Arts

Jun.	Jul.	Aug.	Sep.	Oct.	Nov.	Dec.	Jan.	Feb.	Mar.	Apr.	May
Preparatory							Competitive				Transition
4 AA	3 MxS	2 P	3 MxS	T 3 P	3 MxS	3 P	3 MxS	6 Conv. to P	Maintenance: P		7 Compen.

Note: T = Transition.

Rowing

Rowing requires aerobic endurance and the ability to generate powerful strokes against the water. Starting power and muscular endurance should also be developed.

- Dominant energy systems: anaerobic, lactic, and aerobic
- Limiting factors: M-E medium and long, starting power, MxS
- Training objectives: M-E, P, MxS

Model for Rowing With the Major Regatta in July

Sep.	Oct.	Nov.	Dec.	Jan.	Feb.	Mar.	Apr.	May	Jun.	Jul.	Aug.
Preparatory							Competitive				Transition
6 AA	9 MxS		3 P	3 MxS	3 P	3 MxS	Conv. to M-E	8	Maintenance: M-E/P	10	7 Compen.

© 1991 Beth Schneider

Alpine

Alpine skiers must be able to react quickly to the course flags. Maximum strength development alternates with power development over the long preparation phase.

- Dominant energy systems: anaerobic alactic and lactic
- Limiting factors: reactive power, P-E
- Training objectives: MxS, reactive power, P-E

Model for Alpine Skiing

May	Jun.	Jul.	Aug.	Sep.	Oct.	Nov.	Dec.	Jan.	Feb.	Mar.	Apr.
Preparatory							Competitive				Transition
5 AA	6 MxS	3 P	3 MxS	3 P	3 MxS	6 Conv. to P	Maintenance: P				Compen.

© 1997 Beth Schneider

Nordic (Cross-Country)

Cross-country races require strong aerobic endurance. Maximum strength is converted to muscular endurance toward the end of the preparation phase so the skier is primed to withstand the demands of a long race.

- Dominant energy system: aerobic
- Limiting factor: M-E long
- Training objectives: M-E long, P-E

Model for Nordic Skiing

May	Jun.	Jul.	Aug.	Sep.	Oct.	Nov.	Dec.	Jan.	Feb.	Mar.	Apr.
Preparatory								Competitive			Transition
4 AA	6 MxS	9 M-EL		3 MxS	11 Conv. to M-EL			Maintenance: M-E			Compen.

Swimming

Sprinting

Sprinting swimmers use both their alactic and anaerobic energy systems during a race. They must be able to generate quick, powerful strokes to move efficiently through the water. The model given below is a bi-cycle for a national class sprinter.

- Dominant energy systems: anaerobic alactic and lactic, aerobic (for 100 meters)
- Limiting factors: P, P-E, M-E short
- Training objectives: P, M-E short, MxS

Model for a National-Class Sprinter in Swimming (Bi-Cycle)											
Sep.	**Oct.**	**Nov.**	**Dec.**	**Jan.**	**Feb.**	**Mar.**	**Apr.**	**May**	**Jun.**	**Jul.**	**Aug.**
Preparatory I				Comp. I		T	Prep. II	Comp. II			Transition
4 AA	6 MxS	3 P	3 MxS	4 Conv. to P/P-E	7 Mainten.: P, P-E, M-E	2 3 AA	6 MxS	4 Conv. to to P/P-E, E. M-E	7 Mainten.: P, P-E, M-E		7 Compen.

Long Distance

Long distance swimmers must train for muscle endurance. A long race taxes the aerobic energy system, but proper training will give the swimmer an endurance edge. The model below assumes two competitive phases, one beginning in January and the other beginning in the late spring.

- Dominant energy system: aerobic
- Limiting factor: M-E long
- Training objectives: M-E long, P-E

Model for a National-Class Long-Distance Swimmer

Sep.	Oct.	Nov.	Dec.	Jan.	Feb.	Mar.	Apr.	May	Jun.	Jul.	Aug.
Preparatory I				Comp. I		T	Prep. II		Comp. II		Transition
5 AA	3 MxS	3 M-E	3 MxS	6 Conv. to M-EL	6 Maintenance: M-E	4 AA	3 MxS	6 Conv. to M-EL	7 Mainten.: M-E		6 Compen.

Master Athlete (Short Distances)

Power is the dominant training factor for a master athlete. The long preparatory phase is needed to develop both power and maximum strength. Only one competitive phase is assumed, running from May through late August.

- Dominant energy systems: anaerobic lactic and aerobic
- Limiting factors: P-E, M-E short
- Training objectives: P, P-E

Model for a Master Athlete Short-Distance Swimmer

Oct.	Nov.	Dec.	Jan.	Feb.	Mar.	Apr.	May	Jun.	Jul.	Aug.	Sep.
Preparatory							Competitive				Transition
13 AA			3 MxS	3 P	3 MxS	3 P	3 MxS	6 Conv. to P/P-E	Maintenance: P/P-E		10	8 Compen.

Volleyball

A volleyball player must be able to react quickly and explosively off the ground to spike, block, or dive. Maximum strength, power, and specific endurance are needed to carry a player through the long competitive phase with power and confidence.

- Dominant energy systems: anaerobic alactic and lactic, aerobic
- Limiting factors: reactive power, P-E, M-E medium
- Training objectives: P, M-E, MxS

Model for Volleyball											
Jun.	Jul.	Aug.	Sep.	Oct.	Nov.	Dec.	Jan.	Feb.	Mar.	Apr.	May
Preparatory					Competitive						Transition
6 AA	6 MxS	3 P	3 MxS	7 Conv. to P, P-E, M-E	Maintenance: P, P-E						Compen.

Periodization of Loading Pattern per Training Phase

Loading patterns in training are not standard or rigid. They are not applicable to every sport or every level. Just as loading patterns vary according the sport or level of performance, they also change according to the type of strength being sought in a given training phase. To make this concept easier to understand and use, figures 6.2 through 6.8 show how it is applied in several sports. The examples illustrate the dynamics of loading patterns per training phase for a *mono-cycle* in amateur baseball/softball (figure 6.2), college basketball (figure 6.3), college football (figure 6.4), and an endurance-dominant sport such as canoeing (figure 6.5); and for a *bi-cycle* for sprinting in track and field (figure 6.6) and sprint and long-distance swimming (figures 6.7 and 6.8).

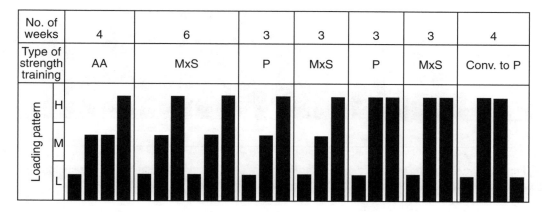

Figure 6.2 Variations of loading pattern for strength training phases for a baseball/softball team. Note that in some phases, the L and M loading is at the upper levels, suggesting a more demanding training regimen. For similar reasons, and to maximize the level of power development, the last three training phases have two adjacent H loads followed by regeneration cycles (L loads).

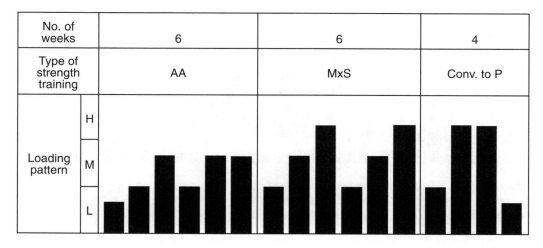

Figure 6.3 Suggested loading pattern for a college basketball team in which the preparatory phase is shorter and must be performed from early July through late October.

The charts indicate (from top to bottom) the number of weeks planned for a particular training phase, the type of training being sought in that phase, and the loading patterns (H = high, M = medium, and L = low). In some cases, the type of contraction being used (concentric and/or eccentric) is also included. The two types of contraction are mainly useful for the MxS phase. Even if your chosen sport is not among the examples, once you understand the concept, it will be easy to apply it to your own particular case. In addition, the examples are so varied that they are applicable through association.

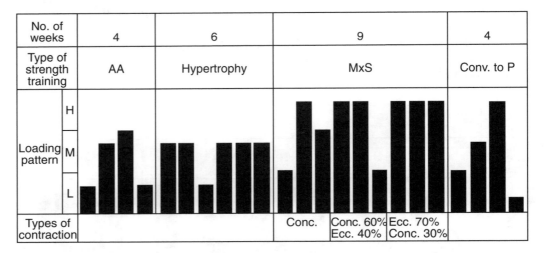

Figure 6.4 Variations of loading pattern for Periodization of Strength for linemen in college football. A similar approach can be used for throwers in track and field and the heavyweight category in wrestling. Note that for the hypertrophy (Hyp) phase, the load is medium (60 to 80 percent of 1RM) but very demanding for 2 to 3 weeks in a row. For the MxS phase, the types of contraction (Con = concentric, Ecc = eccentric) and the percentage per week are also suggested.

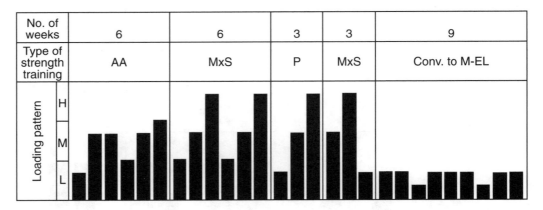

Figure 6.5 Variations of loading pattern for marathon canoeing, a sport where M-EL (muscular endurance long) is the dominant ability. A similar approach can be used for cycling, Nordic skiing, triathlon, and rowing. Note that for conversion to M-EL, the load is low (30 to 40 percent) but very demanding for 2 to 3 weeks in a row.

No. of weeks
5
6
4
Type of strength training
AA
MxS
Conv. to P
Loading pattern
H
M
L

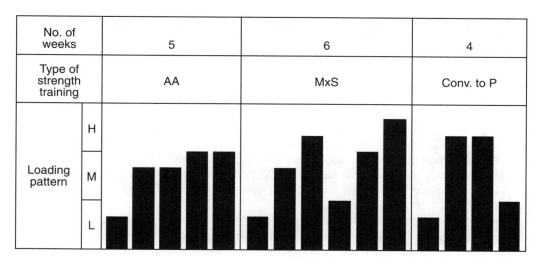

Figure 6.6 Variations of loading pattern for the first peak of a bi-cycle annual plan for sprinting in track and field.

No. of weeks
4
6
3
3
4
Type of strength training
AA
MxS
P
MxS
Conv. to P
Loading pattern
H
M
L

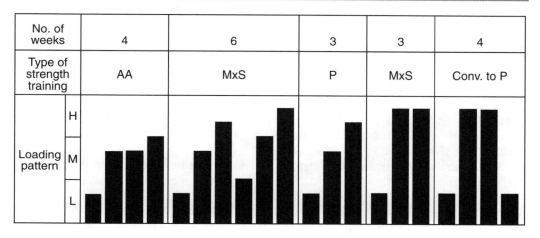

Figure 6.7 Variations of loading pattern for a sprinter in swimming (one peak of a bi-cycle annual plan). Note that training demand for the last two phases is high since the load is high (H) for 2 adjacent weeks.

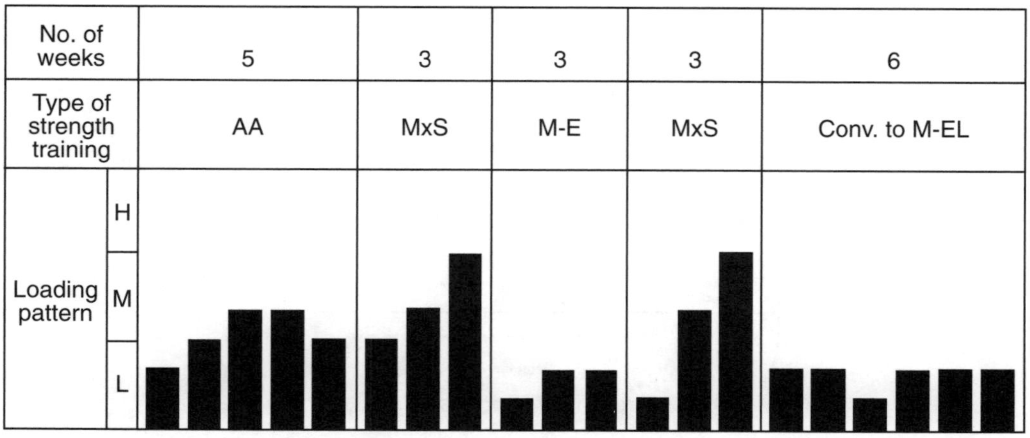

No. of weeks
5
3
3
3
6
Type of strength training
AA
MxS
M-E
MxS
Conv. to M-EL
Loading pattern
H
M
L

Figure 6.8 Variations of loading pattern for swimming for a long-distance event. Note that the load for MxS should not exceed 80 percent of 1RM. Similarly, the load for M-E is low (30 to 40 percent) but the number of repetitions is very high (see chapter 11).

Periodization of Strength and Its Effects on the Force-Time Curve

Due to the influence of bodybuilding, strength training programs often include a high number of repetitions (12 to 15) performed to exhaustion. Such programs mainly develop muscle size, not quickness of contraction. As illustrated in figure 6.9, the application of force in sports is performed very quickly, between 100 and 200 milliseconds. The only type of strength that stimulates such a quick application of force is MxS and P. The curve of force application of such strength components is less than 200 milliseconds, approaching 100 milliseconds.

The opposite is true if a variant of bodybuilding is employed. The total volume of strength training may be higher than MxS and P, but the force application is longer at more than 250 milliseconds and thus is not specific to the needs of most sports. Since the application of force in training is very fast, the main purpose of training is to shift the force-time curve to the left, or as close as possible to the time of the force application (less than 200 milliseconds). Figure 6.10 illustrates the intent of training, namely, that through utilization of MxS and P, the force-time curve can be shifted to the left.

This shift toward the sport-specific time of application of force is not achieved quickly. The whole point of Periodization of Strength is that, as a result of phase-specific strength training, the force-time curve is shifted to the left (i.e., decrease in execution time) before the start of major competitions. This is when the quick application of strength is needed, as well as when athletes will benefit from gains in power. Periodization of Strength was created for this specific purpose.

As explained earlier, each training phase of the Periodization of Strength has certain objectives. By plotting the force-time curve for each training

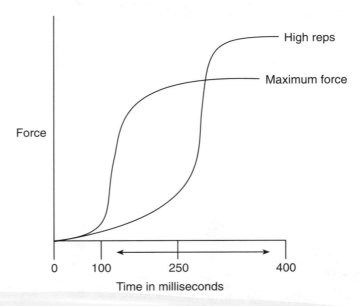

Figure 6.9   The force-time curve of two different weight training programs (from Schmidtbleicher, 1984).

Force
100
250
400
Time in milliseconds

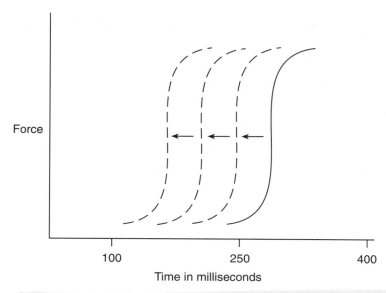

Figure 6.10 The purpose of strength training is to shift the force-time curve to the left.

phase, both coaches and athletes will be able to see from another angle how training influences the force-time curve. Figure 6.11 exemplifies the Periodization of Strength when a hypertrophy phase is also included. Certainly, only some sports may use this model, while many others will exclude hypertrophy from the annual plan.

As figure 6.11 shows, the type of program performed during the AA phase has little effect on the force-time curve. At most, it may shift it slightly to the right (i.e., increase execution time). Typical hypertrophy training methods, however, increase the total volume of strength training performed, as illustrated by the height of the curve. The curve shifts to the right because the load is submaximum and each set is performed to exhaustion and thus not explosively. Such gains in muscle size do not translate into gains in the fast

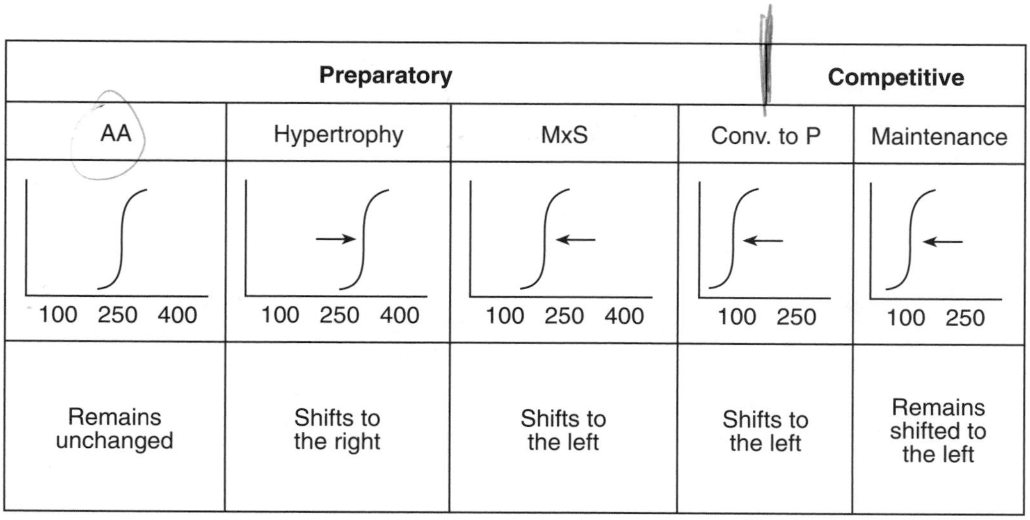

Preparatory
Competitive
AA
Hypertrophy
MxS
Conv. to P
Maintenance
100 250 400
100 250 400
100 250 400
100 250
100 250
Remains unchanged
Shifts to the right
Shifts to the left
Shifts to the left
Remains shifted to the left

Figure 6.11 Graphs showing how the specifics of training for each phase influence the force-time curve.

application of strength. Due to the use of heavy loads from the MxS phase onward, explosiveness during the conversion of MxS to P shifts the curve to the left. As this type of strength training is continued during the maintenance phase, the curve should remain to the left.

When applying Periodization of Strength, you should know that a high level of P, or explosiveness, cannot be expected before the start of the competitive phase. P is maximized only as a result of implementing the conversion phase; thus, high levels of P should not be expected during the H and MxS phases. As mentioned earlier, however, gains in MxS are vital if increments in P are expected from year to year, because P is a function of MxS. Periodization of Strength is the best road to success for both M-E and P development.

PART II

Periodized Strength Training

chapter 7

Phase One: Anatomical Adaptation

Strength training represents an essential element in a coach's quest to produce good athletes. All athletes involved in competitive sports follow an annual program intended to result in peak performance at the time of the main competition(s). Thus, strength training is one of the key ingredients in building the physiological foundation for achieving peak performance.

To achieve peak performance, training must be planned and periodized in a way that ensures performance improvement from phase to phase, leading to the highest levels during the competitive season. The same approach should be applied to strength training as well. Strength should be viewed as an ability to be refined through various methods and phases of training to create a final product—the sport-specific strength combination (figure 1.5, page 9)—rather than as a goal in itself.

As illustrated in table 6.2, strength changes throughout the annual plan according to the concept of Periodization of Strength. As explained earlier, each sport requires a certain type or sport-specific combination of strength, which should represent the physiological base for performance. The transformation of strength into a sport-specific quality is made possible by applying Periodization of Strength and by using training methods specific to the needs of a given strength training phase. Thus, training methods must change as the training phases change.

This and the next four chapters will discuss all available training methods as they relate to Periodization of Strength. Each training phase will be treated separately to show which method best suits that particular phase as well as the needs of athletes. The discussion will also explain the positive and negative aspects of most methods, how to apply the methods, and suggest training programs using a given method.

Key Words

Barbell: A bar to which varying weights are attached; usually held with both arms.

Dumbbell: Small weights of fixed resistance; usually held with one hand.

Elastic cords or surgical tubing: Cords made of rubber or synthetic material used in developing general strength; since the resistance of the material is not difficult to overcome, elastic cords can be used successfully in strength training for endurance sports such as Nordic skiing, marathon canoeing, and triathalon.

Training Methods for Anatomical Adaptation

The goal of the AA phase is to progressively adapt the muscles, and especially muscle attachments to the bone, to cope more easily with heavier loads during the following training phases. As such, the overall load in training must be increased without athletes experiencing much discomfort. The simplest method to consider for AA is *circuit training* (CT), mainly because it provides an organized structure and alternates muscle groups.

Circuit Training

Although CT can be used to develop cardiorespiratory endurance as well as combinations of strength during the AA phase, it should be adjusted to ensure the development of strength. Other variants will be suggested in the section on development of M-E (see chapter 11).

Circuit training was first proposed by Morgan and Adamson (1959) of Leeds University as a method for developing general fitness. Their initial CT routine consisted of several stations arranged in a circle (hence the name "circuit training") so as to work muscle groups alternately from station to station. As CT grew in popularity, other authors began to provide additional information, and perhaps the best book on the market is *Circuit Training for All Sports* (Scholich, 1992).

In developing a CT routine, a wide variety of exercises and devices can be used, such as your own body weight, surgical tubing, medicine balls, light implements, dumbbells, barbells, and any strength training machines. A circuit may be of short (6 to 9 exercises), medium (9 to 12 exercises), or long (12 to 15 exercises) duration and may be repeated several times depending on the number of exercises involved. In deciding the number of circuits, the number of repetitions per station, and the load, you must consider the individual's work tolerance and fitness level. Total workload during AA should not be so high as to cause athletes pain or discomfort. Individual athletes can have input in determining how much work can be performed.

CT exercises must be selected to alternate muscle groups, which affords a better and faster recovery. The rest interval between stations can be anywhere from 60 to 90 seconds, with 1 to 3 minutes between circuits. A typical gym has many different apparatuses, workstations, and strength training machines, so a wide variety of circuits can be created. This constantly challenges the athletes' skills and, at the same time, keeps them interested.

In line with the overall purpose of the preparatory phase, and particularly the goal of AA, exercises should be selected to develop the core area of the body as well as the prime movers.

Young athletes with little or no strength training experience can benefit from circuit training.

Note: CT should not be used as a testing device or to make comparisons between athletes, mainly due to anthropometric differences between athletes. Comparison of athletes is unfair, to say the least, since speed of performance and degree of flexion and extension can vary greatly. On the contrary, achievements should only be compared with an individual athlete's past performance.

Program Design

Circuit training may be used from the first week of AA. Start by testing the athlete for 1RM to calculate the load for the prime movers. Select the CT stations according to the equipment available. A certain progression should be followed, depending on the level of the athletes' classification and training background. For younger athletes with little or no strength training background, start with exercises using their own body weight. Over time, progress to exercises using light implements and weights, then barbells, the Universal gym, and other strength machines. Again, AA phase exercises must be selected to involve most muscle groups irrespective of the needs of the specific sport.

Four circuits using various pieces of equipment are exemplified below. These four circuits, however, far from exhaust all the possible combinations of exercises.

Circuit A (own body weight)
 1. Half squats
 2. Push-ups
 3. Bent-knee sit-ups
 4. Two-legged low hops on spot
 5. Back extensions
 6. Pull-ups
 7. Burpees

Circuit B (using stall bars and gym benches)
 1. Step-ups
 2. Incline push-ups (palms on bench)
 3. Incline bent-knee sit-ups (toes behind third rung)
 4. Chin-ups (gripping highest rung)
 5. Zigzag jumps over benches (long side)
 6. Trunk lifts (hips on bench, feet under low rung)
 7. Jumping on and off a bench

Circuit C (dumbbells and medicine ball)
 1. Half squats
 2. Medicine ball chest throws
 3. Military presses
 4. Bent-knee sit-ups (medicine ball held at chest level)
 5. Medicine ball forward throws (between legs)
 6. Lunges
 7. Back arches, ball behind the neck
 8. Upright rowing
 9. Toe raises
10. Trunk rotations
11. Overhead backward medicine ball throws
12. Jump squats and medicine ball throws

Circuit D (barbells and strength machines)
 1. Leg presses
 2. Bench presses
 3. Incline sit-ups
 4. Good-morning (hip extension with light load)
 5. Upright rowing
 6. Leg curls
 7. Lat pull-downs
 8. Seated bench presses
 9. Toe raises

(handwritten margin note: AA for both / 12-15 reps (not only for circuit))

Table 7.1 Suggested Training Parameters for Circuit Training

Training parameters	Novice athletes	Experienced athletes
Duration of AA	8-10 weeks	3-5 weeks
Load (if weights are used)	30-40 percent	40-60 percent
No. of stations per circuit	9-12 (15)	6-9
No. of circuits per session	2-3	3-5
Total time of CT session	20-25 minutes	30-40 minutes
Rest interval between exercises	90 seconds	60 seconds
Rest interval between circuits	2-3 minutes	1-2 minutes
Frequency per week	2-3	3-4

(handwritten margin note: pretty high for even Athlet)

Table 7.1 suggests the duration of AA, frequency of training sessions per week, and other parameters for CT for both novice and experienced athletes.

As shown in table 7.1, training parameters for experienced athletes are quite different from those for novices. A longer AA phase makes good sense for novice athletes because they need more time for adaptation and for creating a good base for the future. On the other hand, an AA phase much longer than 3 to 5 weeks will not result in visible gains for experienced athletes.

Similar observations can be made regarding the number of stations per circuit. Because novice athletes have to address as many muscle groups as possible, they use more stations and the circuits are longer. Experienced athletes, however, can reduce the number of stations to focus on exercises for the prime movers, compensation, and exercises involving the stabilizers, making for shorter circuits.

The total physical demand per circuit must be increased progressively and individually. The example in table 7.1 illustrates that the load and the

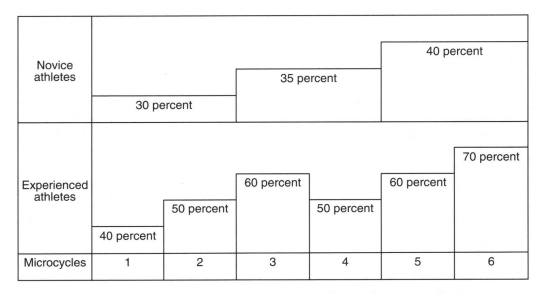

Figure 7.1 Suggested pattern of load increments for CT for novice and experienced athletes.

pattern for increasing it must differ between novice and experienced athletes (figure 7.1). Novice athletes need better adaptation, so the load remains the same for 2 weeks whereas for experienced athletes, it changes from cycle to cycle.

To better monitor improvements in training, as well as to calculate the load every 3 weeks, testing for 1RM should take place in weeks 1, 4, and at the end of week 6.

As illustrated in figure 7.2, toward the end of the AA phase, the load reaches percentages that allow athletes to make an immediate transition to the MxS phase. This approach can be used for all athletes except those requiring increased muscle mass, such as throwers and football linemen. For these athletes, a hypertrophy phase must be planned between AA and MxS (see table 6.4, page 91).

Figure 7.3 demonstrates a AA strength training program designed for a female softball team. Table 7.2 shows a sample 5-week AA training program for a football team (college).

No.	Exercise	Week 1	Week 2	Week 3	Week 4	Week 5	Week 6
1	Leg presses	$\frac{40}{15}$ 2	$\frac{40}{15}$ 3	$\frac{50}{15}$ 3	$\frac{50}{15}$ 2	$\frac{60}{12}$ 3	$\frac{70}{8}$ 3
2	Push-ups	2 × 12	3 × 13	3 × 15	2 × 15	3 × 18	3 × 20
3	Bent-knee sit-ups	2 × 12	3 × 12	3 × 15	2 × 12	3 × 15	3 × 18
4	Upright rowing	$\frac{40}{12}$ 2	$\frac{40}{15}$ 3	$\frac{50}{15}$ 3	$\frac{50}{15}$ 2	$\frac{60}{12}$ 3	$\frac{70}{10}$ 3
5	Back arches (medicine ball)	2 × 10	2 × 12	3 × 12	2 × 12	3 × 12	3 × 15
6	Step-ups	2 × 30 seconds	3 × 30 seconds	3 × 45 seconds	2 × 45 seconds	3 × 45 seconds	3 × 60 seconds
7	Military presses	$\frac{40}{12}$ 2	$\frac{40}{15}$ 3	$\frac{50}{15}$ 3	$\frac{50}{15}$ 2	$\frac{60}{12}$ 3	$\frac{70}{10}$ 3
8	Toe raises	$\frac{40}{15}$ 2	$\frac{50}{15}$ 3	$\frac{50}{20}$ 3	$\frac{50}{15}$ 3	$\frac{60}{20}$ 3	$\frac{70}{15}$ 3
9	Leg curls	$\frac{40}{12}$ 2	$\frac{40}{12}$ 3	$\frac{50}{15}$ 3	$\frac{50}{12}$ 2	$\frac{50}{12}$ 3	$\frac{60}{8}$ 3
10	Burpees	2 × 10	2 × 12	3 × 15	2 × 12	3 × 15	3 × 18

(handwritten notes: "no more than 60%", "AA MxS")

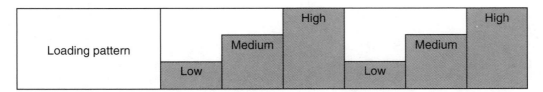

Figure 7.2 Strength training program for the AA phase for a team sport (basketball, ice hockey, volleyball, lacrosse, baseball, etc.). RI: As long as necessary to reach an almost full recovery between stations.

No.	Exercise	Week 1	Week 2	Week 3	Week 4	Week 5	Week 6
1	Half squats	$\frac{40}{12}$ 2	$\frac{50}{15}$ 2	$\frac{60}{10}$ 3	$\frac{60}{12}$ 3	$\frac{70}{10}$ 3	$\frac{70}{10}$ 4
2	Bench presses	$\frac{40}{12}$ 2	$\frac{50}{15}$ 2	$\frac{60}{10}$ 3	$\frac{60}{10}$ 3	$\frac{70}{8}$ 3	$\frac{70}{12}$ 4
3	Leg curls	$\frac{40}{8}$ 1	$\frac{40}{10}$ 2	$\frac{50}{8}$ 2	$\frac{60}{8}$ 2	$\frac{60}{10}$ 3	$\frac{60}{8}$ 3
4	Abdominals (to discomfort)	1×	2×	3×	3×	3×	4×
5	Reverse leg presses	$\frac{50}{12}$ 2	$\frac{50}{12}$ 2	$\frac{60}{12}$ 2	$\frac{60}{10}$ 3	$\frac{70}{10}$ 3	$\frac{70}{12}$ 3
6	Back extensions (to discomfort)	1×	2×	2×	2×	3×	3×
7	Toe raises	$\frac{40}{12}$ 2	$\frac{50}{10}$ 2	$\frac{60}{10}$ 3	$\frac{60}{12}$ 3	$\frac{70}{12}$ 3	$\frac{70}{15}$ 3
8	Front lat pull-downs	$\frac{40}{10}$ 2	$\frac{50}{10}$ 2	$\frac{50}{12}$ 3	$\frac{50}{10}$ 2	$\frac{50}{12}$ 3	$\frac{60}{10}$ 3

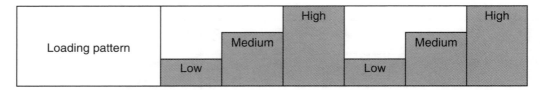

Loading pattern: Low, Medium, High, Low, Medium, High

Figure 7.3 Strength training program for the AA phase for a female softball team. RI: As long as necessary to reach an almost full recovery.

Table 7.2 Example of a 5-Week AA Phase for a College Football Team

Exercise	Week	Percent maximum	Sets	Reps
Half squats	1	40	1	15
		50	1	12
	2	40	1	15
		50	1	15
	3	50	1	12
		60	2	10
	4	50	1	12
		60	2	10
	5	60	2	10
		70	1	8
Bench presses	1	40	1	15
		50	1	12
	2	40	1	15
		50	1	15
	3	50		12
		60	2	10
	4	50	1	12
		60	2	10
	5	60	2	10
		70	1	8

Exercise	Week	Percent maximum	Sets	Reps
Leg curls	1	30	1	15
		40	1	12
	2	30	1	15
		40	1	12
	3	40	2	15
		50	1	12
	4	40	2	15
		50	1	12
	5	50	2	15
		60	1	12
Abdominals	1		2	To discomfort
	2		2	To discomfort
	3	Body	2	To discomfort
	4		2	To discomfort
	5		2	To discomfort
Reverse leg presses	1	40	1	15
		50	1	12
	2	40	1	15
		50	1	12
	3	50	1	12
		60	2	10
	4	50	1	12
		60	2	10
	5	60	2	10
		70	1	8
Back extensions	1		2	To discomfort
	2		2	To discomfort
	3	Body	2	To discomfort
	4		2	To discomfort
	5		2	To discomfort
Military presses	1	40	1	15
		50	1	12
	2	40	1	15
		50	1	12
	3	50	1	12
		60	2	10
	4	50	1	12
		60	2	10
	5	60	2	10
		70	1	8
Upright rowing	1	30	1	15
		40	1	12
	2	30	1	15
		40	1	12
	3	40	1	12
		50	2	10
	4	40	1	12
		50	2	10
	5	50	2	10
		60	1	8
Shoulder shrugs	1	Weight	2	20
	2	that	2	20
	3	allows	3	15
	4	performance	3	15
	5	of 20 reps	3	20

(continued)

Table 7.2 (continued)

Exercise	Week	Percent maximum	Sets	Reps
Diagonal arm pulls	1	Weight	2	20
	2	that	2	20
	3	allows	3	15
	4	performance	3	15
	5	of 20 reps	3	20
Cleans	1	30	1	15
		40	1	12
	2	30	1	15
		40	1	12
	3	40	1	12
		50	2	10
	4	40	1	12
		50	2	10
	5	50	2	10
		60	1	8

Note that the load is expressed in percentage of 1RM and that the load, sets, and reps are presented in separate columns.
RI = to an almost full recovery.

chapter 8

Phase Two: Hypertrophy

Many people think that the larger the body size, the stronger the person, but that is not always the case. For example, a weight lifter may have a smaller body size yet be capable of lifting heavier loads than a larger, bulky-looking bodybuilder. What is necessary in athletics is to have a large, active, fat-free body mass rather than a large body size. The greater the active body mass, the greater the strength, since force depends on muscle density and diameter.

Hypertrophy (Bodybuilding) Method

The enlargement of muscle size (hypertrophy) is best achieved by applying the methodology of bodybuilding. Unlike bodybuilding, however, which focuses on enlarging overall musculature, hypertrophy training for sports focuses mainly on increasing the size of the specific prime movers. The hypertrophy method is better suited to the needs of athletes such as shot-putters, heavyweight wrestlers, and linemen, for whom total body weight is an asset.

Although the application of bodybuilding does produce an important increase in hypertrophy, it does not result in nervous system adaptation such as the stimulation and recruitment of FT fibers. This can be a handicap for most athletes, so bodybuilding is used only in a certain phase of strength development for some athletes (see table 6.4, page 91). Bodybuilding can, however, be used for some novice athletes, provided they do not work to exhaustion in each set, because it is relatively safe and employs moderately heavy loads. It can also be applied when athletes want to move up a weight class in sports such as boxing and wrestling.

The main objective of bodybuilding is to provoke high chemical changes in the muscles. This develops muscle mass as a result of the contracting elements of muscle fibers (myosin filaments), rather than as a result of increased fluid and plasma, as often happens. This is why bodybuilders' strength is not proportional to their size.

As bodybuilders do not employ maximum loads, this method does not provoke maximum tension in the muscles. With the typical submaximum load, athletes contract the muscles to exhaustion and the recruitment of muscle fibers varies; when some begin to fatigue, others start to function.

Key Words

Anabolism: The process of building muscle tissue.

Hypertrophy: Growth of muscle tissue through an increase in the size of the tissue elements, not the number of cells.

Inhibition: Overriding stimulating reflexes of a muscle contraction to produce a voluntary movement.

It is very important in bodybuilding training to reach a maximum number of repetitions within a given set. The number of repetitions can vary between 6 and 12. If a lower number is used, the load should be increased, and vice versa.

During exercise, the resistance of a constant weight varies depending on the number of repetitions. With an increased number of repetitions, weight that feels relatively light at the beginning of an exercise becomes submaximum and then maximum by the last repetition. With increased fatigue, the recruitment and synchronization of motor units are much greater, and the physiological benefits are often similar to those observed when lifting heavy weights.

Program Design

As in any other new training phase, hypertrophy training should begin with a test for 1RM. The athletes then start with a 70 to 80 percent load, or one that allows the performance of 6 repetitions. As they adapt to the load, they will progressively be capable of performing more repetitions. When 12 repetitions are reached, the load is then increased to a level where, again, only 6 repetitions are possible. See table 8.1 for the training parameters of the hypertrophy phase.

To achieve maximum training benefits, it is important for athletes to reach the highest number of repetitions possible in each set. This means they should always reach a degree of exhaustion that prevents them from doing the last repetition, even when maximum contraction is applied. Without performing each individual set to exhaustion, muscle hypertrophy will not reach the expected level since the first repetitions do not produce the stimulus necessary to increase muscle mass. Thus, the key element in hypertrophy training is the cumulative effect of exhaustion in the total number of sets, not just exhaustion per set. This cumulative exhaustion stimulates the chemical reactions and protein metabolism in the body so that optimal muscle hypertrophy will be achieved.

The exercises should be performed at low to moderate speed; however, athletes in sports where speed-power is dominant are strongly advised against slow speed of execution, especially if the hypertrophy phase is longer than 4 to 6 weeks. The primary reason is that the neuromuscular system will adapt to a slow execution and, as a result, will not provide the stimulation for recruitment of FT muscle fibers that is so crucial for speed-power-dominant sports.

Table 8.1   Training Parameters for the Hypertrophy Phase

Training Parameters	Work
Duration of hypertrophy phase	4-6 weeks
Load	70-80 percent
Number of exercises	6-9
Number of repetitions per set	6-12
Number of sets per session	4-6 (8)
Rest interval	3-5 minutes
Speed of execution	Slow to medium
Frequency per week	2-4

Unlike bodybuilding, hypertrophy training for athletics involves a lower number of exercises, a critical factor in that the goal is to involve mainly the prime movers and not all muscle groups. The benefit of such an approach is that more sets are performed per exercise (4 to 6 or even as many as 8), thus stimulating better muscle hypertrophy for the prime movers.

During the rest interval of 3 to 5 minutes, which is longer than in bodybuilding, and at the end of the training session, athletes should stretch the muscles worked. Due to the many repetitions of contractions, the muscles shorten, which in turn produces premature inhibition of contraction of the antagonistic muscles. This results in reduced muscle range of motion and decreased quickness of contraction affecting the overall performance ability of the muscles involved. To overcome this effect, athletes should constantly stretch their muscles to artificially lengthen them to their biological length. In addition, a shortened muscle has a slower rate of regeneration as only the normal biological length facilitates active biochemical exchanges. These exchanges provide nutrients to the muscles and remove the metabolic wastes, facilitating better recovery between sets and after training sessions.

Figure 8.1 shows a sample 6-week program developed for a heavyweight wrestler. The program suggested in each box was repeated four times a week.

No.	Exercise	Week 1	Week 2	Week 3	Week 4	Week 5	Week 6
1	Half squats	$\frac{60}{12}$ 3	$\frac{60}{12}$ 4	$\frac{70}{10}$ 4	$\frac{60}{12}$ 3	$\frac{75}{10}$ 4	$\frac{80}{8}$ 4
2	Seated rows	$\frac{60}{12}$ 3	$\frac{60}{12}$ 4	$\frac{70}{10}$ 4	$\frac{60}{12}$ 3	$\frac{75}{10}$ 4	$\frac{80}{8}$ 4
3	Twisted abdominals	3 × 15	3 × 18	4 × 12	4 × 12	4 × 15	4 × 18
4	Leg curls	$\frac{60}{10}$ 3	$\frac{60}{8}$ 4	$\frac{70}{8}$ 3	$\frac{60}{8}$ 3	$\frac{60}{8}$ 4	$\frac{70}{8}$ 4
5	Dead lifts	$\frac{60}{10}$ 3	$\frac{60}{8}$ 4	$\frac{70}{8}$ 3	$\frac{60}{8}$ 3	$\frac{60}{8}$ 4	$\frac{70}{8}$ 4
6	Bench presses	$\frac{60}{12}$ 3	$\frac{60}{12}$ 4	$\frac{70}{10}$ 4	$\frac{60}{10}$ 3	$\frac{75}{10}$ 4	$\frac{80}{8}$ 4
7	Lateral deltoid raises	$\frac{60}{10}$ 3	$\frac{60}{8}$ 4	$\frac{70}{8}$ 3	$\frac{60}{8}$ 3	$\frac{60}{8}$ 4	$\frac{70}{8}$ 4
8	Shoulder shrugs	$\frac{60}{12}$ 3	$\frac{60}{12}$ 4	$\frac{70}{10}$ 4	$\frac{60}{12}$ 3	$\frac{75}{10}$ 4	$\frac{80}{10}$ 4
9	Toe raises	$\frac{60}{15}$ 3	$\frac{60}{15}$ 4	$\frac{70}{12}$ 4	$\frac{70}{10}$ 3	$\frac{75}{12}$ 4	$\frac{80}{10}$ 4
10	Lat pull-downs	$\frac{60}{12}$ 3	$\frac{60}{12}$ 4	$\frac{70}{10}$ 4	$\frac{60}{12}$ 3	$\frac{75}{10}$ 4	$\frac{80}{10}$ 4
11	Cleans	$\frac{60}{12}$ 3	$\frac{60}{12}$ 4	$\frac{70}{12}$ 4	$\frac{60}{12}$ 3	$\frac{75}{12}$ 4	$\frac{80}{10}$ 4

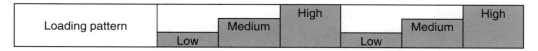

Figure 8.1 Example loading pattern for a 6-week training program for the hypertrophy phase for a wrestler (heavyweight category).

Table 8.2 shows a 6-week hypertrophy training program for a female college basketball player who had a relatively large disproportion between height and weight. This phase was followed by a MxS and P phase, and the player was ready for the league games in early fall. At the end of the summer program, she had gained 14 pounds and had superior levels of MxS and P, factors that helped her visibly improve her game. Table 8.3 shows a sample hypertrophy program for a ice-hockey player who wanted to gain muscle mass. Since the player had only 3 weeks available for training, the schedule was intensive, 6 days a week. Note that the first eight exercises were performed on days 1, 3, and 5, whereas the next eight exercises were performed on days 2, 4, and 6.

Variations of Bodybuilding Methods

As repetitions to exhaustion represent the main element of success in bodybuilding, several variations of the original method were developed. They all have the same objective in that when exhaustion is reached, two to three more repetitions must be attained through blood, sweat, and tears. The expected result is greater muscle growth—increased hypertrophy.

Of the total number of variations (more than 20), the following are considered the most representative.

Split Routine: In bodybuilding, athletes perform two to three exercises per muscle group, and since they address every muscle of the body, they may be

Table 8.2   A Sample 6-Week Hypertrophy Program for a Female College Basketball Player

Exercise	Dates					
	May 13-19	May 20-26	May 27-June 2	June 3-9	June 10-16	June 17-23
Leg presses	$\frac{60}{10}3$	$\frac{60}{12}3$	$\frac{60}{15}3$	$\frac{60}{10}3$	$\frac{60}{15}1\frac{70}{12}2$	$\frac{70}{12}3$
Abdominal curls	3×15	3×18	3×20	3×15	3×18	3×20
Incline bench presses	$\frac{60}{10}3$	$\frac{60}{12}3$	$\frac{60}{15}3$	$\frac{60}{10}3$	$\frac{60}{15}1\frac{70}{12}2$	$\frac{70}{12}3$
Leg curls	$\frac{60}{10}3$	$\frac{60}{12}3$	$\frac{60}{15}3$	$\frac{60}{10}3$	$\frac{60}{15}1\frac{70}{12}2$	$\frac{70}{12}3$
Shoulder shrugs	$\frac{60}{10}3$	$\frac{60}{12}3$	$\frac{60}{15}3$	$\frac{60}{10}3$	$\frac{60}{15}1\frac{70}{12}2$	$\frac{70}{12}3$
Toe raises	$\frac{60}{15}3$	$\frac{60}{15}1\frac{70}{12}2$	$\frac{70}{15}3$	$\frac{60}{15}3$	$\frac{70}{15}3$	$\frac{70}{18}3$
Lat pull-downs (front)	$\frac{60}{10}3$	$\frac{60}{12}3$	$\frac{60}{15}3$	$\frac{60}{10}3$	$\frac{60}{15}1\frac{70}{12}2$	$\frac{70}{12}3$
Preacher curls	$\frac{60}{10}3$	$\frac{60}{12}3$	$\frac{60}{15}3$	$\frac{60}{10}3$	$\frac{60}{15}1\frac{70}{12}2$	$\frac{70}{12}3$

Note: RI = 1 minute between sets.

Table 8.3 Sample Hypertrophy Program for an Ice Hockey Player

Day	Week no. 1			Week no. 2			Week no. 3		
	1	3	5	1	3	5	1	3	5
Half squats	$\frac{60}{12}$3	$\frac{60}{12}$3	$\frac{60}{10}$4	$\frac{70}{10}$4	$\frac{70}{10}$4	$\frac{70}{10}$4	$\frac{80}{8}$4	$\frac{80}{10}$4	$\frac{80}{12}$4
Trunk seated rows	$\frac{60}{12}$3	$\frac{60}{12}$3	$\frac{60}{10}$4	$\frac{70}{10}$4	$\frac{70}{10}$4	$\frac{70}{10}$4	$\frac{80}{8}$4	$\frac{80}{10}$4	$\frac{80}{12}$4
Hip extensions	$\frac{60}{12}$3	$\frac{60}{12}$3	$\frac{60}{10}$4	$\frac{70}{10}$4	$\frac{70}{10}$5	$\frac{70}{10}$5	$\frac{80}{6-8}$5	$\frac{80}{8}$5	$\frac{80}{8}$5
Standing calf raises	$\frac{60}{12}$3	$\frac{70}{12}$3	$\frac{70}{12}$3	$\frac{70}{12}$4	$\frac{70}{10}$5	$\frac{70}{12}$5	$\frac{80}{8}$5	$\frac{80}{8}$5	$\frac{80}{8}$5
Dead lifts	$\frac{60}{10}$3	$\frac{60}{10}$4	$\frac{60}{12}$4	$\frac{70}{10}$4	$\frac{70}{8-10}$5	$\frac{70}{10}$5	$\frac{70}{6-8}$6	$\frac{70}{8}$6	$\frac{70}{8-10}$6
Twisted abdominals	3 × 15	3 × 15	3 × 15	4 × 12	4 × 12	4 × 12	5 × 10	5 × 10	5 × 12
Trunk extensions	3 × 15	3 × 17	3 × 17	4 × 15	4 × 15	5 × 12	5 × 15	5 × 15	5 × 15
Leg curls	$\frac{50}{8}$3	$\frac{50}{8}$3	$\frac{50}{10}$3	$\frac{60}{8}$3	$\frac{60}{8}$3	$\frac{60}{10}$3	$\frac{60}{8}$4	$\frac{60}{8}$4	$\frac{60}{10}$4

Day	Week no. 1			Week no. 2			Week no. 3		
	2	4	6	2	4	6	2	4	6
Shoulder shrugs	$\frac{60}{8-10}$3	$\frac{60}{10}$3	$\frac{60}{10}$3	$\frac{70}{10}$4	$\frac{70}{10}$4	$\frac{70}{10}$4	$\frac{80}{8}$4	$\frac{80}{10}$4	$\frac{80}{10}$4
Bench presses	$\frac{60}{8}$3	$\frac{60}{10}$3	$\frac{60}{10}$3	$\frac{60}{8}$3	$\frac{60}{10}$4	$\frac{60}{12}$4	$\frac{60}{12}$4	$\frac{70}{10}$4	$\frac{70}{12}$4
Preacher curls	$\frac{60}{8}$3	$\frac{60}{10}$3	$\frac{60}{12}$3	$\frac{60}{8}$3	$\frac{60}{10}$3	$\frac{60}{10}$4	$\frac{60}{12}$4	$\frac{60}{12}$4	$\frac{70}{10}$4
Lateral deltoid raises (elbow flexion)	$\frac{60}{8}$3	$\frac{60}{8}$4	$\frac{60}{8}$4	$\frac{70}{8}$4	$\frac{70}{8}$4	$\frac{70}{8-10}$5	$\frac{80}{6-8}$4	$\frac{80}{8}$5	$\frac{80}{8}$6
Triceps cable extensions	$\frac{60}{8}$3	$\frac{60}{8}$4	$\frac{60}{8}$4	$\frac{70}{8}$4	$\frac{70}{8}$4	$\frac{70}{8}$5	$\frac{80}{6}$4	$\frac{80}{8}$5	$\frac{80}{8}$6
Lat pull-downs (front)	$\frac{60}{12}$3	$\frac{60}{12}$3	$\frac{60}{12}$4	$\frac{70}{12}$4	$\frac{70}{12}$4	$\frac{70}{10}$5	$\frac{80}{6-8}$4	$\frac{80}{8}$4	$\frac{80}{8}$4
Seated military presses	$\frac{60}{12}$3	$\frac{60}{12}$3	$\frac{60}{12}$4	$\frac{70}{12}$4	$\frac{70}{12}$4	$\frac{70}{10}$5	$\frac{80}{6}$4	$\frac{80}{8}$4	$\frac{80}{8}$4
Seated rows	$\frac{60}{12}$3	$\frac{60}{12}$3	$\frac{60}{12}$4	$\frac{70}{12}$4	$\frac{70}{12}$4	$\frac{70}{10}$5	$\frac{80}{6}$4	$\frac{80}{8}$4	$\frac{80}{8}$4

Note: RI = 1 minute, except for standing calf raises, where it is 30 seconds.

Repetitions beyond exhaustion result in increased hypertrophy.

in the gymnasium for at least half a day to finish the entire program. Even if athletes have the energy to do this, time constraints represent an important limitation. The solution is to divide the total volume of work into parts and address one part of the body each day, hence the "split routine." This means that even if an athlete trains five to six times a week, an actual muscle group is worked only one to two times a week.

Assisted Repetitions: As an athlete performs a set to temporary exhaustion of the neuromuscular system, a partner assists by providing sufficient support to enable two to three more repetitions.

Resisted Repetitions: The athlete performs a set to temporary exhaustion. The partner then assists the athlete in performing two to three more repetitions concentrically while providing some resistance during the eccentric segment of contraction for each additional repetition (hence "resisted repetitions"). As such, the eccentric part of the contraction is performed twice as long as the concentric part, which overloads the muscles involved beyond the standard level.

Athletes who perform resisted repetitions should be forewarned that the longer the active muscle fibers are held in tension, the higher the nervous tension and energy expenditure. If normal contraction time is 2 to 4 seconds, a repetition performed against resistance can be 6 to 8 seconds long, consuming 20 to 40 percent more energy (Hartmann & Tünnemann, 1988). As the muscles are held in tension longer, the muscles' metabolism is more strongly activated, which stimulates muscle growth beyond standard norms.

Supersets: The superset represents a method in which an athlete performs a set for the agonistic muscles of a given joint, followed without a rest period by a set for the antagonistic muscles (for example, an elbow flexion followed immediately by an elbow extension).

Variation: The athlete performs a set to exhaustion and, after 20 to 30 seconds, follows with another set for the same muscle group. Of course, due to exhaustion, the athlete may be unable to perform the same number of repetitions as in the first set.

Note: Resisted repetitions and supersets should only be performed by experienced athletes with a lengthy training background, due to the higher demands in training.

Cheated Repetitions: This method is normally used when lacking a partner. The athlete performs an exercise to exhaustion, and when unable to perform another repetition through the entire range of motion, the athlete tries to complement the action by jerking another segment of the body toward the performing limb. For example, elbow flexions are performed to exhaustion and then the trunk is jerked toward the forearm. In this way, the athlete is able to exert additional tension in the exhausted muscle. By using the jerking action, the muscles are "cheated" into maintaining a longer contraction time. This method is limited to certain limbs and exercises.

Pre-exhaustion: This method suggests that (1) before large muscle groups are contracted, the small muscles have to be pre-exhausted so that during the actual work, the entire load is taken only by the large muscle groups; and (2) before performing a set involving two to three joints (e.g., half squats), the muscles of a given joint have to be prefatigued and then further exhausted in the complete motion of all the other joints.

This method probably evolved from weight lifting and was then used in bodybuilding. As with the superset, this method is not yet proven and is still at the stage of speculation.

Bodybuilding books, and especially some magazines, refer to many other methods, some of which are said to "work miracles" for athletes. A word to the wise regarding such claims is to be cautious in distinguishing the fine line that separates fact from fantasy.

Bodybuilding workouts are very exhausting even if the split routine method is employed, and often some 75 to 160 repetitions are performed in a single training session. Such high muscle loading requires a long recovery. Due to the type of work specific to bodybuilding, most if not all the ATP/CP and glycogen stores are exhausted after a demanding training session. Although the restoration of ATP/CP occurs very quickly, the exhausted liver glycogen requires some 46 to 48 hours to replenish. Thus, heavy workouts to complete exhaustion should not be performed more than three times per microcycle (refer to planning of microcycles for variation of intensities).

It may be argued that by using a split routine, a given group of muscles is trained every second day, leaving 48 hours between the two training sessions, sufficient time for restoration of energy fuels. Although this may be true for local muscle stores, it ignores the fact that when glucose is exhausted, the body starts tapping the glycogen stores in the liver. If the liver source is tapped every day, 24 hours may be insufficient time to restore glycogen. As a result, if the recovery phase is too short, the overtraining phenomenon may occur.

In addition to exhausting energy stores, constant training also puts wear and tear on the contractile myosins, exceeding their anabolism (the myosin's protein-building rate). The undesirable outcome of such overloading can be that the muscles involved no longer increase in size—there are no gains in hypertrophy. Consequently, one should reassess the application of the overloading principle and start using the step-type method as suggested by the principle of progressive increases of load in training. In addition, the alternation of intensities each microcycle should be considered. The purpose of alternating intensities in training is to alternate work with regeneration because regeneration is just as important as training.

As specified, the duration of the hypertrophy phase can be 4 to 6 weeks depending on the needs of the sport or event and the athlete. The total length of the preparatory phase is also important because the longer it is, the more time there is to work on hypertrophy as well as on MxS.

Table 8.4	Suggested Proportion Between Hypertrophy, MxS, and P for Linemen			
Preparatory				**Competitive**
3 AA	4 Hypertrophy: 3-4 sessions	6 MxS: 2-3 sessions Hypertrophy: 1-2 sessions	5 Conv. to P: 2 sessions MxS: 1 session Hypertrophy: 1 session	Maintenance: P, MxS, hypertrophy

It is equally important to understand that when the hypertrophy phase ends, it does not mean that an athlete who needs to build muscle mass must stop this training. As illustrated by table 8.4, hypertrophy training can be maintained and even further developed during the MxS phase. As such, depending on the needs of the athlete, the proportion between MxS and hypertrophy can be 3:1, 2:1, or even 1:1.

During the maintenance phase, hypertrophy training should be used by very few athletes, such as shot-putters and linemen, and then only during the first half.

As the most important competitions approach, P and MxS should prevail in training.

9

Phase Three: Maximum Strength

*[handwritten: * it determines length of the phase !!!]*

Nearly every sport requires strength, but what each sport really calls for is sport-specific strength. MxS plays an important, if not the determinant, role in creating sport-specific strength. Although the role of MxS varies between sports, it mainly determines the length of the phase. The more important the role of MxS, the longer the phase (e.g., throwers in track and field and linemen in football). The opposite is true if the final performance is not particularly dependent on the MxS contribution (e.g., golf, table tennis). An athlete's ability to generate MxS depends to a great extent on the diameter or cross-sectional area of the muscle involved, more specifically, the diameter of the myosin filaments, including their cross bridges; the capacity to recruit FT muscle fibers; and the ability to synchronize all the muscles involved in an action.

Muscle size depends greatly on the duration of the hypertrophy phase, where the diameter of myosin and the increase in protein content in the form of cross bridges depends on the volume and duration of the MxS phase. The capacity to recruit FT fibers depends on training content, in which maximum loads and explosive power should be dominant. This is the only type of strength training that activates the powerful FT motor units. Improving muscle synchronization depends strictly on learning, which means many repetitions of the same exercise.

[handwritten right margin: MxS, P result in load: ≥ 80-85%]

Strength improves as a result of creating high tension in the muscle, which is directly related to the training method employed. MxS increases as a result of activating a large number of FT motor units. An athlete does not necessarily have to develop large muscles and body weight to become significantly stronger. Throughout MxS and P training, athletes should learn to better synchronize the muscles involved and use loads that result in higher FT muscle fiber recruitment (loads greater than 80 to 85 percent). By using these methods for the MxS phase, especially the maximum load method, athletes will improve MxS with insignificant gains in muscle mass.

*[handwritten right margin: NO * gain muscle mass]*

Of the three contractions, eccentric contractions create the highest tension, followed by isometric and concentric. Concentric strength must be devel-

[handwritten: eccentric create the highest tension ↓ isometric ↓ concentric]

Key Words

Free weights: Weights not a part of an exercise machine (i.e., barbells and dumbbells).

Isometric (static) contraction: Tension is developed with no change in the length of the muscle.

Maxex Training: Combines maximum force exercises with explosive, maximum speed exercises.

Relative strength: The relationship between body weight and MxS.

oped at the highest levels, since most sport actions are concentric. Also, by applying other types of contraction, especially eccentric, athletic performance will benefit as a direct result of improvements in concentric force.

Exercises used for the development of MxS are not performed under conditions of exhaustion as in bodybuilding. Due to maximum activation of the CNS, including factors such as concentration and motivation, MxS training improves links with the CNS, thus improving muscle coordination and synchronization. High CNS activation (e.g., muscle synchronization) also results in adequate inhibition of the antagonistic muscles. This means that when maximum force is applied, these muscles are coordinated in such a way that they do not contract to oppose the movement.

Little is known about the involvement of the nervous system in MxS. Rising interest in the implications of the nervous system in strength training suggests that the CNS acts as a stimulus for strength gains. The CNS normally inhibits the activation of all the motor units available for contraction. Under extreme circumstances, such as fear or life-and-death situations, the inhibition is removed and all the motor units are activated (Fox et al., 1989). One of the main objectives of MxS training is to learn to eliminate CNS inhibition. A reduction in CNS inhibition accompanied by an increase in strength would result in the greatest improvement of strength potential.

Maximum Load Method (Isotonic)

In Periodization of Strength, MxS improved through the maximum load method (MLM) is probably the most determinant factor in developing sport-specific strength. The improvement of MxS using maximum loads has the following advantages:

- It increases motor unit activation, resulting in high recruitment of FT muscle fibers.

- It represents the determinant factor in increasing P. As such, it has a high neural output for sports where speed and power are dominant.

- It is a critical element in improving M-E, especially M-E of short and medium duration.

- It is important in sports where relative strength is crucial, such as the martial arts, boxing, wrestling, jumping events, and most team sports, since it results in minimal increase in hypertrophy. (Relative strength is the relationship between one's body weight and MxS, meaning the higher the relative strength, the better the performance.)

- It improves the coordination and synchronization of muscle groups during performance. The MLM has a learning component because, in physical actions, the muscles are involved in a certain sequence. The better the muscles involved in contraction are coordinated and synchronized and the more they learn to recruit FT muscle fibers, the better the performance.

The MLM positively influences speed- and power-dominant sports by increasing the myosin diameter of the FT fibers and recruiting more FT fibers. The MLM can result in MxS gains that are up to three times greater than the proportional gain in muscle hypertrophy. Although large increases in muscle size are possible for athletes who are just starting to use the MLM, they are less visible for athletes with a longer training background. The greatest gains

handwritten notes in margins:

inhibition accompained

* ↑ myosin diameter of the FT fibers
* recruiting more FT fibers

New   more visible
old   less

Exercises that improve MxS also increase CNS activation.

in MxS occur as a result of better synchronization and increased recruitment of the FT muscle fibers.

The main factors responsible for hypertrophy are not fully understood, but researchers increasingly believe that increased muscle size is stimulated mainly by a disturbance in the equilibrium between consumption and remanufacture of ATP known as the *ATP deficiency theory* (Hartmann & Tünnemann, 1988). During and immediately following MxS training, the protein content in the working muscles is low, if not exhausted, due to the depletion of ATP. As an athlete recovers between training sessions, the protein level exceeds the initial level, resulting in an increase in the size of the muscle fiber, especially if a protein-rich diet is followed.

In practice, this theory means that the muscles' store of ATP/CP should be constantly taxed, not only for gains in hypertrophy, which eventually will level off, but mostly for constant increases of MxS. Loads of 80 to 90 percent seem to be the most effective. Equally important, though, a long enough rest interval must be allowed for the full restoration of ATP/CP. Higher loads of 85 to 100 percent, which permit only two to four repetitions, are of short duration and allow complete restoration of ATP. As such, the ATP deficiency and the depletion of structural protein are too low to activate the protein metabolism that stimulates hypertrophy. Consequently, maximum loads with long rest intervals result in an increase of MxS, and not in hypertrophy.

The MLM also increases testosterone level, which further explains improved MxS. Male athletes with higher testosterone levels have better trainability; female athletes with lower testosterone levels have lower trainability. During the MxS phase, the testosterone level increases only in the first 8 weeks then decreases yet is still higher than at the start (Häkkinen, 1991). This is one reason for limiting MxS phases to no longer than 9 weeks. Apparently the level of testosterone in the blood also depends on the fre-

[Handwritten notes in margins: "testosteron ↑ when MLM is low." "↓ MLM '2 time a day'" "80" "85% - recruit" "15% - latent reserve" "MxS = P" "MxS = H"]

quency of MLM sessions per day and week. Testosterone increases when the number of MLM sessions per week is low and decreases when MLM training is planned twice a day. Such findings substantiate and further justify the suggestions made earlier regarding the frequency of high-intensity training sessions per microcycle.

Program Design

The MLM can be used only after a minimum of 2 to 3 years of general strength training (AA) using lighter loads because of the strain of training and the use of maximum loads. Strength gains can be expected even during long-term AA, mainly due to motor learning as athletes learn to better use and coordinate the muscles involved in training.

Highly trained athletes with 3 to 4 years of MLM are so well adapted to such training that they are able to recruit some 85 percent of their FT fibers. The remaining 15 percent represents a "latent reserve" that is not easily tapped through training (Hartmann & Tünnemann, 1988).

Once an athlete reaches such a level, further increases in MxS may be difficult to achieve. If further MxS development is necessary, alternate methods must be found to overcome this stagnation and continue improvement. New options include the following:

- Apply the principle of progressive increase of load in training. Every athlete who has done so has experienced improvements without the pain of exhaustion.
- Immediately begin an annual plan for strength training based on the concept of Periodization. By following this phase-specific training method, athletes will achieve the highest sport-specific strength at the time of the main competitions or league games.
- If an athlete has used Periodization of training for 2 to 4 years and cannot overcome a plateau, alternate various stimulations of the neuromuscular system. Following AA and the first phase of MxS, alternate 3 weeks of MxS with 3 weeks of P. Power training, with its explosiveness and fast application of force, represents a desired stimulation for the CNS.
- For power sports, another option can be used for stimulation: alternate 3 weeks of hypertrophy training with 3 weeks of MxS. The additional hypertrophy phases will result in a slight enlargement in muscle size or an increase in "active muscle mass." This additional gain in hypertrophy will provide a new biological base for further improvement of MxS.
- Increase the ratio between concentric and eccentric types of contraction (see chapter 12). The additional eccentric training will produce a higher stimulation for MxS improvement, since eccentric contraction creates higher tension in the muscle.

Among the most important elements of success for MLM training are the load used, the loading pattern, and the rhythm or speed of performing the contraction.

The Load

MxS is developed only by creating the highest tension possible in the muscle. Though lower loads engage ST muscle fibers, if most muscle fibers, especially FT fibers, are to be recruited in contraction, loads greater than 85 percent are necessary. Maximum loads with low repetitions result in significant nervous system adaptation, better synchronization of the muscles involved, and an increased capacity to recruit FT fibers. That is why MxS and explosive power are also called nervous system training (Schmidtbleicher, 1984). If, as suggested by Goldberg et al. (1975), the stimulus for protein synthesis is the tension developed in the myofilaments, it is further proof that MxS training should be carried out only with maximum load.

To produce the highest MxS improvements, the prime movers must do the greatest amount of work. Plan training sessions with the highest number of sets the athlete can tolerate (8 to 12). Since this is possible only with a low number of exercises (no more than 3 to 5), choose only exercises for the prime movers. Resist the temptation to use higher numbers of exercises.

Order exercises to ensure better alternation of muscle groups, facilitating local muscle recovery between sets. Even when exercises are ordered to maximize muscle group involvement, there appear to be two approaches regarding the sequence of performing them. Some prefer to perform one set of each exercise starting from the top (vertically). Others choose to perform all sets for the first exercise before moving on to the next (horizontally; see table 9.1). The vertical approach provides better recovery between sets and less fatigue. Minimizing fatigue is important because, in most sports, strength training is just one of the elements that lead to better performance. Thus, attention must be paid to how energy is spent, especially during the competitive phase. Also consider the overall fatigue experienced in training. The horizontal approach is discouraged because it results in higher local fatigue and exhausts the muscles much faster. Working the muscles in a state of exhaustion results in hypertrophy rather than MxS. MxS will benefit only during the early sets, and once exhaustion is reached, muscle mass will benefit.

Since a maximum load is used in MLM training, the number of repetitions per set is low (1 to 4), and the suggested number of repetitions per exercise for a training session is between 15 and 80. The number of repetitions per exercise varies depending on the athlete's classification, training background, and training phase. Hartmann and Tünnemann (1988) proposed the following number of repetitions per exercise per training session for highly trained athletes:

- 100 to 95 percent: 15 to 25 repetitions
- 95 to 90 percent: 20 to 40 repetitions
- 90 to 80 percent: 35 to 85 repetitions
- 80 to 75 percent: 70 to 110 repetitions

Table 9.1 Suggested Training Parameters for the MLM

Training parameters	Work
Load	85-100 percent
Number of exercises	3-5
Number of repetitions per set	1-4
Number of sets per session	6-10 (12)
Rest interval	3-6 minutes
Frequency per week	2-3 (4)

The number of exercises dictates whether to use the lower or higher number of repetitions. If four exercises are selected, use the lower number; for two exercises, the higher number. If the number of repetitions is much lower than recommended, MxS benefits will seriously decline. These suggestions should reinforce the wisdom of selecting a low number of exercises. The lower the number of exercises, the more sets and repetitions can be performed and the greater the MxS improvement per muscle group.

The rest interval (RI) between sets is a function of the athlete's fitness level and should be calculated to ensure adequate recovery of the neuromuscular system. For the MLM, a 3- to 6-minute RI is necessary because maximum loads involve the CNS system, and it takes longer to recover. If the RI is much shorter, CNS participation in terms of maximum concentration, motivation, and the power of nerve impulses sent to the contracting muscles could plummet. Complete restoration of the required fuel for contraction (ATP/CP) may also be jeopardized.

Speed of Contraction

Speed of contraction plays an important role in MLM training. Athletic movements are often performed fast, explosively. To maximize speed, the entire neuromuscular system must adapt to quickly recruiting FT fibers, a key factor in all sports dominated by speed and power. Even with the maximum loads typical of the MLM, the athlete's force application against resistance must be exerted as quickly as possible, even explosively.

To achieve explosive force, maximize the athlete's concentration and motivation before each set. The athlete must concentrate on activating the muscles quickly even though the barbell is moving slowly. Only a high speed of contraction performed against a maximum load will quickly recruit FT fibers resulting in increased MxS. For maximum training benefits, mobilize all strength potentials in the shortest time possible and from the early part of the lift.

Considering the high demand placed on the neuromuscular system, the frequency of MLM training should be no more than two to three times per week. Only elite athletes, particularly linemen in football or shot-putters in track and field, should train four times a week. During the competitive phase, the frequency can be reduced to one to two MLM sessions per week, often in combination with other strength components such as power.

Figure 9.1 shows the MxS phase of a strength training program for an Olympic-class sprinter. This program was used successfully by Ben Johnson in the mid-1980s. To better exemplify the step method for load increment, the bottom of the chart graphically illustrates the step method loading pattern. This 9-week program was repeated twice a year as sprinters usually follow a bi-cycle annual plan. Program weeks are numbered from 1 to 9. A testing (T) session was planned in each of the low steps and was performed in the latter part of the week when the athlete had better recovered from the strain of a high step. Obviously, the goal of the test was to determine the new 100 percent (1RM) and then use it to calculate the load for the following 3-week cycle. You may notice a discrepancy in the number of sets. Some exercises are a high priority and others a lower priority. This way, most of the energy and attention are focused on the high-priority exercises.

The vertical arrows indicate that the same loading pattern was used for the exercise below. The load is lower for leg curls than for most exercises simply because the knee flexors are often more prone to injury, not because this exercise represents a lower priority. In addition, the athlete had not

No.	Exercise	T	Week 1	Week 2	Week 3	T	Week 4	Week 5	Week 6	T	Week 7	Week 8	Week 9
1	Half squats	✓	$\frac{70_1}{8}\ \frac{80_2}{6}$	$\frac{80_2}{6}\ \frac{85_3}{5}\ \frac{90_1}{3}$	$\frac{85_2}{5}\ \frac{90_3}{3}\ \frac{95_1}{2}$	✓	$\frac{80_2}{6}\ \frac{85_1}{4}$	$\frac{85_2}{5}\ \frac{90_3}{3}\ \frac{95_1}{2}$	$\frac{90_3}{3}\ \frac{95_2}{2}\ \frac{100_1}{1}$	✓	$\frac{80_3}{6}$	$\frac{85_1}{5}\ \frac{90_3}{3}\ \frac{95_2}{2}$	$\frac{90_2}{3}\ \frac{95_3}{2}\ \frac{100_2}{1}$
2	Arm pulls	✓	→	→	→	✓	→	→	→	✓	→	→	→
3	Leg curls	✓	$\frac{60_1}{12}\ \frac{70_2}{10}$	$\frac{60_1}{12}\ \frac{70_2}{10}\ \frac{80_2}{6}$	$\frac{70_2}{8}\ \frac{80_2}{6}\ \frac{85_2}{4}$	✓	$\frac{70_3}{8}$	$\frac{70_1}{8}\ \frac{80_2}{6}\ \frac{85_3}{5}$	$\frac{80_1}{6}\ \frac{85_2}{5}\ \frac{90_2}{3}$	✓	$\frac{80_3}{5}$	$\frac{80_1}{6}\ \frac{85_3}{5}\ \frac{90_2}{3}$	$\frac{85_2}{5}\ \frac{90_3}{3}\ \frac{95_2}{2}$
4	Reverse leg presses	✓	$\frac{70_2}{8}\ \frac{80_2}{6}$	$\frac{80_2}{6}\ \frac{85_3}{5}\ \frac{90_1}{3}$	$\frac{85_2}{5}\ \frac{90_3}{3}\ \frac{95_1}{2}$	✓	$\frac{80_2}{6}\ \frac{85_1}{4}$	$\frac{85_2}{5}\ \frac{90_3}{3}\ \frac{95_1}{2}$	$\frac{90_3}{3}\ \frac{95_2}{2}\ \frac{100_1}{1}$	✓	$\frac{80_3}{6}$	$\frac{85_1}{5}\ \frac{90_3}{3}\ \frac{95_2}{2}$	$\frac{90_2}{3}\ \frac{95_3}{2}\ \frac{100_2}{1}$
5	Bench presses	✓	→	→	→	✓	→	→	→	✓	→	→	→
6	Power cleans	–	$\frac{60_1}{10}\ \frac{70_2}{8}$	$\frac{60_1}{8}\ \frac{70_2}{6}\ \frac{80_1}{4}$	$\frac{70_1}{6}\ \frac{80_3}{4}$	–	$\frac{70_3}{6}$	$\frac{70_1}{6}\ \frac{80_4}{4}$	$\frac{80_4}{4}$	–	$\frac{70_3}{6}$	$\frac{70_1}{6}\ \frac{80_3}{4}$	$\frac{80_4}{4}$
	Loading pattern		Low	Medium	High		Low	Medium	High		Low	Medium	High	

Figure 9.1 Example MLM program for an Olympic-class sprinter.

No.	Exercise	Dates					
		May 13-19	May 20-26	May 27-June 2	June 3-9	June 10-16	June 17-23
1	Squats/leg presses	$\frac{70}{8}$ ₃	$\frac{70}{8}$ ₁ $\frac{80}{6}$ ₂	$\frac{80}{8}$ ₁ $\frac{90}{3}$ ₂	$\frac{70}{10}$ ₃	$\frac{80}{8}$ ₁ $\frac{90}{3}$ ₂	$\frac{90}{3}$ ₁ $\frac{95}{2}$ ₂
2	Sit-ups	3 × 15	3 × 18	3 × 20	3 × 15	3 × 18	3 × 20
3	Military presses	$\frac{70}{8}$ ₃	$\frac{70}{8}$ ₁ $\frac{80}{6}$ ₂	$\frac{80}{8}$ ₁ $\frac{90}{3}$ ₂	$\frac{70}{10}$ ₃	$\frac{80}{8}$ ₁ $\frac{90}{3}$ ₂	$\frac{90}{3}$ ₁ $\frac{95}{2}$ ₂
4	Leg curls	$\frac{50}{12}$ ₁ $\frac{60}{10}$ ₂	$\frac{60}{10}$ ₃	$\frac{60}{10}$ ₂ $\frac{70}{8}$ ₁	$\frac{60}{10}$ ₃	$\frac{60}{12}$ ₁ $\frac{70}{10}$ ₂	$\frac{70}{10}$ ₃
5	Toe raises	$\frac{70}{8}$ ₃	$\frac{70}{8}$ ₁ $\frac{80}{6}$ ₂	$\frac{80}{8}$ ₁ $\frac{90}{3}$ ₂	$\frac{70}{10}$ ₃	$\frac{80}{8}$ ₁ $\frac{90}{3}$ ₂	$\frac{90}{3}$ ₁ $\frac{95}{2}$ ₂
6	Front lat pull-downs	$\frac{70}{8}$ ₃	$\frac{70}{8}$ ₁ $\frac{80}{6}$ ₂	$\frac{80}{8}$ ₁ $\frac{90}{3}$ ₂	$\frac{70}{10}$ ₃	$\frac{80}{8}$ ₁ $\frac{90}{3}$ ₂	$\frac{90}{3}$ ₁ $\frac{95}{2}$ ₂
7	Simple dead lifts	$\frac{50}{12}$ ₁ $\frac{60}{10}$ ₂	$\frac{60}{10}$ ₃	$\frac{60}{10}$ ₂ $\frac{70}{8}$ ₁	$\frac{60}{10}$ ₃	$\frac{60}{12}$ ₁ $\frac{70}{10}$ ₂	$\frac{70}{10}$ ₃

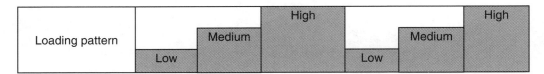

Loading pattern — Low, Medium, High, Low, Medium, High

Figure 9.2 Six-week MxS phase for a college women's volleyball team. *Note:* RI between sets = 3 to 4 minutes.

reached a balanced development between knee extensors and flexors at that point. Notice that for the low step, the load is always decreased and the number of sets reduced. Figure 9.2 shows a 6-week MxS program for a women's volleyball team (college level). In the program, force was applied aggressively, without jerking or snapping. During the RI, the limbs used were shaken to relax the muscles. Dumbbells were used for dead lifts. The program was repeated three times a week.

Partial Extension Variation

When the traditional method of contraction through the entire range of motion no longer improves MxS, the partial extension method can enable athletes to achieve additional improvement in maximum strength. Partial extension is performed by flexing the targeted joint approximately one-quarter of its entire range of motion (see figure 9.3).

When using the entire range of motion, the most difficult part in overcoming the weight of the barbell is at the lowest end. In the bench press, this occurs when the barbell is close to or touching the chest. At this point, the muscles are at their shortest and weakest because the overlap between actins and myosins is greatest. The highest force of pull of both actins and myosins occurs at the opposite end, the beginning of overlapping. This is the point at which the cross bridges are capable of displaying maximum force. Partial extension, therefore, results in maximizing force capabilities. Through partial extension, athletes can lift heavier loads than 1RM, creating higher tension in the muscles and improving maximum force. When the highest loads are used and maximum concentration is necessary, the partial extension method is advisable only for elite athletes or those with an extensive strength training background.

Drop Jumps With Light Loads

A drop jump (figure 9.4) is a depth jump performed by jumping from a height while tightly holding the limb at a given angle without flexing further. In most cases, the angle could be between one-quarter to one-half the total range of flexion. To create the high tension necessary to improve MxS, athletes must land on the floor on the balls of the feet with the knees or elbows at a predetermined angle. This angle is held tightly for 2 to 3 seconds. For drop jumps performed with the arms, a heavy vest may be worn to increase the load.

Figure 9.3   Example of the partial extension method.

The high stress and tension of performing a drop jump are felt in the muscle tissue as well as in ligaments and tendons. Unless athletes have at least 4 to 5 years of strength training or are well adapted to heavy loads and have strong ligaments and tendons, they should not perform higher drop jumps or use weights. Pay maximum attention to the landing. For drop jumps on the legs, keep the spine as tight and as vertical as possible. Do not bob forward and backward, especially if a weight is used, since this may result in low back problems. When using a barbell, the athlete and barbell should form a single, compact unit. A towel can be used over the shoulders to avoid bruises. The progression from free drop jumps to higher jumps, or to using weights, should take

Figure 9.4   Two examples of drop jumps, one for the legs and one for the arms.

place over several years of training. Be conservative in progressing. It is always better to underload athletes than to overload them.

Drop jump progression goes as follows:

- Free drop jumps from a low height (60 centimeters or 2 feet)
- Free drop jumps from a higher point (80 centimeters or 3 feet)
- Drop jumps from a low height (25 to 60 centimeters or 1 to 2 feet) with a low load (a light dumbbell in each hand, a heavy vest over the torso using the lightest load the vest can accommodate, or a light barbell on the shoulders)
- Drop jumps from a higher point (60 to 80 centimeters or 2 to 3 feet) with low loads
- Drop jumps from a higher point (60 to 80 centimeters or 2 to 3 feet) while increasing the load slightly (20 to 30 percent of 1RM)

 Isometric Method

This training method was known and used for some time before Hettinger and Müler (1953) and again Hettinger (1966) scientifically justified the merits of static contractions in the development of maximum strength. This method climaxed in the 1960s then faded in popularity. Although static contraction has little functional effect for muscular endurance, it is still useful for the development of MxS and can be used by throwers in their strength training efforts. Static conditions can be realized through two techniques: (1) by attempting to lift a weight heavier than one's potential and (2) by applying force (push or pull) against an immobile object.

An isometric contraction produces high tension in the muscle, making this method most useful during the MxS phase. With disputed merits, it can also be used in the maintenance phase to preserve MxS. Even if, as some enthusiasts claim, isometric training can increase MxS by 10 to 15 percent more than other methods, it has clear limitations in the development of P and M-E.

As isometric force is applied against a given resistance, the tension in the muscle builds progressively, reaching maximum in about 2 to 3 seconds and, toward the end, decreasing in a much shorter time (1 to 2 seconds). Since training benefits are angle specific, each group of muscles must be trained at different angles. For instance, if the range of motion of a joint is 180 degrees, to achieve benefit throughout this range, angles of 15, 45, 75, 105, 135, and 165 degrees must be used. Only then does the tension cover the entire range of motion. Reservations can also be expressed regarding transferability of angle-specific strength gains into dynamic or explosive athletic actions, which often involve muscles throughout the entire range of motion.

The isometric method has both advantages and disadvantages. Isometric exercises can be performed with simple apparatus or equipment and can result in rapid increases in strength, especially for beginners. A partner is not needed. It can be used to rehabilitate injured muscles. Since no joint motion occurs, "the athlete may continue training even with a joint or bone injury" (Hartmann & Tünnemann, 1988). This can certainly reduce the risk of muscular atrophy. Isometric training produces negligible increase in muscle hypertrophy. This can be an advantage for athletes in sports dominated by relative strength. The duration of a training session is short (20 to 30 minutes). Well-trained athletes may be able to contract most if not all the motor units. Fatigue experienced at the end of a training session may be no higher than that for the MLM.

Isometric training has disadvantages, too. Since strength development is angle specific, contractions must be performed at different angles (every 30 degrees) to cover the entire range of motion. MxS gains cannot be applied readily to dynamic contractions. There is no learning component of the technical skills involved in the selected sport or muscle memory. Because isometric contraction is static, it does not develop flexibility, so training may affect muscle elasticity. Since isometric contraction is performed in a state of apnea (breath holding), an oxygen debt is acquired during work. This must be compensated for by breathing at a higher rate during the rest interval. Gains in MxS may be lost as quickly as they are gained. Although isometric training may add to overall gains in MxS, it does not shift the force-time curve to the left, a disadvantage that must not be ignored. Finally, isometric contractions have little, if any, cardiorespiratory benefit. In fact, blood circulation may be restrained during a contraction, hampering the supply of nutrients. Athletes with heart and circulation problems are strongly discouraged from engaging in isometric training.

Program Design

Achieving maximum gains with isometric training requires exercises as similar as possible to the technical skill. The isometric method should be used primarily by advanced athletes in combination with other MxS methods. See table 9.2 for training parameters.

Isometric contraction can be performed with all limbs using angles from completely open to fully bent. The following aspects should be considered:

- Isometric training is most effective when contraction is near maximum (80 to 100 percent).
- The duration of contraction can be between 6 and 12 seconds, a total of 60 to 90 seconds per muscle per training session.
- The training load is intensified by increasing the number of exercises and sets, not by increasing the duration of contractions.
- During the 60- to 90-second RI, relaxation and breathing exercises are recommended. The latter is a compensatory necessity because static

Table 9.2 Suggested Training Parameters for Isometric Training

Training parameters	Work
Load	80-100 percent
Number of exercises	4-6
Duration of contraction per set	6-12 seconds
Duration of contraction per session	60-90 seconds
Number of sets per session	6-9
Rest interval	60-90 seconds
Frequency per week	2-3

contraction is performed in apnea. In addition, the intrathoracic pressure is elevated, which restricts circulation and thus oxygen supply.

- For a more effective program, alternate static contractions with isotonic contractions, especially for sports that require speed and power.
- A more effective variant of the isometric method is the functional isometric contraction, which involves free weights. This variant combines isotonic with isometric exercises in that the athlete lifts an object to a certain angle, where it is stopped for 6 to 8 seconds. While working through the entire range of motion, the athlete may stop two to four times, which combines the isotonic and isometric methods. This variant has a better physiological benefit, hence the term "functional," especially for M-E short.

③ Isokinetic Method

Isokinetic means "equal motion," or maintaining the same speed of movement throughout the range of motion. Specially designed equipment allows muscles to encounter the same resistance for both concentric and eccentric contractions. Although the equipment can provide maximum activation of the muscles involved, training velocity is very important because benefits are proportional to velocity. Training at slower speeds seems to increase strength only at the speed of contraction employed, resulting in major gains in muscle hypertrophy. On the other hand, training at a higher speed may increase strength at all speeds of contraction at or below the training speed, with major benefits for MxS and even some gains in P.

More advanced motor-driven computerized equipment can be used to set the desired velocity and measure strength. Although isokinetic equipment has yet to fulfill the major requirement in strength training, namely, to constantly increase acceleration, it can be used as a training method as long as its advantages and disadvantages are taken into account.

The isokinetic method offers athletes a safe training environment and is appropriate for novice athletes. It is well suited for the AA phase when overall strength development and muscle attachment adaptation is the main purpose, and can be used for rehabilitation of injuries. Athletes can achieve gains in hypertrophy depending on the load and number of repetitions. At higher velocities that create increased resistance, athletes may experience gains in MxS.

Isokinetic training has its disadvantages, too. The equipment is expensive and permits only a constant exercise speed, contrary to most athletic movements. In athletics, the application of force is progressively increased to reach maximum acceleration toward the end of the action. This element cannot be duplicated with isokinetic equipment. Finally, the force-velocity curve does not shift left because of the constant resistance and the nonexplosive actions.

Program Design

A training program designed for isokinetic contraction must follow the same methodology as the MLM. Resistance must be close to or at maximum so that the highest strength mobilization will occur. With the load (resistance of the machine) set to maximum, an athlete obviously will be unable to perform more than 3 to 4 repetitions. See table 9.3 for training parameters.

Table 9.3 Suggested Training Parameters for the Isokinetic Method	
Training parameters	**Work**
Load	Maximum
Number of exercises	3-5
Number of repetitions per set	1-4
Number of repetitions per session	40-60
Number of sets per session	3-5
Rest interval	3-6 minutes
Frequency per week	1-2

Isokinetic equipment allows the athlete to preset the speed of performance. With maximum resistance provided by the machine, the movement cannot be performed quickly. To achieve MxS benefits, however, the athlete must attempt to apply force as dynamically as possible to recruit the highest proportion of FT muscle fibers. All other training parameters must follow the suggestions made for the MLM (see table 9.1).

Again, due to its disadvantages, the isokinetic method should be used in conjunction with the MLM. That is why some of the training parameters are lower than for the MLM, as well as the frequency per week. The balance is performed with other methods, primarily the MLM.

Eccentric Method

Any strength exercise performed with free weights or most isokinetic equipment employs concentric and eccentric contractions. During the concentric phase, force is produced while the muscle shortens; during the eccentric segment, it is produced as the muscle lengthens.

Practice has demonstrated that the eccentric phase always seems to be easier than the concentric phase. When a bench press is performed, the return of the barbell to the starting point (the eccentric part of the lift) always seems easier than the lift itself. Thus, one could logically conclude that since an athlete can work with heavier loads during the eccentric contraction, strength is certainly improved to higher levels by using the eccentric method alone.

Researchers have concluded that eccentric training creates higher tension in the muscles than isometric or isotonic contractions. Furthermore, since higher muscle tension normally means higher strength development (Goldberg et al., 1975), eccentric training could logically be considered a superior training method.

Komi and Buskirk (1972) demonstrated the superiority of the eccentric method over the isokinetic method. Other researchers have found that gains in maximum strength appear to result mostly from changes in neural activation rather than hypertrophic response (Dudley & Fleck, 1987). This means that MxS improvements do not result from gains in muscle mass, but rather from specific neural adaptations such as an increase in FT muscle fiber recruitment, increased strength with little or no hypertrophy, and modifications in the neural commands used to control the movement. The nervous system commands the eccentric contraction differently. This occurs mostly as grading, or ranking the amount of muscle activation necessary to complete a task (Enoka, 1996). The amount of muscle activation and the number of fibers involved are proportional to the training load. The neural command for eccentric contraction is unique in that it decides: (1) which motor units should be activated; (2) how much they have to be activated; (3) when they should be activated; and (4) how the activity should be distributed within a group of muscles (Abbruzzese et al., 1994).

Muscles resist fatigue during eccentric contraction, and activity can be longer than for concentric contraction (Tesch et al., 1978), possibly because of the altered recruitment order of motor units. As the load in eccentric training is much higher than in the maximum concentric contraction, the speed of performance is quite slow. Since such a slow rate of contraction does not result in higher neural activation, it stimulates protein synthesis at a higher rate, resulting in muscle hypertrophy. However, if the eccentric contraction is performed faster, the muscle force is higher than the concentric method (Astrand & Rodahl, 1985). This can create a major difficulty in training, especially if free weights are employed. Two spotters are needed to help the athlete lift the barbell for the concentric phase because the load for eccentric training is higher than 1RM. The spotters should also ensure that as the bar is lowered, the athlete does not drop it onto the chest, causing injury. The need for such careful assistance as the bar is being slowly lowered makes it impossible to perform the exercise quickly. Unless one has access to special isokinetic equipment, or can stop the barbell before it reaches the chest (security pins or keys), fast eccentric contraction is difficult and unsafe.

Athletes may experience muscle soreness during the first few days of eccentric training. This is to be expected, since higher tension provokes some muscle damage. As athletes adapt, the muscle soreness will disappear (7 to 10 days). Short-term discomfort can be avoided if the load is increased in steps.

As expected, the eccentric method shifts the force-time curve to the left. Heavy loads that generate high tension in the muscles improve strength because they result in high recruitment of the powerful FT motor units. Strength gains are even greater if the force is exerted faster.

Program Design

Only athletes with 3 to 5 years of strength training background should use the eccentric training method since it employs the heaviest loads (110 to 160 percent). The eccentric method can be used alone in a training session or a short training phase, or can be combined with other methods, especially the MLM. Eccentric contractions should not be used excessively. Every time maximum or supermaximum loads are employed, maximal mental concentration is required, which can be psychologically wearing. Use the eccentric method carefully no more than once or twice a week, or in combination with power training.

To achieve maximum training benefits, athletes should use the MLM for as long as practically possible. When a plateau is reached where little or no improvement is being achieved, the coach should turn to the eccentric method. Remember to balance the antagonistic muscles by exposing them to the same methods, but not necessarily the same number of sets. To avoid injury, use two spotters. Active recovery techniques should be used to elimi-

Table 9.4 Suggested Training Parameters for the Eccentric Method

Training parameters	Work
Load	110-160 percent
Number of exercises	3-5
Number of repetitions per set	1-4
Number of sets per exercise	4-6 (8)
Number of sets per session	20-36
Rest interval	3-6 minutes
Speed of execution	Slow
Frequency per week	1

nate discomfort, reduce soreness, and encourage faster regeneration (for additional information, see chapter 13).

Table 9.4 presents training parameters for the eccentric method. The range of the load is presented as the percentage of maximum strength capacity for the concentric contraction and suggests a resistance between 110 and 160 percent. Lower loads should be used for less experienced athletes. The most effective load for highly trained athletes is around 130 to 140 percent. Such loads should be used only after at least two seasons of MxS training in which the eccentric contraction method is also employed. The suggested number of sets per exercise should be used as a guideline for experienced athletes. This number should be lowered for other athletes according to their training potential. The same applies to the number of sets per training session, which also depends on the number of exercises. The rest interval is an important element in the capacity to perform highly demanding work. If athletes do not recover well enough between sets to complete the next set at the same level, the RI must be increased slightly.

The speed of execution is slow because the load is supermaximum. The athlete's motivation and concentration capacity are important factors in eccentric training. Because eccentric contractions use such heavy loads, athletes must be highly motivated and able to concentrate. By being mentally and psychologically prepared, they will be capable of performing eccentric contractions effectively. The eccentric method is rarely performed in isolation from the other MxS methods. Even during the MxS phase, the eccentric method is used with the MLM; therefore, only one eccentric training session per week is suggested. For elite athletes, the frequency may eventually be

Table 9.5 Example of the Progression and Proportions Between Concentric and Eccentric Contraction for a 6-Week MxS for a College Football Team

Week	1	2	3	4	5	6
Types of training and frequency per week	Concentric 3×	Concentric 4×	Concentric 3× Eccentric 1×	Concentric 1× Eccentric 2×	Concentric 2× Eccentric 2×	Concentric 2× Eccentric 2×

No.	Exercise	Week 4	Week 5	Week 6
1	Squats (eccentric)	$\frac{120}{6}$ 4	$\frac{130}{4}$ 4	$\frac{140}{3\text{-}4}$ 4
2	Incline bench presses (eccentric)	$\frac{120}{6}$ 4	$\frac{130}{4}$ 4	$\frac{140}{3\text{-}4}$ 4
3	Dead lifts (concentric)	$\frac{75}{8}$ 3	$\frac{75}{8}$ 3	$\frac{75}{8}$ 3
4	Toe raises (concentric)	$\frac{90}{3}$ 3	$\frac{90}{4}$ 3	$\frac{90}{5}$ 3
5	Jump squats (takeoff=concentric, landing=eccentric)	$\frac{70}{5\text{-}6}$ 3	$\frac{70}{6}$ 3	$\frac{70}{6}$ 3

Loading pattern		High	High
	Low/Medium		

Figure 9.5   A sample MxS phase for the last 3 weeks of a 6-week competitive phase for an international-class shot-putter.

increased during the third step in the pattern to increase the load in training. See table 9.5 for a sample six-week program designed for a college football team. Figure 9.5 shows the last 3 weeks of a 6-week program developed for an international-class shot-putter. A 3-week conversion to power phase followed, then a week of unloading prior to an important competition.

⑤ Maxex Training

The above methods for development of MxS should not be applied rigidly or in isolation, especially for sports where speed and power are dominant. For all team sports, sprinting, jumping, and throwing events in track and field, the martial arts, boxing, wrestling, Alpine skiing, ski-jumping, fencing, diving, figure skating, sprinting in swimming, etc., MxS methods can be combined with plyometrics. Maximum-tension exercises can be combined with exercises requiring explosiveness. This new method combining maximum force with exercises for explosiveness will be called *Maxex Training.*

The variations of training methods proposed (figures 9.6 through 9.15) need not be performed year-round. They can be planned at the end of the preparatory phase or, in the case of several MxS phases, during the last phase. An MxS phase is still necessary before any power training, as power is a function of MxS. The incorporation of power training during the MxS phase enhances speed and explosiveness to ready athletes for the competitive phase.

Combining MxS with power must be done carefully and conservatively. Although many combinations are possible, remember that training has to be simple so athletes can focus on the main task of the workout or training phase. The more variations you use, the more you may confuse your athletes and disrupt the way their bodies adapt.

Figure 9.6 shows a variation of Maxex Training using slow eccentric with fast concentric contractions. The suggested program includes the following:

Load: 60 to 80 percent of 1RM, depending on how important MxS is to the sport; heavier loads are for football and throwing events

Number of reps: 6 to 8

Number of sets: 1 to 3, depending on how many other activities are performed in the workout

RI between sets: 2 to 4 minutes

Another variation is a slow eccentric contraction followed by jumping half squats (figure 9.7). The suggested program for this variation is:

Load: 40 to 60 percent, or slightly higher for football and throwing events

Number of reps: 4 to 6

Number of sets: 1 to 4

RI between sets: 2 to 3 minutes

Be sure to keep upper body vertical with the barbell tight on the shoulders. Place a heavy towel on the shoulders to avoid bruising. Absorb the shock of landing by contacting the ground first with the toes and balls of the feet, then the heels.

Another variation is shown in figure 9.8. The athlete performs a drop jump (barbell on shoulders) with a quick concentric contraction followed by box plyometrics. A drop jump from 25-40 cm (10-15 in.) is maintained for 2 seconds. Once the spotters remove the barbell, the jumper performs plyometrics on and off a set of boxes or benches of the same height. The suggested program is:

Figure 9.6 The eccentric contraction (bending the knees) is performed slowly, whereas the concentric contraction (knee extension) is done as quickly as possible.

Figure 9.7 After completing the slow eccentric contraction, the athlete performs a jumping squat (10 to 20 centimeters or 5 to 7.5 inches). The barbell could be replaced with dumbbells held in each hand.

Figure 9.8 Drop jump from 25 to 40 centimeters (10 to 15 inches) is maintained for 2 seconds; as soon as the spotters take the barbell off the shoulders, the athlete does plyometrics on and off a set of boxes or benches of the same height.

Figure 9.9   Same drop jump as in figure 9.8 but this time followed by a series of bounding exercises on alternate legs.

Load: 40 to 80 percent
Number of reps for box plyometrics: 6 to 8
Number of sets: 3 to 6

The variation in figure 9.9 shows a drop jump followed by bounding exercises. The suggested program includes:

Load: 40 to 60 percent
Number of reps: 1 drop jump, 1 jump squat, followed by a series of 8 to 10 bounding exercises
Number of sets: 3 to 6

Figure 9.10 shows a drop jump, jump squat, followed by two-legged jumps over hurdles, benches, or ribbons. The suggested program uses the same load, number of repetitions, and number of sets as were suggested for the variation in figure 9.9. For variety, replace the hurdle jumps with bounding exercises.

Figure 9.11 shows a drop jump, quick concentric contraction, slow eccentric contraction, followed by bounding or jumps over objects. The suggested program also uses the same load, repetitions, and number of sets as in figure 9.9. For variety, replace jumps over objects with bounding.

Figure 9.10   This time the drop jump is followed by one to four jump squats; after removing the barbell, a series of two-legged jumps is performed over hurdles, benches, ribbons, or the like.

Figure 9.11 Combination of a drop jump with quick concentric and slow eccentric contractions followed by a series of hurdle jumps or bounding exercises.

Figure 9.12 One-legged eccentric contraction (on incline leg press machine) followed by a series of jumps and bounds.

The final variation uses an eccentric contraction (one leg) followed by plyometrics (figure 9.12).

The suggested program is:

Load: 110 to 140 percent of 1RM for one leg
Number of reps: 2 to 4 for each leg, followed by 8 to 10 plyometrics
Number of sets: 2 to 3
RI between sets: 2 to 4 minutes

Maxex Training applies to the upper body as well. In sports like basketball, baseball, ice hockey, football, lacrosse, the martial arts, boxing, wrestling, kayaking, squash, European handball, water polo, wrestling, and throwing events in track and field, strong arms and shoulders are essential. Without exhausting all options, the following three examples (figures 9.13 through 9.15) will illustrate how Maxex Training can be applied to the above sports.

Figure 9.13 shows a slow eccentric, fast concentric incline bench press, drop push-ups, shot throw, and medicine ball throw. The suggested program is:

Load: 70 to 90 percent
Number of reps: 2 to 4 for bench press and drop push-up, 4 to 8 for shot and medicine ball throws

Figure 9.13   After two to three slow eccentric, fast concentric incline bench presses, the athlete performs a drop push-up followed by explosive shot and medicine ball throws (one or two arms). Appropriate for shot put, boxing, the martial arts, football, basketball, and so on.

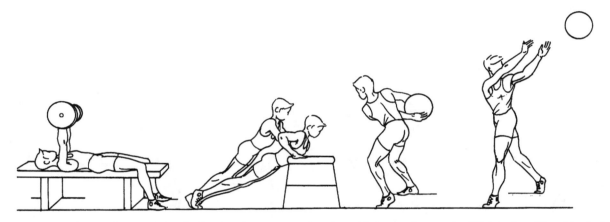

Figure 9.14   Suggested Maxex training for hockey, lacrosse, rugby, discus throw, and so on, in which a slow eccentric, fast concentric bench press is followed by drop push-ups and side medicine ball throws.

Number of sets: 2 to 4
RI between sets: 2 to 3 minutes

In the second variation, the athlete performs slow eccentric, fast concentric bench press, drop push-ups, and side medicine ball throws (figure 9.14). The suggested program is:

Load: 70 to 90 percent
Number of reps: 2 to 4 for bench press and drop push-up, 4 to 8 for shot and medicine ball throws
Number of sets: 2 to 4
RI between sets: 2 to 3 minutes

Finally, the variation in figure 9.15 shows a slow eccentric, fast concentric incline bench press, drop push-up and overhead medicine ball throws. The suggested program includes:

Load: 70 to 90 percent
Number of reps: 2 to 4 for bench press and drop push-up, 4 to 8 for shot and medicine ball throws
Number of sets: 2 to 4
RI between sets: 2 to 3 minutes

Figure 9.15   Example of Maxex Training in which incline bench and drop push-ups are combined with medicine ball overhead throws. Appropriate for basketball, volleyball, football (quarterback), baseball, soccer, lacrosse, and so on.

During the MxS phase, athletes can combine MxS methods with some of the given variations or with plyometrics (either low or medium impact). Table 9.6 suggests such combinations for an athlete who plans three strength training sessions per week.

Table 9.6 Possible Combination of MxS With Maxex Training					
Monday	**Tuesday**	**Wednesday**	**Thursday**	**Friday**	**Saturday**
*T/TA		*T/TA		*T/TA	
*15 minutes Maxex		*15 minutes Maxex		*15 minutes Maxex	
*45 minutes MxS		*60 minutes MxS		*45-60 minutes MxS	

The concept of Maxex Training relies on science, manipulating two physiological concepts to produce speed and explosiveness and improve athletic performance. The first part of the Maxex routine is performed against a heavier load, which stimulates a high recruitment of FT muscle fibers. The follow-up explosive/quickness movements increase the firing rate of the FT muscle fibers, preparing the athlete for the quick, explosive actions required for all speed-power sports during the competitive phase.

chapter 10

Phase Four: Conversion Phase—Conversion to Power

Strength training has become widely accepted as a determinant element in athletic performance. Today almost every athlete uses some sort of strength training program. However, most strength programs fail to transform strength gains into sport- or event-specific strength. The Periodization of Strength method accomplishes this transformation with the conversion phase.

The unrefined, nonspecific gains in strength made during the previous phase are of no direct benefit to athletic performance. Thus, the main objective of the conversion phase is to synthesize those gains into competitive and sport-specific P or M-E that forms the physiological foundation for advancements in athletic performance during the competitive phase. The determining factors in the success of the conversion phase are its duration and the specific methods used to transform MxS gains into sport-specific strength.

Training Methods for Sport-Specific Power

Power is the ability of the neuromuscular system to produce the greatest possible force in the shortest amount of time. Power is simply the product of muscle force (F) multiplied by the velocity (V) of movement: $P = F \times V$. For athletic purposes, any increase in power must be the result of improvements in either strength, speed, or a combination of the two.

An athlete can be very strong, with a large muscle mass, yet be unable to display power due to an inability to contract already strong muscles in a very short time. To overcome this deficiency, the athlete must undergo power training that will result in improving the rate of force production.

The advantage of explosive, high-velocity power training is that it "trains" the nervous system. Increases in performance can be based on neural changes that help the individual muscles achieve greater performance capability (Sale, 1986). This is accomplished by shortening the time of motor unit recruitment, especially FT fibers, and increasing the tolerance of the motor neurons to increased innervation frequencies (Häkkinen, 1986; Häkkinen & Komi, 1983).

Power training exercises must be employed to activate the motor units more quickly to encourage better nervous system adaptation. Training practice and research has shown that muscle adaptation requires considerable time and progresses from year to year. Adaptation, especially in well-trained athletes, shows itself in the form of higher and better synchronization of motor units and their firing pattern. Another physiological adaptation phenomenon, so critical in the display of power, is that muscles discharge a greater number of muscle fibers in a very short time.

Neuromuscular adaptation to power training also results in improved intramuscular coordination—better linkages between the excitatory and inhibitory reactions of a muscle to many stimuli. As a result of such adaptation, the CNS "learns" when and when not to send a nerve impulse that signals the muscle to contract and perform a movement.

A further indication of adaptation to power training is evidenced by better intermuscular coordination or the ability of the agonistic and antagonistic muscles to cooperate to perform a movement effectively. Improved intermuscular coordination enhances the ability to contract some muscles and relax others, namely, to relax the antagonistic muscles, which results in improved speed of contraction of the prime movers, the agonistic muscles.

The human body has the capacity to adapt to any environment and therefore any type of training. If an athlete is trained with bodybuilding methods, which is often the case, the neuromuscular system adapts to them. As a result, the athlete should not be expected to display fast, explosive power because the neuromuscular system was not trained for it.

If the development of power for a given sport, event, or specific skill is the expected outcome, training must be designed to meet that challenge. Such a program has to be specific to the sport or event and use exercises that simulate the dominant skills as closely as possible. When the muscles involved in power training are more specific, intramuscular coordination becomes more efficient and the skill becomes more precise, smoother, and quicker.

During the conversion phase, athletes need to be energy-conscious, using most of their energy for technical and tactical training and much less for power training. Coaches must plan training with the lowest possible number of exercises that closely relate to the skill. Such programs must be efficient, with two to three exercises performed dynamically over several sets for maximum return. Time and energy should not be wasted on anything else.

The program must be performed quickly and explosively to recruit the highest number of motor units at the highest rate of contraction. The entire program should have only one goal: move the force-time curve as far to the left as possible (figure 6.10, page 119) so that the muscles will contract explosively. During MxS conversion to P, select only training methods that fulfill the requirements of power development. These requirements are to enhance quickness and explosive application of force and to make the muscles react quickly to athletic movements.

The methods presented here can be performed separately or in combination. When they are combined, the total work per session must be divided

When strength gains are converted to power gains, the athlete is able to react explosively.

among them. Recommendations for possible combinations appear at the end of chapter 12 (see "Planning the Training Methods").

Isotonic Method

Attempting to move a weight as rapidly and forcefully as possible through the entire range of motion is one of the classical methods of power training. Free weights, or other equipment that can be moved quickly, are good means of developing power. The weight of the equipment used for the isotonic method represents the *external resistance*. The force necessary to defeat the inertia of a barbell or to move it is considered the *internal strength*. The more internal strength exceeds external resistance, the faster the acceleration. If an athlete has to apply 95 percent of 1RM to lift a barbell, she will be incapable of generating any acceleration. If the same athlete works on MxS for 1 to 2 years, her strength will have increased so much that lifting the same weight will require only 30 to 40 percent of 1RM. The athlete will then be capable of moving the barbell explosively, generating the acceleration necessary to increase power. This explains why the Periodization of Strength requires an MxS phase prior to power training. No visible increments of power are possible without clear gains in MxS.

A high level of MxS is also necessary for the early part of a lift or throw. Any barbell or implement (such as a ball) has a certain inertia, which is its mass or weight. The most difficult part of lifting a barbell or throwing an implement explosively is the early part. To overcome the inertia, a high level of tension has to be built in the muscle. Consequently, the higher the MxS, the easier it is to overcome the inertia and the more explosive the start of the movement will be. As an athlete continues to apply force against the barbell or implement, acceleration is created. As more acceleration is developed, less force is necessary to maintain it.

To increase acceleration continuously, limb speed must be constantly increased. This is possible only if one can quickly contract the muscle, which is why athletes involved in speed- and power-dominant sports need to power train during the conversion phase. Without power training, an athlete will never be able to jump higher, run faster, throw farther, or deliver a quick punch. For improvements to occur, more than just MxS is needed. Athletes must also have the capacity to use MxS at a very high rate, which can only be achieved through power training methods.

Program Design

During the MxS phase, the athlete is accustomed to maximum or supermaximum loads. Therefore, using loads between 30 and 80 percent of 1RM to develop power presents no challenge. The challenge is to use this type of load and at the same time create high acceleration.

For most sports involving cyclic motions, such as sprinting, team sports, and the martial arts, the load for the isotonic method can be 30 to 50 percent (maximum 60 percent). For sports involving acyclic motions such as throwing, weight lifting, and line play in football, the load has to be higher (50 to 80 percent) because these athletes have a much higher MxS to start with and must defeat a higher external resistance. See table 10.1 for a summary of training parameters.

A low number of repetitions (4 to 10) is suggested since the key element for power training is how forcefully the repetitions are executed, not how many are performed. For sports where speed with high frequency is an important attribute, such as sprinting in track, swimming, and speed skating, all the repetitions per set have to be performed nonstop, dynamically, and at the highest rate possible. Do not overlook safety. When a limb extends, it should not be snapped. Exercises should be performed as smoothly as possible without jerking the barbell or implement.

For sports that require power and explosiveness, such as throwing, the heavyweight categories in boxing and wrestling, or line play in football, repetitions do not necessarily have to be nonstop. They can be performed with some rest between them so the athlete can concentrate maximally to achieve

Table 10.1 Training Parameters for the Isotonic Method

Training parameters	Work
Load: *Cyclic	30-50 percent
*Acyclic	50-80 percent
Number of exercises	2-4 (5)
Number of repetitions per set	4-10
Number of sets per session	3-6
Rest interval	2-6 minutes
Speed of execution	Dynamic/fast
Frequency per week	2-3

Table 10.2 Sample 3-Week Power Training Program for a Female College Basketball Player			
Exercise	Week 1	Week 2	Week 3
Jump squats	$\frac{60}{8}3$	$\frac{70}{6}4$	$\frac{70}{8}4$
Preacher curls	$\frac{70}{8}3$	$\frac{70}{8}3$	$\frac{70}{10}3$
Military presses	$\frac{60}{6}3$	$\frac{60}{8}3$	$\frac{70}{8}3$
V-sits	3×15	3×15	4×15
Power cleans	$\frac{50}{6}3$	$\frac{60}{6}3$	$\frac{60}{8}3$

the most dynamic move. The athlete can perform 1 to 4 repetitions at a time, as long as they are performed explosively for maximum FT muscle fiber recruitment. When explosiveness is no longer possible, the activity should be stopped, even if the set has not been completed. Only maximum concentration and explosive action will result in the greatest FT fiber recruitment.

Be selective in choosing exercises for power training. They must be very sport-specific to mimic the skills. Exercises such as bench presses and power cleans should not be chosen simply because of tradition. These two exercises have no built-in magic! Power cleans are useful for throwers or linebackers, but not necessarily for tennis, soccer, or ice hockey players. These athletes could better use jumping squats while holding heavier dumbbells (15 percent in each hand).

Also, select the lowest number of exercises (2 to 4, maximum of 5), so athletes can perform the highest number of sets realistically possible (3 to 6) for maximum benefit of the prime movers. When deciding the number of sets and exercises, remember that power training is performed in conjunction with technical and tactical training and only a certain amount of energy is left for it.

A key element in developing power in the isotonic method is the speed of exertion. For maximum power improvement, exertion speed must be as high as possible. Fast application of force against an implement or weight throughout the range of motion is essential and must start from the early part of the movement. To be able to displace the barbell or implement immediately and dynamically, the athlete must apply maximum concentration to the task.

Table 10.2 shows a sample power training program for a college-level female basketball player with 4 years of strength training.

Ballistic Method

Muscle energy can be applied in different forms and against different resistances. When the resistance is greater than the internal force of the athlete, no motion occurs (isometric). If the resistance is slightly less than the maximum capacity of the athlete, the barbell or strength training equipment will move slowly (isotonic). If, however, the athlete's internal force clearly exceeds the external resistance (e.g., a medicine ball), a dynamic motion occurs (ballistic).

For power training purposes, an athlete's internal or muscle force can also be applied against implements such as the shots used in track and field, medicine balls, heavy bells, and rubber cords (surgical tubing). The resulting motion occurs explosively because the force of the athlete far exceeds the resistance of these instruments. The method of employing such instruments to enhance power is called the ballistic method.

During a ballistic action, the athlete's energy is dynamically exerted against the resistance from the beginning to the end of the motion. As a result, the implement is projected a distance proportional to the power applied against it. Throughout the motion, the athlete must be able to develop considerable strength to accelerate the equipment or implement continuously, culminating in the release. To project the implement the maximum possible distance, the highest acceleration must be achieved at the instant of release.

The fast, ballistic application of force is possible as a result of quick recruitment of FT muscle fibers and effective intermuscular coordination of the agonistic and antagonistic muscles. After years of practice, an athlete can contract the agonistic muscles forcefully while the antagonistic muscles reach a high level of relaxation. This superior intermuscular coordination maximizes the force capabilities of the agonistic muscles because the antagonistic muscles exert no opposition to their quick contraction.

Program Design

Ballistic exercises can be planned at the end of a training session or following the warm-up depending on training objectives. If technical and tactical work has been planned on a given day, the development and improvement of power becomes a secondary goal. However, for sprinting, field events in track and field, and the martial arts, where speed and power are dominant, power work can often be planned immediately after the warm-up, especially in the late preparatory phase. Table 10.3 summarizes the training parameters for a ballistic program.

Power training of an explosive nature is enhanced if performed when physiologically fresh. A well-rested CNS can send more powerful nerve impulses to the working muscles for quick contractions. The opposite is true when the CNS and muscles are exhausted and inhibition is dominant as this pre-

Table 10.3   Suggested Training Parameters for the Ballistic Method

Training parameters	Work
Load	Standard
Number of exercises	2-5
Number of repetitions per set	10-20
Number of sets per session	3-5
Rest interval	2-3 minutes
Speed of execution	Explosive
Frequency per week	2-4

vents effective involvement of the FT muscle fibers. When intensive work is performed prior to explosive power training, the athlete's energy supplies (ATP/CP) are exhausted. If energy is not available, quality work is impossible because FT fibers fatigue easily and will hardly be activated. Consequently, the movements will be performed without vigor.

Speed of performance is paramount when using the ballistic method. Each repetition should start dynamically with the athlete attempting to increase the speed constantly as the release or end of the motion approaches. This enables a higher number of FT motor units to become involved. The critical element is not the number of repetitions and sets. To increase power, it is not necessary to perform many repetitions. The determining factor is speed of performance, which dictates the speed of muscle contraction. Therefore, exercises should be performed only as long as quickness is possible. *Repetitions must discontinue the moment speed declines.*

The speed and explosiveness of an exercise are guaranteed only as long as high numbers of FT fibers are involved. When they fatigue, speed decreases. Continuing an activity after speed declines is futile because at this point the ST fibers might be called into action, an unwanted situation for athletes seeking power development.

The training load is dictated by the standard weight of the implements. Medicine balls weigh from 2 to 6 kilograms (4.4 to 13 pounds), whereas heavy bells weigh between 10 and 32 kilograms (22 to 70 pounds). The resistance provided by rubber cords or surgical tubing depends on how far they are stretched—the greater the stretch, the greater the resistance.

As in other power-related methods, the number of exercises must be as low as possible so that a high number of sets can be performed to achieve maximum power benefits. Again, exercises should closely mimic technical skills, but if this is impossible, the coach should select exercises that involve the prime movers.

For any explosive power method, the RI should be as long as necessary to reach almost full recovery so the same quality of work can be repeated in each set. Since most ballistic exercises require one or more partner(s), a short interval between each repetition is dictated by necessity. For instance, a shot has to be fetched, a position taken, and a few preparatory swings made before the shot is heaved back to the first athlete. By that time, some

Table 10.4 Example of the Ballistic Method Combined With Maximum Acceleration

Exercise	Week 1	Week 2	Week 3
Medicine ball chest throws	2 × 10	3 × 12	3 × 15
Jump squats and medicine ball chest throws	2 × 8	3 × 10	3 × 15
Medicine ball overhead backward throws	2 × 10	3 × 12	3 × 15
Medicine ball side throws (for each side)	2 × 12	3 × 15	3 × 20
Medicine ball forward overhead throws	2 × 10	3 × 10	3 × 12
Two-handed shot throws from chest followed by 15-meter/yard sprint	4×	6×	6×
Push-ups followed by 15-meter/yard sprint	4×	6×	8×

15 to 20 seconds have elapsed, which facilitates better rest, so the number of repetitions is higher than in other power training methods.

The frequency per week of using the ballistic method depends on the training phase. In the late preparatory phase, it should be low (one to two sessions); during the conversion phase, it should be higher (two to four). The sport or event must also be considered. The frequency will be higher for speed- and power-dominant sports than for sports where power is of secondary importance. Table 10.4 shows a sample combined ballistic—maximum acceleration program. This program has been used successfully with football, baseball, lacrosse, soccer, and hockey players.

Power-Resisting Method

This method represents a three-way combination of the isotonic, isometric, and ballistic methods. The following description of an exercise will help explain this method. An athlete lies down to perform a sit-up, with his toes held against the ground by a partner. The coach stands behind the athlete. The athlete begins the sit-up. When he reaches approximately a quarter of the hip flexion (135 to 140 degrees), the coach places his palms on the athlete's chest or shoulders, stopping the movement. At this point, the athlete is in a maximum static contraction, trying to defeat the resisting power of the coach by recruiting most or all the motor units possible. After 3 to 4 seconds, the coach removes his hands and the maximum static contraction is converted into a dynamic ballistic motion for the rest of the sit-up. The athlete slowly returns to the starting position and rests for 10 to 30 seconds before another repetition is performed.

The most important parts of this method are the maximum isometric contraction and the ensuing ballistic action. The ballistic-type motion, with its quick muscle contraction, results in power development. The types of actions for this method are similar to a catapult machine. The initial isotonic action must be performed slowly. Following the stop, the maximum isometric contraction represents a high pre-tension (the loading phase) of the muscles involved. As the chest or shoulders are released, the trunk is catapulted forward (the ballistic phase). Figure 10.1 shows a sample 5-week power training program with a combined isotonic and ballistic emphasis. This program was designed for a rugby team.

Similar power-resisting exercises can be performed for other parts of the body, such as the following:

- Pull-ups in which the athlete performs an early elbow flexion, at which point the coach or partner stops the action for a few seconds; a dynamic action then follows.
- Dips.
- Jumping squats with no weights.
- Half squats with weights.
- Bench presses.
- Trunk rotations with a medicine ball held sideways in the hands. The athlete performs a backward rotation, and as the rotation comes forward, the athlete is stopped for 2 to 4 seconds; the ballistic action that follows culminates with the release of the ball.

Any other movements that duplicate the above phases of action can be categorized under the ballistic method, with similar effects on power development.

No.	Exercise	Week 1	Week 2	Week 3	Week 4	Week 5
1	Jumping half squats	$\frac{40}{6}$ 4	$\frac{50}{5}$ 5	$\frac{60}{5}$ 5	$\frac{50}{6}$ 5	$\frac{60}{5}$ 5
2	Medicine ball side throws	4 × 10	5 × 10	5 × 12	5 × 10	5 × 12
3	Between-the-legs, two-handed overhead throws	4 × 6	4 × 8	5 × 10	5 × 8	5 × 10
4	Reactive jump plyometrics	4 × 6	5 × 6	5 × 8	4 × 6	5 × 8

Loading pattern	Low	Medium	High	Medium	High

Figure 10.1   Five-week power training program (combining isotonic and ballistic methods) for a rugby team. RI = 3 to 4 minutes.

Another type of power stimulation can be achieved through isotonic weight training by alternating the loads. The athlete first performs 2 to 4 repetitions with a load of 80 to 90 percent, followed immediately by a similar number of repetitions performed with a low-resistance load of 30 to 50 percent. The heavy-load exercises represent a neuromuscular stimulation for the low-resistance repetitions, and the athlete can perform the last repetitions more dynamically.

A large variety of exercises, from bench pulls to bench presses, can be used with this method. A note of caution regarding motions involving knee and arm extensions. Snapping or jerking actions (forced, snapped extensions) should be avoided as they can result in joint damage.

Program Design

The load for the power-resisting method is related to the exercise performed. For the isometric phase, the contraction should last 3 to 4 seconds, or the duration necessary to reach maximum tension. For exercises where the

Table 10.5 Suggested Training Parameters for the Power-Resisting Method

Training parameters	Work
Load	Exercise related
Number of exercises	2-4
Number of repetitions per set	4-8
Number of sets per session	3-5
Rest interval	2-4 minutes
Speed of execution	Explosive
Frequency per week	1-2

resistance is provided by a barbell, the load should be 80 to 90 percent for the stimulating phase and 30 to 50 percent for the explosive repetitions. Select excercises carefully to match the direction of prime mover contraction. For maximum power benefit, keep the number of exercises low (two to four) so that a large number of sets (three to five) can be performed.

This training can be performed separately or combined with other power training methods. The latter is preferable, since other power training methods may be more beneficial for certain sports or athletes. Table 10.5 summarizes the training parameters for the power-resisting method.

Plyometric Method

Since ancient times, athletes have explored a multitude of methods designed to enable them to run faster, jump higher, and throw an object farther. To achieve such goals, power is essential. Strength gains can be transformed into power only by applying specific power training. Perhaps one of the most successful methods is training that employs plyometric exercises.

Also known as the stretching-shortening cycle, or myotatic stretch reflex, plyometrics refers to exercises in which the muscle is loaded in an eccentric (lengthening) contraction, followed immediately by a concentric (shortening) contraction. Research has demonstrated that a muscle stretched before a contraction will contract more forcefully and rapidly (Bosco & Komi, 1980; Schmidtbleicher, 1984). For example, by lowering the center of gravity to perform a takeoff or swing a golf club, the athlete stretches the muscle, resulting in a more forceful contraction.

Plyometric action relies on the stretch reflex found in the belly of the individual muscle. The main purpose of the stretch reflex is to monitor the degree of muscle stretch and prevent overstretching. When an athlete jumps, a great amount of force is required to propel the body upward. The body must be able to flex and extend quickly to leave the ground. A plyometric exercise relies on this quick body action to attain the power required for the movement.

Plyometric movement is based on the reflex contraction of the muscle fibers resulting from the rapid loading of these same fibers. When excessive stretching and tearing become a possibility, the stretch receptors send proprioceptive nerve impulses to the spinal cord. Then the impulses rebound back at the stretch receptors. Through this rebounding action, a braking effect prevents the muscle fiber from stretching farther, releasing a powerful muscle contraction.

Plyometric exercises work within complex neural mechanisms. Plyometric training causes muscular and neural changes that facilitate and enhance the performance of more rapid and powerful movements. The contractile elements of the muscles are the muscle fibers; however, certain noncontractile parts of the muscles create what is known as the "series elastic component." Stretching the series elastic component during muscle contraction produces elastic potential energy similar to that of a loaded spring. This energy augments the energy generated by the muscle fibers. This action is visible in plyometric movements. When the muscle is stretched rapidly, the series elastic component is also stretched and stores a portion of the load force in the form of elastic potential energy. The recovery of the stored elastic energy occurs during the concentric or overcoming phase of muscle contraction triggered by the myotatic reflex.

In plyometric training a muscle will contract more forcefully and quickly from a prestretched position. The more rapid the prestretch, the more forceful the concentric contraction. Correct technique is essential. Make sure the athlete lands in a prestretched position (legs and arms bent). The shortening contraction should occur immediately after completion of the prestretch phase. The transition from the prestretch phase should be smooth, continuous, and as swift as possible.

Plyometric training results in the following:

- The quick mobilization of greater innervation activities.
- The recruitment of most, if not all, motor units and their corresponding muscle fibers.
- An increase in the firing rate of the motor neurons.
- The transformation of muscle strength into explosive power.
- Development of the nervous system so it will react with maximum speed to the lengthening of the muscle; this will develop the ability to shorten (contract) rapidly with maximum force.
- Fatigue induced by repeated reactive training that affects eccentric and concentric work capacity. Fatigue is characterized by increased contact time (Gollhofer et al., 1987).

A good strength training background of several years will help an athlete progress faster through plyometric exercises. Prior experience is also an important factor in preventing injury. In terms of establishing a good base of strength and developing shock-absorbing qualities, the benefits of introducing children to plyometric exercises should not be dismissed; however, these exercises must be performed over several years and the principle of progression must be respected. The key element of this approach is *patience*.

A healthy training progression for children would be to first expose them to low-impact plyometrics over several years, say, between the ages of 14 and 16. After this initial period, they can be introduced to more demanding reactive jumps. Throughout these years of long-term progression, teachers and coaches should teach young athletes the correct plyometric techniques in which the "hop" and "step" from the triple jump are the *ABCs* of plyometric training.

Several points of controversy surround plyometric exercises. One is the amount of strength that should be developed before doing plyometrics. Some authors consider the ability to perform half squats with a load twice the body weight a safe guide. Others include the type of training surface, what equipment to use, and whether additional weights such as heavy vests and ankle and waist belts should be worn when performing these exercises.

Where injury is a concern, exercises should be performed on a soft surface, either outdoors on grass or soft ground or indoors on a padded floor. Although this precaution may be appropriate for beginners, a soft surface can dampen the stretch reflex; only a hard surface can enhance the reactivity of the neuromuscular system. Thus, athletes with an extensive background in sports and/or strength training should use a hard surface.

Finally, weighted ankle and waist belts should not be used during plyometric drills. These weights tend to decrease the reactive ability of the nerve-muscle coupling and obstruct the reactivity of the neuromuscular system. Furthermore, although such overloading may result in increased strength, it certainly slows the speed of reaction and the rebounding effect.

Some Mechanical Characteristics of Plyometrics

Plyometric action relies mechanically on the stretch reflex found in the belly of each muscle. The main purpose of the stretch reflex is to monitor the degree of muscle stretch and thereby prevent overstretching and possible tearing of any muscle fiber. When jumping off the ground, a large amount of force is required to propel the entire body mass upward. To leave the ground, the body must be able to flex and extend the limbs very quickly. A plyometric exercise relies on this quick body action to attain the power required for the movement.

Mechanically, when the takeoff leg is planted, athletes must lower their center of gravity, creating a downward velocity. This "amortization phase" is an important component of any jumping activity, for during this phase athletes prepare for takeoff in a different direction. A long amortization phase, also called the "shock-absorbing phase," is responsible for a loss of power. For example, if long jumpers do not plant their takeoff leg properly, the result will be loss of both the upward and horizontal velocity required to propel them forward. Athletes who perform jumping actions must work toward a shorter and quicker amortization phase. The shorter this phase, the more powerful the concentric muscle contraction when the muscle has previously been stretched during the eccentric contraction or amortization phase (Bosco & Komi, 1980). This action is possible due to recovery and utilization of all the energy that has been stored in the elastic components of the muscle during any stretching action.

All jumping motion can be improved through analysis of each biomechanical component of the jump. An example of this is improvement in a high jumper's technique. High jump performance can be enhanced by eliminating the deep knee bend phase and shortening the time interval between the eccentric and concentric contractions. Elimination of a deep flexion utilizes the elastic qualities of the muscle more efficiently.

First jumpers need to lower their center of gravity, creating a downward velocity. They must then produce forces to counter the downward motion (amortization phase) to prepare for the upward thrusting phase. Remember that force equals mass times acceleration ($F = m \times a$). Greater force is required to decelerate the body more quickly and result in a shorter amortization phase. From this, a second equation can be derived:

Average force of amortization = body mass × change in velocity/time of amortization

This equation shows that if athletes want to decrease the time of amortization, they must generate a greater average force. If they are unable to do so, a longer, less efficient amortization phase will result, with a loss of horizontal velocity due to the weakened concentric contraction.

The equation also points out the importance of maintaining a low level of body fat and a high power-weight ratio. An increase in body mass requires an even greater average force of amortization. A greater downward velocity at impact requires an increase in the average force produced during the amortization phase. For example, when long or high jumpers lower their center of gravity before takeoff, they reduce the impact of the forces.

The entire body must be used efficiently to maximize jumping ability. The upward acceleration of the free limbs (e.g., the arms) after the amortization phase acts to increase the vertical forces placed on the takeoff leg. For example, triple jumpers must be able to apply peak force as great as four to six times their body weight to compensate for the inability to lower their center of gravity during the more upward hopping phase. Long jumpers, on the other hand, can manipulate their bodies more easily just before takeoff. An effective takeoff will only be achieved if jumpers can apply large forces on impact and produce a shorter, quicker amortization phase.

It is sometimes difficult to train for this specific phase of the jump, as few conventional exercises apply. Many jumpers use traditional weight training (e.g., squats) to train for the takeoff phase of their jumps. This type of weight training places a large load on the leg extensors, which over time will provide an adequate strength training base. The main problem with using only weight training, however, is that a heavy squat lift is unlikely to be fast enough to utilize the elastic qualities of the muscles.

Bounding exercises, on the other hand, can simulate successfully an effective takeoff and improve overall jumping ability. Bounding has the potential to possess similar force-time characteristics to the takeoff. It also allows athletes to practice resisting large impact loads on the takeoff leg and to exert force in a short time interval. Bounding exercises will also involve multijoint movement and make it possible to develop the required muscle elasticity.

Program Design

To design a plyometrics program properly, one must be aware that the exercises vary in level of intensity and are classified in different groups for better progression. The level of intensity is directly proportional to the height or length of an exercise. High-intensity plyometric exercises such as reactive or drop jumps result in higher tension in the muscle, which recruits more neuromuscular units to perform the action or to resist the pull of gravitational force.

Plyometric exercises can be categorized into two major groups that reflect their degree of impact on the neuromuscular system. Low-impact exercises include skipping; rope jumps; jumps with low and short steps, hops, and jumps; jumps over rope or low benches 25 to 35 centimeters (10 to 15 inches) high; throws of a 2- to 4-kilogram (5- to 9-pound) medicine ball; tubing; and throwing light implements (e.g., a baseball). High-impact exercises include standing long and triple jumps; jumps with higher and longer steps, hops, and jumps; jumps over rope or high benches 35 centimeters (15 inches) or higher; jumps on, over, and off boxes 35 centimeters (15 inches) or higher; throws of a 5- to 6-kilogram (11- to 13-pound) medicine ball; throwing heavy implements; drop jumps and reactive jumps; and "shock" muscle tension induced by machines.

From a more practical viewpoint, plyometric exercises can be divided into five levels of intensity (see table 10.6). This classification can be used to plan better alternation of training demand throughout the week. In table 10.6, the suggested number of repetitions and sets is for advanced athletes. Coaches should resist the temptation to apply these numbers to beginners or athletes with an insufficient foundation in sports and/or strength training.

Any plan to incorporate plyometric exercises into a training program should consider the following factors:

- The age and physical development of the athlete
- The skills and techniques involved in plyometric exercises
- The principal performance factors of the sport
- The energy requirements of the sport
- The particular training phase of the annual plan
- The need to respect methodical progression over a long period (2 to 4 years), progressing from low impact (levels 5 and 4 in table 10.6), to simple bounding (level 3), and then to high-impact exercises (levels 2 and 1)

Table 10.6 Five Levels of Intensity of Plyometric Exercises

Intensity level	Type of exercises	Intensity of exercises	No. of reps and sets	No. of reps per training session	RI between sets
1	Shock tension, high reactive jumps >60 centimeters (>24 inches)/(200)	Maximum	8-5 x 10-20	120-150	8-10 minutes
2	Drop jumps 80-120 centimeters (32-48 inches)	Very high	5-15 x 5-15	75-150	5-7 minutes
3	Bounding exercises *Two legs *One leg	Submaximum	3-25 x 5-15	50-250	3-5 minutes
4	Low reactive jumps 20-50 centimeters (8-20 inches)	Moderate	10-25 x 10-25	150-250	3-5 minutes
5	Low-impact jumps/throws *On spot *Implements	Low	10-30 x 10-15	50-300	2-3 minutes

Although plyometric exercises are fun, they demand a high level of concentration and are deceptively vigorous and taxing. The lack of discipline to wait for the right moment for each exercise can result in athletes performing high-impact exercises before they are ready. The injuries or physiological discomforts that result are not the fault of the plyometric exercises. Rather they are the result of the coach's or instructor's lack of knowledge and application. The five levels of intensity will help coaches select appropriate exercises that follow a consistent, steady, and orderly progression and incorporate appropriate rest intervals.

Progression through the five levels of intensity is long-term. The 2 to 4 years spent incorporating low-impact exercises into the training programs of young athletes is necessary for progressive adaptation of ligaments, tendons, and bones. It also allows for the gradual preparation of the shock-absorbing sections of the body, such as the hips and spine.

Table 10.7 illustrates a long-term comprehensive progression of strength and power training including plyometric training. It is important to observe the age suggested for the introduction of plyometrics, as well as the precept that high-impact plyometrics should only be introduced after 4 years of training. This period indicates the time required to learn proper technique and to allow for progressive anatomical adaptation. From this point on, high-impact plyometrics can be part of an athlete's normal training regimen.

The intensity in plyometric exercises—the amount of tension created in the muscle—depends on the height of the exercise performed. Although the height is determined strictly by the individual qualities of the athlete, the following general principle applies: The stronger the muscular system, the greater the energy required to stretch it to obtain an elastic effect in the shortening phase. Thus, what is optimal height for one athlete may not generate enough stimulation for another. Therefore, the following information should be treated only as a guideline.

According to Verkhoshanski (1969), to make gains in dynamic strength (power), the optimal height for depth (reactive) jumps for speed training is between 75 and 110 centimeters (30 and 43 inches). Similar findings were reported by Bosco and Komi (1980). The latter authors concluded that above

Table 10.7 Long-Term Strength Development and the Progression of Plyometric Training

Age groups	Forms of training	Method	Volume	Intensity	Means of training
Prepuberty (12-13 years)	*General exercises only *Games	*Muscular endurance	*Low *Medium	Very low	*Light resistance exercises *Light implements *Balls/medicine ball
Beginners (13-15 years)	*General strength *Event-oriented exercises	*M-E (CT)	*Low *Medium	Low	*Dumbbells *Tubing *Balls *Universal gym
Intermediate (15-17 years)	*General strength *Event-oriented exercises	*Bodybuilding *M-E (CT) *Power	*Low *Medium *High	*Low *Medium	*All the above *Free weights
Advanced (>17 years)	*Event-oriented exercises *Specific strength	*Bodybuilding *M-E *Power *MxS *Low-impact plyometrics	*Medium *High *Maximum	*Medium *High	*Free weights *Special strength equipment
High performance	*Specific	*All the above *Eccentric *Plyometrics *Low impact *High impact	As above	*Medium *High *Supermaximum	As above

110 centimeters (43 inches) the mechanics of the action are changed; the time and energy it takes to cushion the force of the drop on the ground defeats the purpose of plyometric training. Exceptional heights were tried by other authors. Zanon (1977) employed the following heights for elite long jumpers: 2.5 meters (8.2 feet) for men and 2.1 meters (7 feet) for women. The landing from boxes of these heights was immediately followed by a long jump for distance!

As far as the number of repetitions is concerned, plyometric exercises fall into two categories: single-response (SR) and multiple-response (MR) drills. The former consist of a single action such as a high reactive jump, shock tension (level 1 in table 10.6), or a drop jump (level 2), where the main purpose is to induce the highest level of tension in the muscles. The objective of such exercises is to develop maximum strength and power. Repetitive exercises such as bounding (level 3) and low reactive (level 4) and low-impact (level 5) jumps result in the development of power and power endurance. As suggested in table 10.6, the number of repetitions can be between 1 and 30, with the number of sets ranging from 5 to 25 depending on the goal of training, the type of exercise, and the athlete's background and physical potential.

Often, especially for MR exercises, it is more convenient and practical to equate the number of repetitions with a distance, for example, 5 sets of 50 meters rather than 5 sets of 25 repetitions. This eliminates the need to count the number of repetitions constantly.

An important factor for high-quality training is adequate physiological recuperation between exercises. Often athletes and coaches either pay too little attention to the duration of the RI or are simply caught up in the traditions of a given sport, which often dictate that the only RI required is the time needed to move from one station to another. This amount of time is inadequate, especially when the physiological characteristics of plyometric training are considered.

Fatigue consists of local fatigue and CNS fatigue. Local fatigue results from depletion of the energy stored in the muscle (ATP/CP) (the fuel necessary to perform explosive movements) and the production of lactic acid from repetitions longer than 10 to 15 seconds. During training, athletes also fatigue the CNS, the system that signals to the working muscle to perform a given amount of quality work. Plyometric training is performed as a result of these nerve impulses, which have a certain speed, power, and frequency. Any high-quality training requires that the speed of contraction, its power, and its frequency be at the highest level possible.

When the RI is short (1 to 2 minutes), the athlete experiences local and CNS fatigue. The working muscle is unable to remove lactic acid and has insufficient time to replenish the energy necessary to perform the next repetitions with the same intensity. Similarly, a fatigued CNS is unable to send the powerful nerve impulses necessary to ensure that the prescribed load is performed for the same number of repetitions and sets before exhaustion sets in. Exhaustion is often just a short step away from injury, so utmost attention should be paid to the RI.

As suggested in table 10.6, the RI is a function of the load and type of plyometric training performed—the higher the intensity of the exercise, the longer the RI should be. Consequently, for maximum intensity (high reactive jumps), the RI between sets should be 8 to 10 minutes or even longer. The suggested RI for intensity level 2 is 5 to 7 minutes; for levels 3 and 4, it should be between 3 and 5 minutes, and for low-impact activities (level 5), around 2 to 3 minutes.

Application of Power Training to the Specifics of Sports

Power is not a combined ability that suits the needs of every sport or event. It must be developed so it meets the needs of a given sport, event, or team position. To further illustrate the need for sport-specific application of power, definitive examples are presented in this section. Many elements of the previously described power training methods are also applicable. The following discussion further explains the need to develop power according to the specific requirements of each sport, event, and skill.

Landing/Reactive Power

In several sports, not only is landing an important skill, but it is often followed by performance of another skill (e.g., another jump in figure skating or a quick move in another direction, as in tennis or many team sports). Thus, the athlete must have the power to control the landing as well as the reactive power to perform another move quickly.

The power needed to control and absorb the shock of landing is related to the height of the jump. Landings such as drop or depth jumps from 80 to 100 centimeters (32 to 40 inches) often load the ankle joints with six to eight times the athlete's body weight. To absorb the shock from a figure skating jump, a power of five to eight times one's body weight is required. Muscles must be trained for shock-absorbing power to reduce impact forces at the instant of landing.

Landing involves an eccentric contraction. Without proper training, the result will be an incorrect landing and exposure to injury, since higher tension is produced with the same amount of muscle fiber activity, and the elastic tissue of the tendons is placed under greater stress. To overcome this, eccentric contraction as well as plyometrics should be applied in training.

Schmidtbleicher (1992) specifies that at the instant of ground contact, athletes experience an *inhibitory effect*. He noted that well-trained athletes cope with impact forces much better, and that drop jump training reduced inhibitory effects. He concluded that the inhibitory mechanisms represent a protection system, especially for novice athletes, that shields them against injury.

To enhance landing/reactive power, make concentric and eccentric contractions a part of training. Use eccentric strength training and plyometrics, primarily drop jumps, that mimic the desired landing skill. Drop/reactive jumps are performed from a raised platform (box, bench, or chair), with the athlete landing in a flexed position (knees slightly bent) to absorb the shock. Landing is performed on the balls of the feet without touching the ground with the heels.

During the dropping phase, the muscles adopt a reflex or ready-to-work position, which enhances the tension and the elastic properties of the muscles. At landing, especially if the athlete is quickly preparing for another action, energy is stored in the elastic elements of the muscle. At the ensuing takeoff or quick move in another direction, this readily available energy releases a stretching reflex that recruits more FT fibers than under normal strength training conditions. This enables the athlete to perform another quick and explosive action immediately. It is important for practitioners to understand that these reflexes (including the muscle spindle reflex) are trainable, and that drop/reactive jumps can be improved as a result of a well-periodized training.

Specific exercises for developing landing and reactive power are illustrated in the following sections. These example combinations are not meant to be an exhaustive list, but to inspire you to devise your own versions.

Exercises for Landing Power. For *landing power*, the exercise should mimic sport-specific landing skills, such as in figure skating, ski jumping, free-style skiing, and Australian football. Figures 10.2, 10.3, and 10.4 illustrate three sample exercises for developing landing power.

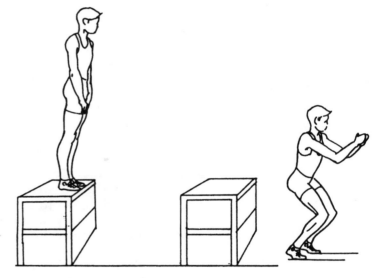

Figure 10.2 Standard drop jump in which the athlete lands on the balls of the feet, with knees and hips bent, and holds for 1 to 2 seconds.

Figure 10.3 Drop jump with a one-legged landing.

Figure 10.4 Drop jump from a lower height using a 10- to 15-kilogram (20- to 30-pound) heavy vest, dumbbell, or even a barbell.

Figure 10.5 Standard reactive jump in which the athlete lands on the balls of the feet, then instantly jumps upward in a springlike takeoff.

Exercises for Reactive Power.   For *reactive power*, the athlete should continue with another jump or plyometric movement, or run as quickly as possible after landing (as in figure skating, volleyball, jumping events, basketball, gymnastics, and Alpine skiing). Figures 10.5 through 10.11 illustrate seven sample exercises for developing reactive power.

Training for reactive power progresses from lower to higher heights; from two-legged to one-legged landings; from free drops to drop jumps using heavy vests, dumbbells, and even light barbells; and from a low number of sets and repetitions to higher numbers. This progression must take place over several years. These exercises are for mature, well-trained athletes. A good strength training background of 3 to 4 years is strongly advised. Exposing junior athletes to some of these exercises may result in muscle, ligament, and tendon strains or injuries. The program must also consider the athlete's classification and working potential.

Figure 10.6 Reactive jump followed by several double-speed hops.

Figure 10.7 Reactive jump from a high box (60-90 centimeters or 2 or 3 feet) followed by a series of reactive jumps over lower boxes, benches, hurdles, cones, or the like.

Figure 10.8 Reactive jump from a high box onto another high box.

Figure 10.9 One-legged reactive jumps over several boxes or benches.

Figure 10.10   Combination of a two-legged reactive jump from a box followed by a series of bounding exercises.

Figure 10.11   Suggested variation of a two-legged reactive jump followed immediately by slalom jump or jumps performed sideways or backward.

Throwing Power

For a pitcher in baseball, a quarterback in football, or a thrower in track and field, throwing power is generated mostly by FT muscle fibers. The larger the diameter of the individual fiber, the faster it contracts. Similarly, the more fibers involved in a simultaneous contraction, the greater the power for delivery of an implement.

Throwers and athletes in sports such as fencing, boxing, and baseball must be able to develop considerable power to accelerate the implement or the equipment they use. It is often necessary to overcome the inertia of an implement or piece of equipment with the greatest possible speed from the beginning of the movement, increasing acceleration throughout the movement especially before the release. To achieve this, internal strength must exceed the resistance of the implement. The more one exceeds the weight of the implement, the higher the acceleration. A well-planned MxS and power training phase is required for sports that utilize throwing power. The greater the difference between the MxS of the athlete and the resistance of the implement, the higher the acceleration.

Specific power training for throwing events and movements must concentrate on the maximum application of force and use the isotonic and ballistic methods. For the isotonic method, the repetitions (4 to 10) need not be performed nonstop and at a high rate. For maximum benefit of explosive contraction where the greatest number of FT fibers are recruited at once, it is more important to perform 1 repetition at a time while achieving the highest mental concentration before each of them.

Exercises for Throwing Power.   Figures 10.12 through 10.15 illustrate several exercises for throwing power. Training for throwing power progresses from lighter to heavier implements, then lighter again 1 to 2 weeks prior to competition or the start of league games in team sports. Ending with lighter implements ensures explosiveness and high speed of contraction of the muscles involved. The plan should move from a reduced number of sets and reps to higher numbers. Before competitions, the number of sets and reps are again reduced to avoid fatigue and enhance explosiveness. The training program includes 4 to 6 sets of 6 to 10 repetitions with a 1 to 2 minute RI.

Figure 10.12 Catch-and-drop push-up followed immediately by a two-arm chest shot/medicine ball throw.

Figure 10.13 Combination of a drop push-up followed by several medicine ball overhead throws.

Figure 10.14 Incline bench press followed by a two-arm chest shot throw.

Figure 10.15 Combined drop push-up/bench press with: a between-the-legs forward throw; back or side throws of shots or medicine balls.

Takeoff Power

In many sports (jumping events in track and field, ski jumping, volleyball, basketball, soccer, figure skating, and diving), good performance is possible only if the athlete is capable of an explosive takeoff. In many cases, takeoff occurs following a short-distance, high-velocity run, during which the muscles prestretch and store energy. At takeoff, this energy is used as an acceleration thrust, producing a powerful jump.

The depth of the crouch needed at the instant of joint flexion depends on leg power. The deeper the crouch, the greater the force required from the leg extensors. The crouch is a mechanical necessity, though, because it puts the muscles in a state of stretch, giving them a greater distance to accelerate, culminating in a takeoff. To be more effective, the depth of the crouch must be proportional to the power of the legs. If the flexion is too great, the extension (or shortening phase) will be performed slowly, and as a result, the jump will be low.

Many jumpers use traditional weight training (e.g., squats) to train for the takeoff phase. This type of weight training places a large load on the leg extensors and, over time, will provide an adequate strength training base. The main problem with using only weight training is that a heavy squat lift is unlikely to be fast enough to utilize the elastic qualities of the muscles. The single-leg takeoff, however, uses multiple joint movements, all happening simultaneously.

Plyometric and bounding exercises can be used to simulate an effective takeoff and improve the athlete's overall jumping ability. Bounding has the potential to possess force-time characteristics similar to the takeoff. In addition, it allows the athlete to practice resisting large impact loads on the takeoff leg and exert force in a short time interval. Bounding exercises also involve multijoint movements and provide the opportunity to develop the required muscle elasticity.

Exercises for Takeoff Power. Several exercises can be used to develop takeoff power, such as two- or one-legged reactive jumps followed by any type of plyometrics. Most of the exercises suggested here (figures 10.16 through 10.19) combine a reactive box jump with a one-legged takeoff or bounding routine. Takeoff power exercises, especially the one-legged reactive jump, are strongly recommended for figure skating, jumping events, team sports, Alpine skiing, racquet sports, sprinting in track and field, cycling, and speed skating. They can also be performed with a two-legged takeoff, important for sports such as volleyball, soccer, basketball, and diving.

Athletes with a broad strength training background will have an easier time performing the suggested exercises or other possible combinations. To observe the necessary progression for less experienced athletes, select the height of the box or bench very carefully. Do not immediately challenge them with boxes that are 60 to 90 centimeters (2 to 3 feet) in height. Start conservatively with low benches and, in time (1 to 2 years), move to higher boxes.

Training for takeoff power progresses from lower to higher heights; from two legs to one leg; and from a lower to a higher number of sets and reps. One to 2 weeks before competitions or league games, reduce the number of sets and reps, but look for explosive takeoff/reactive power. The training program consists of 3 to 5 (6 maximum) sets or 4 to 6 repetitions. The RI should be 3 to 4 minutes long.

Figure 10.16 One-legged reactive jump stressing the takeoff part of the exercise.

Figure 10.17 The same exercise but reaching out for a more distant (150 centimeters or 5 feet) landing and takeoff.

Figure 10.18 One-legged landing followed by several bounding exercises.

Figure 10.19   One-legged landing followed immediately by a jump onto a lower box.

Starting Power

Starting power is an essential and often determinant ability in sports where the initial speed of action dictates the final outcome (boxing, karate, fencing, the start in sprinting, or the beginning of an aggressive acceleration from standing in team sports). The athlete's ability to recruit the highest possible number of FT fibers to start the motion explosively is the fundamental physiological characteristic necessary for successful performance.

In sprinting, starting is performed with the muscles in the prestretched position (both knees bent), from which they can generate greater power than when relaxed or shortened. In this position, the elastic elements of the muscles store kinetic energy that acts like a spring at the sound of the gun. The power used by national-class athletes is very high at the start: 132 kilograms (290 pounds) for the front leg and 102 kilograms (225 pounds) for the back leg. The higher the starting power, the more explosive and faster the start.

In boxing and martial arts, a quick and powerful start of an offensive skill prevents an opponent from using an effective defensive action. The elastic, reactive component of muscle is of vital importance for delivering quick action and powerful starts. The more specific the power training during the conversion phase, the better a muscle's stretch reflex and the greater the power of the FT fibers.

The stretching and reactive components of the muscle that are key to starting a motion quickly and powerfully are trainable through isotonic, ballistic, and especially Maxex and plyometric exercises. They can be performed in a set of repetitive motions or separately. In the latter case, exercises in a set are performed one at a time so the athlete has enough time to reach maximum mental concentration to perform them as explosively as possible. These conditions make it possible to recruit a high number of FT fibers, and consequently, the athlete can perform the action with the greatest power available.

Exercises for Starting Power.   The key element to look for in a training program aimed at developing power is a quick and powerful application of force against the ground. Several types of exercises (see figures 10.20 through 10.23) can enhance the power of force application.

Figure 10.20 Jumping half squats followed by jumps over hurdles. After completing the jumping half squats, the weight of either a heavy vest, dumbbells, or a barbell is taken by two spotters so that the athlete can continue with the loadless exercises.

Figure 10.21 Reverse leg press followed by a quick acceleration of 20 to 25 meters/yards.

Figure 10.22 Set of three to five half squats with a load of 60 to 80 percent of 1RM followed by 25 meters/yards of powerful bounding jumps.

Figure 10.23 Series of four to five knee tuck jumps followed by several powerful alternative single-leg jumps over boxes or benches.

Training for starting power progresses from exercises without additional load to the use of barbells, heavy vests, or dumbbells; from two-legged to one-legged exercises; and from a reduced to an increased number of sets and repetitions, which are again reduced before competitions. The training program consists of 4 to 6 sets of 8 to 12 (15 maximum) repetitions with a 3 to 4 minute RI. For additional variations, refer to Maxex Training in chapter 9.

Acceleration Power

In sprinting, swimming, cycling, rowing, and most team sports, the athlete's ability to accelerate to develop high speed is crucial for achieving improved performance. Power is an essential attribute for every sport that requires high acceleration. Without power, an athlete cannot perform the powerful push against the ground that is needed for the propulsion phase in running or overcome water resistance in sports performed in water.

In sprinting, for instance, the force applied against the ground is two to three times that of the athlete's body weight. In rowing, the oarsperson must use a constant blade pressure of 40 to 60 kilograms (88 to 132 pounds) per stroke to maintain high acceleration. In all sports requiring acceleration power, the forceful actions involved must be performed repetitively and very rapidly. The greater the difference between MxS and, in the above instances, water resistance or the power applied against the ground, the higher the acceleration.

To achieve high acceleration, the development of MxS is essential. A key physiological requirement for the ability to display power is a relatively large diameter of the contracting muscle filaments. These filaments, primarily the protein-rich myosin cross bridges, can increase their size or hypertrophy only as a result of using MxS training methods. Since this is achieved during the MxS phase, the gains have to be converted into power through specific power training methods. The isotonic, ballistic, power-resisting, and plyometric methods can assist athletes in successfully applying the series of muscle impulses that will activate a great number of FT fibers. When this is achieved, acceleration power reaches the desired high levels.

These methods can be done using either a low number of repetitions (6 to 10), performed explosively and with high frequency, or individually, 1 repetition at a time. In the first case, the goal is repeated displays of power; in the second case, the objective is to apply the highest amount of power in a single attempt. In sports where acceleration power is required, athletes must be capable of performing powerful actions with high frequency, so both methods must be used. By applying Periodization of Strength, athletes increase the likelihood of achieving the above as well as reaching peak acceleration power before major competitions or events.

Exercises for Acceleration Power. Several exercises for developing acceleration power are illustrated in figures 10.24 through 10.27. For variation, use any of the Maxex exercises suggested in chapter 9. Acceleration training progresses from free exercises to using a heavy vest, barbell, or dumbbells and from two-legged jumps to one-legged bounding/plyometrics. The training program consists of 6 to 8 sets with a 2- to 3-minute RI.

Figure 10.24 Two-handed medicine ball chest throw followed immediately by a powerful acceleration.

Figure 10.25 After a drop push-up, the athlete stands up quickly and performs a 25-meter/yard powerful acceleration.

Figure 10.26 Series of five to six reactive box or bench jumps followed by 15 to 20 meters/yards of bounding, ending in a 20-meter/yard acceleration.

Figure 10.27 Drop jump with a barbell on the shoulders followed by three to five drop jumps from a high box.

Deceleration Power

In several sports, especially tennis and team sports, deceleration is as important as acceleration. To overtake an opponent or make oneself available to receive a pass, a team sport player must accelerate and run as quickly as possible. In sports such as soccer, basketball, lacrosse, or ice hockey, they also need to decelerate, decreasing speed very quickly to stop, and then quickly change running direction or jump to rebound an oncoming ball. Often an athlete who can decelerate fast can create a tactical advantage. Performing a quick deceleration can require leg power up to twice as high as one's body weight.

Deceleration is performed through eccentric contraction of the leg muscles. This is facilitated by placing the feet ahead of the center of gravity and leaving the upper body behind it. Strong legs and good biomechanics enable one to decelerate quickly. Muscles developed to decelerate quickly from a fast sprint rely on their elastic properties to amortize and reduce impact forces. The ability to amortize these forces requires power and degrees of leg flexion similar to those needed for absorbing shock while landing.

To train the muscles to decelerate quickly, athletes must employ several training methods such as eccentric contraction and plyometrics. For eccentric contraction, the MxS method (eccentric) must be applied with progression from medium to supermaximum loads. For plyometrics, after a few years of normal progression from low- to high-impact exercises, drop (depth) and reactive jumps should be used. Athletes will successfully develop the needed deceleration power by following the methodology described for these methods.

Exercises for Deceleration Power. Exercises for deceleration power are illustrated in figures 10.28 through 10.30. Variations include a drop jump followed by acceleration and then quick deceleration or combinations of drop jump and "stop and go" (a quick stop followed by a quick acceleration in the other direction). Training progresses from free drop jumps to drop jumps using heavy vests, dumbbells, and for experienced athletes (3 to 4 years of strength training), even barbells, and from two-legged to one-legged drop jumps. Increase the number of sets and reps, and decrease again before competitions. The training program consists of 6 to 8 sets with a 2- to 3-minute RI.

Figure 10.28 Drop jump from a high box followed by several short jumps, emphasizing the landing (land on balls of feet, knees bent, and hold).

Figure 10.29 Drop jump on one leg, emphasizing the landing, followed by 8 to 10 alternate one-legged bounds with the same emphasis.

Figure 10.30 Set of 3-5 jump squats followed by a series of alternate one-legged bounding exercises.

chapter 11

Conversion to Muscular Endurance

No matter how intensive or comprehensive it is, strength training cannot result in adequate adaptation and have a positive influence in every sport or event unless the specific physiological needs of the given sport are addressed. Most training specialists might agree with this statement, but in reality, strength training programs for sports and events in which endurance is either dominant or an important component are still inadequate. Weight-lifting and bodybuilding training methods still unduly influence these programs. Many researchers and strength training specialists still consider 15 to 20 repetitions to be an effective way to train M-E. Such a training regimen is grossly inadequate for sports such as mid- and long-distance swimming, rowing, canoeing, boxing, wrestling, cross-country skiing, speed skating, and triathlon.

If a low-repetition strength training program with submaximum or maximum loads is employed, the energy supply, recovery, and physiological functioning of the organs and the neuromuscular system adapt to such loading. All the physiological parameters of such a program differ fundamentally from those required for effective physiological behavior of athletes involved in endurance-dominant sports. Thus, it would result in strength increments but would inhibit the endurance component of athletes' adaptation for such sports.

A strength training program for endurance-dominant sports requires a load closely matching the resistance that must be overcome while competing, relatively low muscle tension, and a high number of repetitions that approach the duration of the event. This trains athletes to cope with the fatigue specific to the sport and utilize simultaneous stimuli for both specific strength and endurance. Adaptation to such training will be very similar to the physiological requirements of competition. Fortunately, the neuromuscular system is capable of adapting to any type of training. It will, however, adapt to whatever it is exposed to.

The importance of MxS for endurance-dominant sports increases in proportion to external resistance. For instance, 400-meter swimmers swim with a higher velocity than 800- to 1,500-meter swimmers. To create the higher velocity, 400-meter swimmers have to pull against the water resistance with greater force than 1,500-meter athletes. Consequently, MxS is more important for 400-meter than for 1,500-meter swimmers. In both cases, MxS must be improved from year to year if athletes expect to cover the distance faster. Such improvement is possible only if swimmers improve their aerobic endurance and increase the force used to pull against the water resistance. Only this increased force will push the body through the water faster.

M-E is best increased through a strength training program that emphasizes a high number of repetitions. The selected exercises and the number of repetitions have to result in the desired adaptation to the physiological requirements of the sport or event. If an adequate method is not applied during the conversion of MxS to M-E, positive transfer from one type of training to a different physiological requirement cannot be expected. In other words, if a bodybuilding or weight-lifting methodology with 20 repetitions is applied, improvement cannot be expected in a sport where 200 nonstop strokes are performed during a race.

For endurance sports, aerobic endurance and M-E have to be trained at the same time. This can be done either by training each of them on separate days or by combining them in the same training session. In the latter case, M-E should be performed at the end of the session, since the specific endurance work includes technical training. Fatigue can limit combined workouts, and if the total work per day has to be decreased, M-E is normally reduced. Athletes with proper technique and aerobic endurance will find training M-E separately is more beneficial.

The strength-endurance axis refers to four types of combinations between the two abilities: power-endurance (P-E) and M-E short, medium, and long. Each strength combination is required for certain sports, so the training methods for each are presented separately.

Power-Endurance Method

Sports like sprints in track and field, swimming, and wrestling, and positions like running back or pitcher, require a high degree of power applied several times repetitively. Sprinting, including that in all team sports requiring explosive running (football, baseball, ice hockey, rugby, and Australian football), is often misjudged. When sprinters cover the classical 100 meters in 10 to 12 seconds, they have trained to perform powerful leg actions throughout the entire race, not just at the start and for the following 6 to 8 strides. In a 100-meter race, athletes take 48 to 54 strides, depending on stride length; thus each leg makes 24 to 27 contacts with the ground. In each ground contact, the force applied is approximately two times body weight!

Consequently, athletes who compete in these sports need to perform powerful actions over and over. In football, rugby, and Australian football, athletes are often required to repeat a strenuous activity after only a few seconds of game interruption. To do this successfully, these athletes need a high power output and the ability to repeat it 20 to 30 times. This constitutes power-endurance (P-E). Athletes with a high level of P-E will have the capacity to avoid a decrease in stride frequency and velocity at the end of a race or a longer sprint.

Sprinters must maintain their powerful strides throughout the race.

Program Design

P and P-E are the determinant abilities in several sports, and MxS is a determinant factor in both abilities. This section describes the training methodology for developing muscle endurance in an explosive manner, or P-E.

P-E requires 50 to 70 percent of MxS repeated rhythmically and explosively. Such a load requires dynamic repetitions executed explosively 20 to 30 times nonstop. Such an important training requirement can be achieved progressively, starting with a lower number of repetitions (8 to 15) and increasing over 4 to 6 weeks, the duration of the conversion phase for such sports.

Early in the conversion phase, the FT muscle fibers were trained to instantaneously display the highest possible level of power. Now, for P-E purposes, the FT fibers are trained to resist the fatigue induced by performing many repetitions dynamically. Training is now aimed at developing the endurance component of speed, which is accomplished by progressively increasing the number of repetitions and sets. This requires athletes to exert maximum willpower to overcome fatigue and to reach optimum mental concentration before each set is performed.

To perform a high number of sets for each prime mover, the number of exercises must be as low as possible (two to three). At the same time, each repetition in a set of 20 to 30 repetitions has to be performed explosively, and the RI has to be 5 to 7 minutes long.

During this type of work, athletes will experience a high level of lactic acid buildup. Unless this buildup is disposed of, it will impair the ability to repeat quality work. Thus, sufficient time must be allowed for removal of at least 50 percent of the total lactic acid before the next set is performed. Normally, it takes 15 to 25 minutes to remove 50 percent of the lactic acid accumulation. Since the muscle groups involved in training are being constantly alternated, by the time the same exercise is repeated, removal will take at least 20 minutes.

Speed of performance must be dynamic and explosive. Unless this rule is strictly observed, the training will be bodybuilding rather than P; the outcome will be hypertrophy rather than P-E! It will take a few weeks before athletes can perform 20 to 30 repetitions explosively nonstop. In the meantime, athletes should stop when they become incapable of performing a repetition of a set dynamically because P-E is no longer being trained. A summary of training parameters for P-E is listed in table 11.1. Figure 11.1 shows a sample 4-week training program for a tennis player.

Table 11.1 Suggested Training Parameters for P-E

Training parameters	Work
Load	50-70 percent
Number of exercises	2-3
Number of repetitions per set	15-30
Number of sets per session	2-4
Rest interval	5-7 minutes
Speed of execution	Very dynamic
Frequency per week	2-3

No.	Exercise	Week 1	Week 2	Week 3	Week 4
1	Jumping half squats	$\frac{50}{15}$ 2	$\frac{50}{20}$ 2	$\frac{50}{20}$ 2	$\frac{60}{25}$ 3
2	Medicine ball side (right and left) throws	3 × 25	3 × 30	3 × 25	4 × 30
3	Medicine ball overhead forward throws	3 × 25	3 × 30	3 × 25	4 × 30
4	Reactive jumps	2 × 15	3 × 15	2 × 15	3 × 20

	Week 1	Week 2	Week 3	Week 4
Loading pattern	Medium	High	Medium	High

Figure 11.1   Four-week P-E training program for an international-class tennis player. RI = 5 minutes.

Muscular Endurance of Short Duration Method

In the world of sports, there are several events with a duration between 30 seconds and 2 minutes, such as in track and field, swimming, canoeing, speed skating, and skiing. There are also sports in which intense activity of this duration is constantly required during a game or match, as in ice hockey, soccer, rugby, basketball, boxing, wrestling, and the martial arts. During such intense activity, athletes build up a high level of lactic acid, often more than 12 to 15 millimoles per liter, which shows that the lactic acid energy system is either dominant or an important component in the overall performance of the sport or event. Most of these sports require very strong anaerobic power as well as very good aerobic endurance.

Strength training must complement overall physiological demands. One of the key objectives for endurance sports is to train athletes to tolerate fatigue, so strength training should have the same goal. As the competitive phase approaches, strength training must be designed so that it challenges athletes' ability to tolerate a high buildup of lactic acid.

The specifics of M-ES are similar to the intensive interval training method used in circuit training (CT) where an oxygen debt is developed during the RI, which is typical for activities where the anaerobic energy system prevails. After 60 to 90 seconds of such activity, the heart rate can be as high as 180 to 200 beats per minute and blood lactic acid concentration between 12 and 15 millimoles per liter, or even higher. The energy sources for M-ES are blood and muscle glucose and, in particular, the glycogen stored in the liver.

The structure of M-ES can follow the format of CT, in which the repetitions are performed rhythmically and at a fast pace. The load is not very high, 50 to 60 percent, but is performed at a high intensity, at or close to the rate in competition, and thus the lowest number of exercises (three to six) should be selected.

The number of repetitions can be set precisely, but as in interval training, it is more appropriate to decide the duration of each set and the speed of performance (30 to 60 seconds). If the number of exercises is low, three to six sets or circuits can be performed. The speed of performance and the duration and number of sets have to be increased progressively over time from a lower level to that suggested in figure 11.2. To train athletes to tolerate lactic acid buildup, the RI must be short (60 to 90 seconds). Table 11.2

Table 11.2 Suggested Training Parameters for M-ES

Training parameters	Work
Load	50-60 percent
Number of exercises	3-6
Duration of activity	30-60 seconds
Number of sets per session	3-6
Rest interval	60-90 seconds
Speed of execution	Medium to fast
Frequency per week	2-3

No.	Exercise	Week 1	Week 2	Week 3	Week 4	Week 5	Week 6
1	Bent-over arm pulls; load 50%	2 × 30 seconds	2 × 30 seconds	2 × 45 seconds	2 × 30 seconds	2 × 45 seconds	3 × 45 seconds
2	Abdominal V-sits (reps)	2 × 20	2 × 25	2 × 30	2 × 25	2 × 30	2 × 35
3	Lay on back, arms above head, hold; medicine ball forward throws	1 × 25	2 × 25	2 × 30	2 × 25	2 × 30	2 × 30
4	Leg extensions; load 50%	2 × 30 seconds	2 × 30 seconds	2 × 45 seconds	2 × 30 seconds	2 × 45 seconds	2 × 45 seconds
5	Cable elbow extensions; load 60%	2 × 30 seconds	2 × 30 seconds	2 × 45 seconds	2 × 30 seconds	2 × 45 seconds	2 × 45 seconds

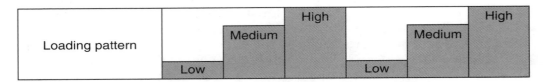

Figure 11.2 Six-week training program for M-ES for a national-class 100-meter fly swimmer.

lists the training parameters for M-ES training. Figure 11.2 is a sample 6-week program for a national class 100 meter fly swimmer.

Muscular Endurance of Medium and Long Duration Method

The development of M-E is one of the main factors in improving performance for all sports where performance time is greater than 2 minutes. A specific strength training program has to relate to the nonstop duration of activity for sports where aerobic endurance is either dominant or an important component of the final performance.

M-E training is of major benefit for boxing, wrestling, rowing, swimming (400 to 1,500 meters), kayaking/canoeing (1,000 to 10,000 meters), road cycling, cross-country skiing, biathlon, and triathlon. The incorporation of M-E of medium duration during the preparatory phase is also beneficial for some team sports, especially rugby, ice hockey, basketball, soccer, and Australian football.

M-E training can be performed as CT following the principles of interval training of long duration. This training method can also be called "extensive interval training," because the term *extensive* implies a high-volume, long-duration type of activity. The main objective of training for M-E is to increase the ability to cope with fatigue. Athletes improve anaerobic and aerobic endurance, since M-E training employs a high number of repetitions, often more than 100. In the early part of a nonstop set with many repetitions, energy is provided by the anaerobic system. This produces a buildup of lactic acid that creates physiological and psychological problems for athletes as they attempt to continue the activity. As these challenges are overcome and athletes continue to work, energy is supplied by the aerobic system. Repetitive M-E training results in specific adaptation that improves cardiovascular regulation and aerobic metabolism.

Physiological adaptations promote better oxygen and energy supply and increase the removal of metabolic wastes. Repetitive M-E training increases glycogen stores in both muscles and liver. Thus, the specific benefit of M-E training is an overall increase in physiological efficiency.

Because M-E employs such a relatively low load (around 30 to 50 percent), the muscles improve their long-term contracting capability without any evident increase in muscle fiber diameter. Only a certain number of motor units are active at one time; the others are at rest and are activated only when and where the contracting fibers become fatigued. Improvement of MxS during that phase is also beneficial for sports where M-E represents an important training method. If the diameter of an individual muscle fiber has increased as a result of MxS, a smaller number of motor units are needed to perform an M-E training task.

This type of strength reserve is critical and increases the muscle's capacity to produce work more effectively since fewer fibers are involved to overcome the resistance. Thus, MxS should not be minimized. On the contrary, it should, within limits, be used for all the sports mentioned above. However, for sports of long duration, such as a marathon, or sports that require less than 30 percent of MxS to perform the activity, further increments of MxS have negligible, if any, benefits (Hartmann & Tünnemann, 1988).

M-E medium and M-E long training have similar physiological bases. M-E medium (M-EM) is, however, suggested for sports where the duration of competition is between 2 and 10 minutes, whereas M-E long (M-EL) is suggested for sports where the duration is 10 minutes or longer. This distinction is necessary because M-EM has a stronger anaerobic component, whereas M-EL is clearly aerobic. The program designs for each type of M-E will be described separately since the load, duration of a set, and speed of execution are clearly different.

Program Design for Muscular Endurance of Medium Duration

The M-EM training program can be designed either as CT or as interval training. The first option is suggested for sports where it is necessary to train more muscle groups (wrestling, boxing), whereas the second is advisable for sports where one limb prevails (speed skating, canoeing). An example will be presented for each option.

The load for M-EM is 40 to 50 percent (table 11.3), performed progressively over a longer duration. As shown in tables 11.4 and 11.5, the duration and number of repetitions are increased progressively over a longer period. The duration of the conversion phase for M-E must be 8 to 10 weeks. This length of time is necessary for physiological adaptation to such high training. Throughout the M-EM phase, the load, number of exercises, rest interval, and speed of execution remain constant. The number of repetitions, however, increases every second week (table 11.4).

As shown in table 11.3, the rest interval between sets is short, so athletes have insufficient time to recover adequately. However, the program considers the physiological characteristics of the sports employing M-EM and is designed precisely to expose athletes to high levels of fatigue constantly so they learn to cope with the pain and exhaustion of competitions.

Table 11.3 Training Parameters for M-EM

Training parameters	Work
Load	40-50 percent
Number of exercises	4-8
Number of sets per session	2-4
Rest interval between sets	2 minutes
Rest interval between circuits	5 minutes
Speed of execution	Medium
Frequency per week	2-3

Table 11.4 Hypothetical CT for a Wrestler

Exercise	Number of weeks			
	2	2	2	2
Half squats	30	40	50	60
Arm curls	30	40	50	60
Leg curls	30	40	50	60
Bench presses	30	40	50	60
V-sits	15	20	25	30
Dead lifts	15	18	20	25

Table 11.4 shows a difference in number of reps between the first four exercises and the last two. The latter exercises are considered a lower priority. The ability to perform more repetitions of these exercise requires a solid training background of several years. The load for a dead lift must be lower (30 to 40 percent) and used carefully with beginners (long-term progression).

A CT designed for either M-EM or M-EL can use a barbell or any other piece of equipment. The advantage of using a barbell is that different limbs can be exercised without stopping to rest, as required in the circuit shown in table 11.5.

The circuit in table 11.5 includes eight exercises performed as follows. Place a barbell of 40 percent of MxS on the shoulders and perform 50 half squats. After completing the last repetition, sit on a bench and perform 40 arm curls. Then lie on the bench and do 50 bench presses. Quickly place the barbell back on the shoulders and perform 50 half squats. Follow this with 50 vertical rowing actions. Again, quickly place the barbell back on the shoulders and perform 60 toe raises followed by 50 dead lifts. Now place the barbell on the floor and perform 50 V-sits for the abdominal muscles. The total number of repetitions performed in our hypothetical circuit is 400!

The advantage of this method is that as training alternates different muscle groups, the cardiorespiratory system is involved throughout the circuit. This develops M-E and aerobic endurance, the two crucial abilities for any of the

Table 11.5 Example of an M-EM for a Rower

Exercise	Number of weeks			
	3-4	3	3	2
Half squats Arm curls Bench presses Half squats Seated rows Toe raises Dead lifts V-sits	Take a load of 30-50 percent and progressively aim to perform 50-60 reps nonstop per exercise.	Perform two exercises nonstop, or 100 reps together; for instance, 50 half squats followed by 50 arm curls. Pair the remaining six exercises.	Perform four exercises nonstop, or 200 repetitions. After a rest interval, repeat the other four exercises in the same manner.	Perform all exercises nonstop: eight exercises × 50 repetitions = 400 repetitions nonstop.
Rest interval between exercises	1 minute	1-2 minutes between each group of two.	2 minutes between each group of four.	—
Rest interval between circuits	—	—	—	4-5 minutes

A similar program can be developed for 400- to 1,500-meter swimming, middle-distance events in speed skating, kayaking/canoeing, and so on.

sports discussed in this chapter.

To further clarify the information in table 11.5:

- The number of repetitions is progressively increased to reach 40 to 60 or even higher; 2 to 4 weeks may be needed to accomplish this.
- The number of exercises may vary depending on the needs of the sport.
- The same exercise can be repeated twice in the same circuit to emphasize the importance of that group of muscles in a given sport (half squats in our example).
- The number of exercises may not be the same for every limb. This decision should be based on the strengths and weaknesses of the athletes involved.
- Observe a steady speed throughout the circuit; it will be easier on the cardiorespiratory system.
- Set up all the equipment needed before training, so the least amount of time is wasted changing from one exercise to another.
- Perform two exercises nonstop in the second phase, four exercises in the third phase, and all of them in the last phase.
- It may take 6 to 8 minutes or longer to perform an eight-exercise circuit nonstop, depending on the classification of the athlete involved. An even longer circuit can be designed for better improvement of M-EL.
- Since the physiological demands of M-E and M-EL are severe, this method should be applied only to athletes with a strong background in both strength and endurance training (national-class athletes and higher). For a less demanding circuit (for juniors), include only four to six exercises.
- It is best to use an even number of exercises because of the way they are performed—two, then four, then all together nonstop.

- As athletes adapt to performing the total number of exercises nonstop during the last phase, the coach can use a stopwatch to monitor improvement. As a result of adaptation, the time of performance may decrease continuously.

This type of M-EM training should not be used for testing purposes or for comparing the achievements of two or more athletes. Since anthropometrics (size or length of limbs) differ from athlete to athlete, such a comparison would be unfair, especially for tall athletes.

Program Design for Muscular Endurance of Long Duration

Sports of longer duration require a different kind of physiological training. In most of these sports, athletes apply force against a given resistance, for example: water in swimming, rowing, and canoeing; the pedals in cycling (body weight applied as strength, especially uphill); ice in speed skating; or snow and various terrains in cross-country skiing and biathlon.

The dominant energy system in these sports is aerobic endurance. Since improved performance is expected to come from increments in aerobic power, strength training must be designed to enhance this. To increase M-EL, therefore, the key training ingredient is a high number of repetitions performed nonstop. The other training parameters remain constant, as indicated in table 11.6.

Since one of the training goals of M-EL is to cope with fatigue, the RI does not allow full recovery. Only a very short rest is afforded as athletes change stations, usually 2 to 5 seconds.

Table 11.7 exemplifies a typical training program for M-EL for sports such as triathlon, marathon, kayaking/canoeing (10,000 meters and marathon), long-distance swimming, road cycling, and cross-country skiing. Note that the work is expressed in minutes rather than number of repetitions to make it easier to monitor the many minutes of steady work.

The first four exercises can be performed with a Universal gym or any similar training machine. The last two exercises must be performed using rubber cords, often called elastic cords, which are available in many sporting goods stores. Since this particular program is for long-distance kayaking or canoeing, the elastic cords must be anchored before training so that arm pulls or elbow extensions, typical motions for these two sports, can be performed from a seated position.

Table 11.6 Suggested Training Parameters for M-EL

Training parameters	Work
Load	30-40 percent
Number of exercises	4-6
Number of sets per session	2-4
Rest interval	See table 11.5
Speed of execution	Medium
Frequency per week	2-3

Table 11.7 Suggested Training Program for M-EL for an Experienced Marathon Canoeist

Exercise	Number of weeks					
	2	2	2-3	2	2	2-3
Leg presses Arm pulls Bench presses Leg presses Arm pulls (cords) Elbow extensions (cords)	Take a load of 30 percent and progressively perform 4 minutes of nonstop work for each exercise.	Perform the same work for 7 minutes nonstop for each exercise.	Perform 10 minutes of nonstop work for each exercise.	Perform two exercises nonstop, or 20 minutes of work. Repeat for exercises 3 and 4, and again for exercises 5 and 6.	Perform three exercises nonstop, or 30 minutes of work. Repeat for the other three exercises.	Perform all six exercises nonstop, or 60 minutes of work.
RI between exercises	1-2 minutes	2 minutes	2 minutes	—	—	—
RI between circuits	—	—	—	2-4 minutes	3-4 minutes	5 minutes

A similar concept of training can be applied to long-distance cross-country skiing, kayaking, marathon swimming, triathlon, and so on.

The number of sets per group of two, three, or all six exercises together, performed nonstop, must be determined based on the work tolerance and performance level of each athlete.

chapter 12

Strength Training During the Competitive and Transition Phases

Strength training is an important physiological contributor to overall athletic performance. The more explosive a skill, the more important the role of MxS and P; the longer the duration of an activity, the more determinant the role of M-E. Superior performance levels cannot be achieved without the vital contribution of strength.

The benefits of strength to athletic performance are felt as long as the neuromuscular system maintains the cellular adaptations induced by training. When strength training stops, benefits decrease as the contractile properties of the muscles diminish. The consequence is detraining, or a visible decrease in the contribution of strength to athletic performance. During the competitive phase, a sport-specific strength program is needed to avoid detraining.

Peaking, or the ability of an athlete to perform at peak performance during the main competitions or games of the year, is also related to strength training. In several sports, especially power sports, peak performance is often achieved in the early part of the competitive phase. Coaches tend to overlook strength training as specific technical and tactical training become dominant. Unfortunately, lack of strength training causes decreased performance as the season progresses. In the early part of the season, while strength benefits remain, performance is as expected. However, when the muscles' ability to contract powerfully diminishes, so does performance.

According to the theory of Periodization of Strength, gains in MxS during the MxS phase should be transformed into either M-E or P during the conversion phase so athletes acquire the best possible sport-specific strength and are equipped with the physiological capabilities necessary for good performance during the competitive phase. To maintain good performance throughout the competitive phase, this physiological base must be maintained. This means that a coach must plan a sport-specific maintenance program throughout the competitive phase. MxS is a crucial ingredient for sport-specific strength programs. Many sports require maintenance of some MxS during the competitive season, mostly as a result of employing the maximum load method.

Gains in MxS decline faster if they resulted from processes dependent on the nervous system, such as recruitment of large motor units (Hartmann & Tünnemann, 1988). Often such gains result from power training without a strong MxS base. In many sports, the type of strength performed is event-specific power training. MxS using the MLM is often overlooked and gains are short-lived. Most strength training gains deteriorate as the competitive phase progresses and approaches its peak, because strength training is done mostly during the preparatory phase.

The maintenance of strength during the competitive phase is not a question of *whether* to do it, but *how* it should be done. A coach must keep in mind the dominant ability of the sport and carefully consider what types of strength athletes should maintain. Most sports require some elements of MxS, P, and M-E. The most important decision, therefore, is what *proportion* of each to maintain and how best to integrate them into training, *not* which of the three to maintain.

In power sports, both MxS and P should be maintained. Since these abilities cannot substitute for each other, but rather are complementary, one should not be maintained at the expense of the other. For instance, throwers in track and field and linemen in football must maintain MxS during the competitive phase, with a proportion between MxS and P of approximately 50-50. Most team sport athletes should maintain P and either P-E or M-ES, depending on the position played. For endurance sports, however, the proportion among MxS, P, and M-E depends on the duration of the event and on which energy system is dominant. For the majority of endurance sports, M-E is the dominant component of strength.

The duration of the competitive phase is equally important in determining the proportion of different types of strength to be maintained. The longer the competitive phase, the more important it is to maintain some elements of MxS, as this type of strength is an important component of both P and M-E. If this fact is overlooked, as MxS is detrained, it will affect both P and M-E. Table 12.1 shows the proportions of different types of strength to be maintained during the competitive phase for various sports and positions.

The same training methods suggested in previous chapters should be applied during the maintenance phase. What differs during this phase is the volume of strength training compared to the technical, tactical, and other elements of physical training—not the training methodology.

Remember that the strength maintenance program is subordinate to other types of training during the competitive phase. Use the lowest number of exercises (2 to 3, maximum of 4) to address the prime movers. This expends the least possible energy for maintenance of strength, leaving the majority available for technical and tactical training.

The two (maximum three) strength training sessions per week should be as short as possible. A good maintenance program can often be accomplished in 20 to 30 minutes of specific work. Obviously, the frequency of strength training sessions also depends on the competition schedule. If no competitions are scheduled on the weekend, a microcycle may have two (three maximum) strength training sessions. If a game or competition is

Table 12.1 Suggested Proportion Among Different Types of Strength to Be Maintained During the Competitive Phase

Sport/event	MxS Concentric %	MxS Eccentric %	P %	P-E %	M-E %
Athletics: *Sprinting	20	—	60	20	—
*Jumping	20	10	70	—	—
*Throws	30	20	50	—	—
Baseball: *Pitcher	40	—	40	20	—
*Field players	20	—	70	10	—
Basketball	10	—	50	20	20
Biathlon	—	—	—	20	80
Boxing	20	—	20	30	30
Canoeing/kayaking: *500 meters	40	—	30	20	10
*1,000 meters	20	—	20	20	40
*10,000 meters	—	—	—	20	80
Cycling: *Track 200	20	—	70	10	—
*4,000-meter pursuit	10	—	30	20	40
Diving	—	10	90	—	—
Fencing	—	—	60	30	10
Figure skating	20	20	40	10	10
Field hockey	—	—	40	20	40
Football: *Linemen	30	20	50	—	—
*Linebackers	20	—	60	20	—
*Running backs	20	—	60	20	—
*Wide receivers	20	—	60	20	—
*Defensive backs	20	—	60	20	—
*Tailbacks	20	10	40	20	10
Football (Australian)	20	10	40	20	10
Ice hockey	10	—	50	30	10
Martial arts	—	—	60	30	10
Rowing	10	—	—	20	70
Rugby	20	—	40	30	10
Skiing: *Alpine	20	20	30	30	—
*Nordic	—	—	—	20	80
Soccer: *Sweepers/goalie	20	10	60	10	—
*Other positions	—	—	60	20	20
Speed skating: *Sprinting	20	—	60	20	—
*Distance	—	—	10	20	70
Swimming: *Sprinting	20	—	50	20	10
*Middle distance	10	—	10	20	60
*Long distance	—	—	—	20	80
Tennis	—	—	60	30	10
Volleyball	15	5	50	20	10
Water polo	10	—	20	20	50
Wrestling	—	—	30	10	60

planned on the weekend, one or at most two short strength training sessions can be planned, normally in the early part of the week.

The number of sets is usually low (1 to 4), depending on whether P or M-E is trained. For P and MxS, 2 to 4 sets are possible, as the number of repetitions is usually low. For M-E, 1 to 2 sets are suggested, as the number of repetitions is higher. During the competitive phase, the number of repetitions for M-EM and M-EL should not exceed 20 to 30, as these two components of M-E are also developed during the technical, tactical, or conditioning program specific to the sport. The RI should be longer than usual, so athletes can recover almost entirely during the break. The intent of the maintenance phase is to stabilize performance, not create fatigue.

The planning for each microcyle of a maintenance program depends on the type of strength sought. For power training, look for exercises that enhance explosiveness by using resistance close to that encountered in competitions. Two types of resistance are suggested. *Increased load*, or a resistance slightly higher than in competition, enhances both specific MxS and P. Exercises should be specific to the prevailing skills of the particular sport. This type of exercise is suggested mostly for the early part of the competitive phase as a transition from MxS to P. *Decreased load*, or a resistance below that encountered in competition, enhances explosiveness and should prevail in the phase prior to the main competitions. Both loads increase the ability to recruit a high number of FT fibers and improve synchronization of the muscles involved. If the competitive phase is longer than 4 to 5 months, dedicate 25 percent of the total work to the maintenance of MxS since the detraining of MxS will negatively affect overall M-E capacity.

The maintenance of MxS is more elaborate since its effectiveness depends on the proportion between the types of contraction. Often a combination between concentric and eccentric contraction can be more effective than using only concentric contraction. A combination of 75 percent concentric, 15 percent eccentric, and 10 percent P seems most effective.

Variations of Loading Pattern for the Competitive Phase

Planning in training and the loading patterns used in strength training are not rigid processes. On the contrary, they should be flexible and adaptable to the athlete's well-being and progress in training, the requirements of the sport, and the schedule of competitions or games. To illustrate this, the following sections present several practical examples of the dynamics in loading pattern for both individual and team sports for the competitive phase.

Individual Sports

For speed-power sports (sprinting, jumping and throwing events in track and field, 50-meter swimming, the martial arts, fencing, etc.), the suggested plan for strength training in figure 12.1 implements the following important training concepts valid for the competitive phase. For the first 2 to 3 days following competition, the objective of training is regeneration. Only two strength training sessions are planned, both later in the week, the first of low intensity. The only time strength training is challenging is during week 2. The third week is a peaking week, so only two strength training sessions are planned, the second of low intensity. To ensure that the Wednes-

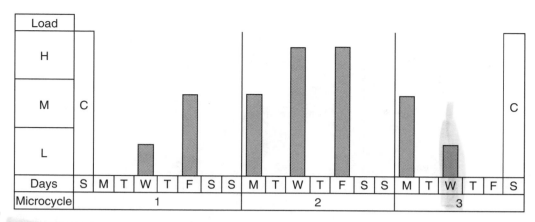

Figure 12.1 Suggested plan for strength training (and its loading) for a speed-power-dominant sport where competitions (C) are planned 3 weeks apart. *Note:* Load could also mean training intensity/overall demand.

day session is of low load/demand, the rest interval between two to three sets of strength-power training should be long (4 to 5 minutes) for full regeneration. This will avoid any residual fatigue before the upcoming competition.

Figure 12.2 addresses similar concerns for a situation where competitions are planned 2 weeks apart. Note that in designing such a plan, you should allow 2 to 3 days of regenerative, low-intensity training following the first competition. Training must again be of low intensity on the last 2 to 3 days before competition to facilitate peaking.

In individual sports, scheduling weekly competitions is far from ideal simply because the more you compete, the less time there is for training. During periods of weekly competitions, especially when fatigue is high, most coaches look for training elements to be cut, and unfortunately strength training is often the first to go.

For situations where weekly competitions are the norm, figure 12.3 illustrates a strength training plan that can be altered to accommodate high levels of fatigue. But remember, planning too many training cycles with weekly

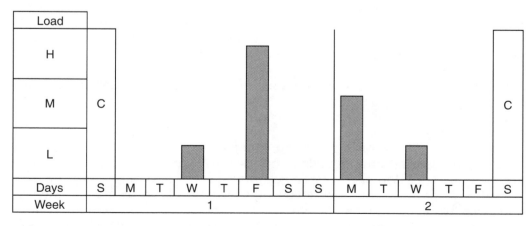

Figure 12.2 Proposed strength training days (and their loading magnitude) for a situation where competitions are planned 2 weeks apart.

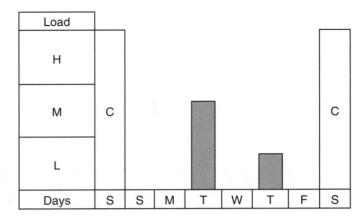

Figure 12.3 Possible scenario for planning strength training for a situation where weekly competitions are the norm. In case of high-level fatigue; the plan can be altered to either reduce Tuesday's load to low intensity or schedule only one workout on Wednesday.

competitions will have a predictable outcome: detraining with its ensuing loss of speed-power.

Team Sports

Without negating the importance of specific endurance, power is the dominant ability for most team sports. Consequently, to avoid detraining of power, a maintenance program must be planned throughout the competitive phase.

The examples presented in this section are for two competitive schedules: one and two games per week. They are valid for baseball, basketball, volleyball, football, ice hockey, field hockey, Australian football, soccer, rugby, lacrosse, and water polo, where specific endurance is an important component.

Despite other pressures on the team (the need for more technical or tactical training, placement in league standings, etc.), the coach must find the time and the athletes must find the energy for maintenance of power. The longer the duration of the competitive phase, the more important the need to maintain power training.

Figure 12.4 suggests a plan for a cycle with a game (G) scheduled every Saturday (can be adjusted for any other day of the week). Note that a strength training session of medium demand is proposed for Tuesday. If the athletes' level of fatigue is higher than expected, the overall demand can be reduced by using a low load.

Even for team sports with two games per week, a maintenance program for strength training is still possible; however, it should be limited to one to two sets of three exercises at 70 percent of 1RM, or a maximum of 15 to 20 minutes (figure 12.5).

The content of a training session must be related to the load used in training, the overall intensity/demand used in that session, and the proximity of a competition or game. The examples suggested below assume that strength training is performed following specific work on technique, tactics, and drills for speed and specific endurance. Consequently, since there is little time and energy to spare, strength training must be short and sport specific.

The suggested program for a heavy load/demand strength training session lasts 20 to 30 minutes. MxS or P, or combinations of the two, are trained.

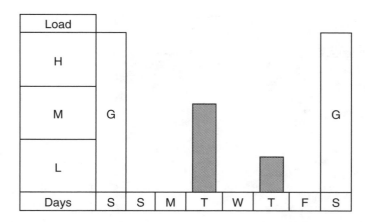

Figure 12.4 Suggested schedule for strength training for a team sport with a game every weekend.

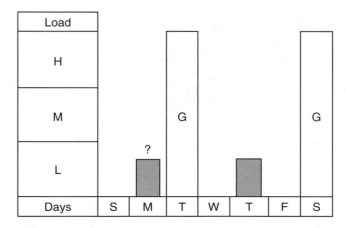

Figure 12.5 Suggested maintenance program for strength training for a team sport playing two games per week. The main workout is on Thursday, with fatigue and the importance of the Tuesday game dictating the fate of Monday's strength training.

Four to five exercises specifically for the prime movers with a load of 70 to 80 percent are performed as fast and dynamically as possible. Five to eight repetitions are performed within two to four sets with a RI of two to four minutes.

The suggested program for a medium load lasts 20 to 30 minutes. MxS or P are trained. Three to four exercises using a load of 70 percent are performed explosively. Five to eight repetitions are performed in two to three sets with a RI of two to three minutes.

The suggested program for a low load lasts 15 minutes. MxS or P are trained. Two to three exercises using a 60 to 70 percent load are performed explosively. Four to six repetitions are performed over one to two sets with a RI of two to three minutes.

Athletes in some sports, such as linemen in football, throwers in track and field, and heavyweight boxers and wrestlers, have to train quite differently from the programs proposed above. The suggested program for such athletes lasts 60 to 75 minutes. The strength sought is 40 to 50 percent MxS and 50 to 60 percent P. Four to six exercises using a load of 70 to 90 percent

Minimize plyometric exercises to alleviate stress on a basketball player's leg during the season.

are performed as explosively as possible. Five to eight repetitions are performed over three to six sets with a RI of 3 to 4 minutes.

For team sports where many jumps are performed during training and games (basketball, volleyball), plyometric training should be reduced to a minimum compared to the end of the preparatory phase. This will alleviate the strain on the athlete's legs throughout the season.

The strength maintenance program should end 5 to 7 days before the most important competition of the year, so that all the energies are used to achieve the best performance possible.

Strength Training During the Transition Phase

Following a lengthy period of hard work and stressful competitions, when determination, motivation, and willpower are tested, athletes experience a high degree of physiological and psychological fatigue. Although muscular fatigue may disappear in a few days, fatigue of the CNS and the psyche can be observed through an athlete's behavior much longer.

The more intensive the training and the more competitions athletes are exposed to, the greater the fatigue. Any athlete would have difficulty beginning a new annual training cycle under such conditions. Athletes must rest themselves physically and psychologically before another season of training starts. When the new preparatory phase begins, they should be completely regenerated and ready to participate in training. In fact, following a successful transition phase, athletes should feel a strong desire to train again.

The transition phase, inappropriately called the off-season, represents a link between two annual cycles. Its major objectives are psychological rest, relaxation, and biological regeneration and maintainance of an acceptable level of general physical preparation. This phase should last no longer than 4 to 5 weeks because athletes will detrain, visibly losing most of their fitness.

To maintain a decent level of fitness, athletes should train two to three times a week during the transition phase. Remember that it takes less effort to maintain 40 to 50 percent of the previous fitness level than to start redeveloping it from zero.

During transition, athletes should perform compensation work to involve muscle groups that receive little attention throughout the preparatory and competitive phases. This means paying attention to the antagonistic muscles and stabilizers. For example, following any informal physical training such as a pickup game or recreational play, 20 to 30 minutes can be dedicated to activating these two muscle groups. The program can be relaxed, with athletes working at their own pace for as long as they desire. The program need not be stressful. In fact, stress is undesirable during transition. Forget the formal program with its specific load, number of repetitions, and sets; for once, athletes should do as they please.

Planning the Training Methods

In the illustrations accompanying the discussions on planning-periodization and training methods (chapter 6), a vertical bar was used to separate training phases. This may have implied that a certain type of training ends on the last day of one phase and a completely different type begins on the first day of the next. In reality, the transition between phases is not quite so abrupt. There is always an overlap, with a training method to be used in a given phase progressively introduced in the previous phase. Similarly, the method used in a previous phase is usually maintained for a short time in the next phase while progressively reducing its emphasis.

Each training phase has a dominant method(s) and another that may be progressively introduced. This allows for a more effective transition from one method to the next. For instance, the transition from MxS to P is performed progressively by introducing some elements of power training during the MxS phase and maintaining some MxS training during the conversion phase (figure 12.6).

A transition between two training methods or phases can take place over two microcycles. Figure 12.6 shows that as power is progressively introduced, MxS is progressively reduced. This is accomplished by creating different

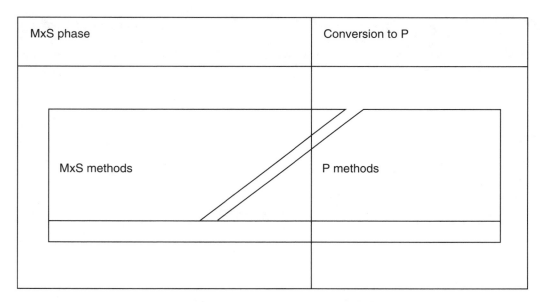

Figure 12.6   Illustration of the transition between two training methods or phases.

Table 12.2 Progressive Transition From an MxS-Dominant Training Phase to P

Training day		Microcycle 1			Microcycle 2		
		1	2	3	1	2	3
Sets	MxS	5	4	3	2	1	0
	P	0	1	2	3	4	5

Table 12.3 Suggested Progressive Transition From MxS to P

Microcycles		1	2	3	4
Training days	MxS	3	2	1	0
	P	0	1	2	3

combinations between sets of MxS and P, as illustrated in table 12.2. For easier presentation, it is assumed that three strength training sessions of five sets per day are planned in each microcycle.

Another method of transition from MxS to P is through the number of training sessions dedicated to each ability. Table 12.3 illustrates such an example. All three training sessions in microcycle 1 are dedicated to MxS; then MxS is decreased as P is increased until all three training sessions in microcycle 4 are dedicated to P.

The transition from one type of training to another can be planned more elaborately, as illustrated in table 12.4. This chart shows the Periodization

Table 12.4 Example of Transition to Different Types of Strength for Synchronized Swimming

Dates		Sep.	Oct.	Nov.	Dec.	Jan.	Feb.	Mar.	Apr.	May
Periodization	Competition	—				Provincial	Division			Natl. Champ.
	Training phase	Preparatory				Competitive				
	Periodization of strength	AA core strength	MxS Maintenance of core strength			Conversion: *P *M-E *Maintenance of core strength		Maint.	Cessation	
No. of workouts per week		3	3-4			4			2	
Duration in weeks		5	9			4	4	4	4	4	1
Type of strength		2AA 1 core	2-3 MxS 1 core			2 M-E 1P 1/2 MxS 1/2 core	→	3 M-E 1 P	2 M-E 1 P	1 M-E 1 P	

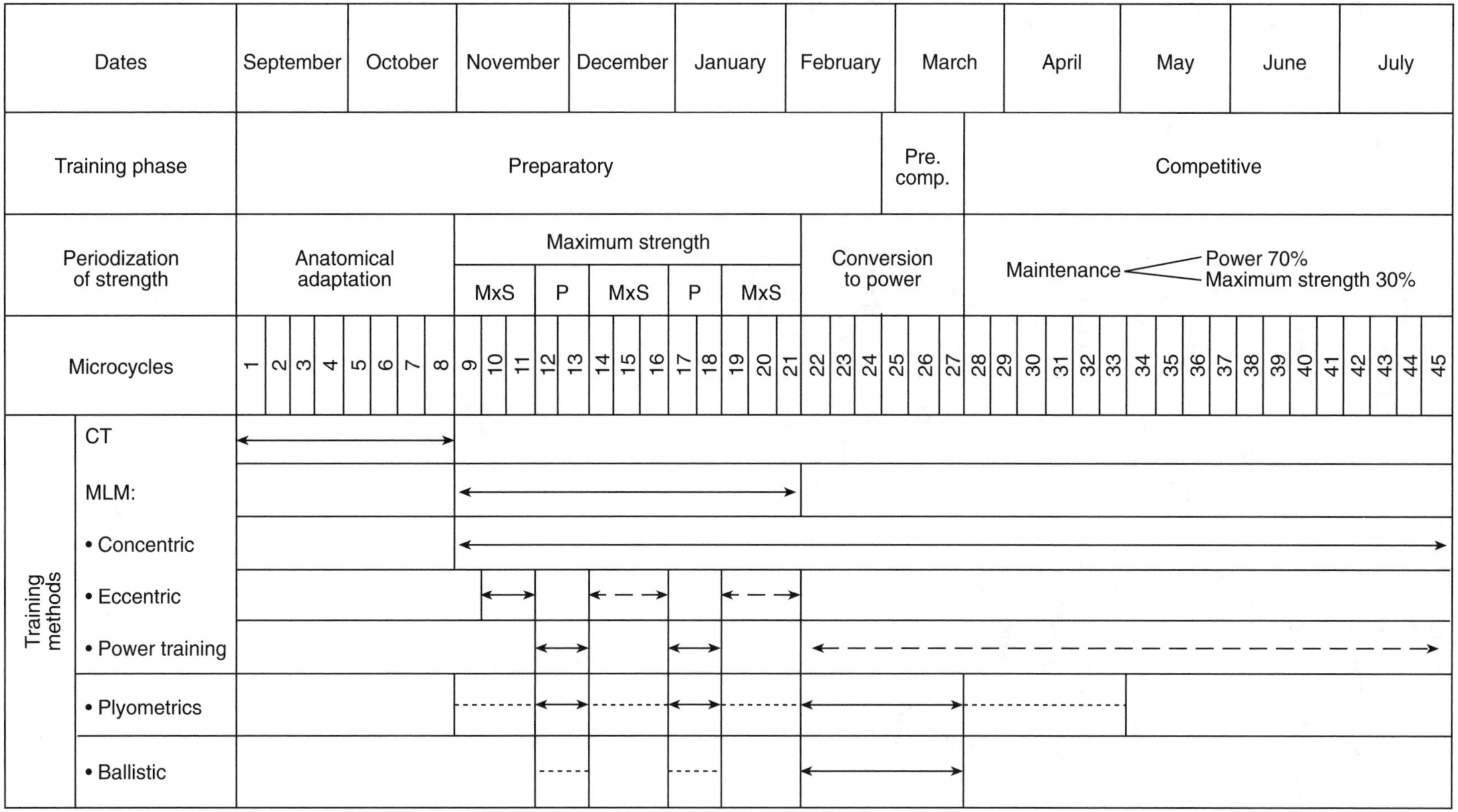

Figure 12.7 A hypothetical example of planning the training methods for a power-dominated sport.

of Strength, the number of workouts per week, the duration of each phase in weeks, and the transition from one type of strength to another. Note that in this case, the core strength for synchronized swimming, which is the strength of the hips, abdominals and lower back, was emphasized or maintained throughout the annual plan.

A well-organized coach will also structure a plan that shows how to use a certain type of training method and for how long. In doing so, the coach will plan the most appropriate methods for each training phase, showing the duration of each as well as which method is dominant.

Figure 12.7 illustrates how training methods can be planned. The example refers to hypothetical sports where power is the dominant ability. As usual, the top of the chart shows the training phases of a mono-cycle, and below is the Periodization of Strength.

The bottom part of the chart lists several methods. Three types of symbols are used since in a given training phase, a certain method can have a higher priority than the others. The solid line indicates the method with the highest priority, the dashed line shows second priority, and the dotted line, third priority. For instance, during the AA phase, CT is the dominant training method. When the MxS phase begins, MLM (maximum load method) concentric prevails, while the eccentric method is of secondary priority during some segments of the program.

In power training, only the ballistic method and plyometrics are presented. The dotted line shows that these methods are a third priority in some phases. Figure 12.7 is only a hypothetical example and does not exhaust all available methods or all possibilities of showing how they are used.

chapter 13

Fatigue, Muscle Soreness, and Recovery

Athletes are constantly exposed to various types of training loads, some of which exceed their tolerance threshold. As a result, adaptation decreases, affecting overall performance. When athletes drive themselves beyond their physiological limits, they risk fatigue. The greater the fatigue, the greater the negative training aftereffects such as low rate of recovery, decreased coordination, and diminished power output. Fatigue from training can increase if an athlete is undergoing other personal stresses.

Muscle fatigue and overreaching commonly associated with exercise-induced muscle damage are complex physiological and psychological phenomena. Fatigue can affect an athlete's force-generating capacity or result in the inability to maintain a required force. Though much research has been devoted to muscle fatigue, neither the exact sites nor the exact causes are well known. Coaches and instructors should become as informed as possible in this area so they can create better plans to avoid fatigue and overreaching. Considering the complexity of this topic, reference will be made mainly to fatigue induced by strength training.

To improve performance, training loads must be high enough to stimulate adaptation. For adaptation to occur, training programs must intersperse work periods with rest and alternate various levels of intensity while avoiding large increments in training load. This practice creates a good work-to-rest balance; exposing athletes to loads beyond their capacity or underestimating the necessary rest will result in decreased ability to adapt to a new load. Failure to adapt triggers biochemical and neural reactions that take athletes from fatigue to chronic fatigue and ultimately to the undesirable state of overtraining. Fatigue is the consequence of physical work and reduces the capacity of the neuromuscular and metabolic systems to continue physical activity. The focus of this section will be the two main sites of fatigue: the neuromuscular and metabolic systems.

Neuromuscular Fatigue

Though fatigue is assumed to originate in the muscles, the CNS plays an important role, since incentive, temperament, stress, and other psychological factors affect fatigue. Increasing evidence suggests that the CNS limits performance to a greater extent than once thought.

The CNS has two basic processes: *excitation* and *inhibition*. Excitation is a stimulating process for physical activity; inhibition is a restraining process. Throughout training, these two processes alternate. For any stimulation, the CNS sends a nerve impulse to the working muscle, causing it to contract. The speed, power, and frequency of the nerve impulse depends directly on the state of the CNS.

Nerve impulses are most effective when (controlled) excitation prevails, resulting in a good performance. When fatigue inhibits the nerve cell, the muscle contraction is slower and weaker. Thus, the electrical activation of the CNS is responsible for the number of motor units recruited and the force of the contraction. Recruitment of motor units decreases as fatigue increases.

Nerve cell working capacity cannot be maintained for very long. Under the strain of training or competition it decreases. If high intensity is maintained, the nerve cell will assume a state of inhibition to protect itself from external stimuli. Consequently, fatigue should be viewed as a self-protecting mechanism against damage to the contractile mechanism of the muscle.

In speed-power sports, fatigue is visible to the experienced eye. Athletes react more slowly to explosive activities and show a slight coordination impairment and an increase in the duration of the contact phase in sprinting, bounding, rebounding, jumping, and plyometrics. These activities rely on the activation of FT fibers, which are more easily affected by fatigue than ST fibers. Thus, even a slight inhibition of the CNS affects their recruitment.

Skeletal muscle produces force by activating its motor units and regulating their firing frequency, which progressively increases to enhance force output. Fatigue that inhibits muscular activity can be neutralized to some extent by a modulating strategy of responding to fatigue through the ability of the motor units to alter firing frequency. As a result, the muscle can maintain force more effectively under a certain state of fatigue. However, if the duration of sustained maximum contraction increases, the frequency of the motor units' firing decreases, signaling that inhibition will become more prominent (Bigland-Ritchie et al., 1983; Hennig & Lomo, 1987).

Marsden et al. (1971) demonstrated that end firing frequency decreased by 80 percent compared to the start of a 30-second maximum voluntary contraction. Grimby (1992) reported similar findings: as contraction duration increased, activation of large motor units decreased, lowering the firing rate below the threshold level. Any contraction beyond that level was possible through short bursts (phasical firing) but was not appropriate for a constant performance.

These findings should alarm those who promote the theory (especially in football) that strength can be improved only by performing each set to exhaustion. The fact that the firing frequency decreases as a contraction progresses discredits this highly acclaimed method.

As a contraction progresses, fuel reserves deplete, resulting in longer motor unit relaxation time and a lower frequency of muscle contraction. Fatigue is the suspected cause of such neuromuscular behavior. This

Coaches and trainers should watch for signs of fatigue and overreaching so corrective measures can be taken before an injury occurs.

should warn practitioners that short rest intervals (the standard 1 to 2 minutes) between two sets of maximum load are insufficient to relax and regenerate the neuromuscular system to produce high activation in subsequent sets.

When analyzing the functional capacity of the CNS during fatigue, the athletes' perceived fatigue and past physical capacity achieved in training must be considered. When physical capacity is above the level of fatigue experienced in testing or competition, it enhances motivation and, as a result, the capacity to overcome fatigue. Thus, the level of motivation must be related to past experience and the state of training.

Metabolic Sources of Fatigue

Muscle fatigue may be associated with calcium flux in skeletal muscle although this relationship remains a mystery. The complex cycle of muscle contraction is triggered by the nerve impulse that depolarizes the surface membrane of the muscle cell and is then conducted into the muscle fiber. This is followed by a series of events in which calcium is bound together with protein filaments (actin and myosin), resulting in contractile tension. The functional site of fatigue is suggested to be the link between excitation and contraction, resulting in either reducing the intensity of these two processes or decreasing the sensitivity to activation. Changes in the flux of calcium ions affect the operation of excitation-contraction (Tesch, 1980).

Fatigue Due to Lactic Acid Accumulation

The buildup of lactic acid in the muscle decreases its ability to contract maximally (Fox et al., 1989). Any athletic movements requiring quickness or force of contraction must rely on the contraction of FT fibers. Since such actions are anaerobic, they rely on anaerobic types of fuel, resulting in increased production and accumulation of lactic acid. During the performance of high-intensity (heavy-load) sets, FT fibers produce high levels of lactates, blocking any immediate excitation-stimulation coming from the CNS. The next high-intensity set can be performed only after a longer rest period (see "Rest Interval" in chapter 4).

The biochemical exchanges during muscle contraction result in the liberation of hydrogen ions that in turn produce acidosis or the not yet clearly understood "lactate fatigue," which seems to determine the point of exhaustion (Sahlin, 1986). The more active a muscle, the greater its hydrogen ion concentration and thus the higher the level of blood acidosis.

Increased acidosis also inhibits the binding capacity of calcium through inactivation of troponin, a protein compound. Since troponin is an important contributor to muscle cell contraction, its inactivation may expand the connection between fatigue and exercise (Fabiato & Fabiato, 1978). The discomfort produced by acidosis can also be a limiting factor in psychological fatigue (Brooks & Fahey, 1985).

Fatigue Due to the Depletion of ATP/CP and Glycogen Stores

Fatigue occurs when creatine phosphate in the working muscle is depleted, muscle glycogen is consumed, or the carbohydrate store is exhausted (Sahlin, 1986). The end result is obvious: the work performed by the muscle decreases. The possible reason is that in a glycogen-depleted muscle, adenosine triphosphate is produced at a lower rate than it is consumed. Studies show that carbohydrates are essential to the ability of a muscle to maintain high force (Conlee, 1987) and that endurance capabilities during prolonged moderate to heavy physical activity are directly related to the amount of glycogen in the muscle prior to exercise. This indicates that fatigue occurs as a result of muscle glycogen depletion (Bergstrom et al., 1967).

For high-intensity activities of short duration, such as high-intensity sets, the immediate sources of energy for muscular contraction are ATP and CP. Total depletion of these stores in the muscle will certainly limit its ability to contract (Karlsson & Saltin, 1971).

With prolonged submaximum work such as muscular endurance of medium or long duration, glucose and fatty acids are used to produce energy. The availability of oxygen is critical in this type of strength training. When the supply of oxygen is limited, carbohydrates are oxidized instead of free fatty acids. Maximum free fatty acid oxidation is determined by the inflow of fatty acids to the working muscle and the aerobic training status of the athlete since aerobic training increases both the availability of oxygen and the power of free fatty acid oxidation (Sahlin, 1986). Lack of oxygen, oxygen-carrying capacity, and inadequate blood flow all contribute to muscular fatigue (Bergstrom et al., 1967). This demonstrates the need for decent aerobic conditioning, even for speed-power sports.

Muscle Soreness

Muscle soreness after training can occur when first starting a strength training program, when unfamiliar exercises are performed that work muscles other than those normally used, or any time heavy loads are employed for a prolonged period. Beginners exposed to heavy loads without adequate adaptation will also experience muscle soreness.

Two basic mechanisms explain how exercise initiates damage: the disturbance of metabolic function and the mechanical disruption of the muscle cell.

The metabolic mechanism of muscle damage is at work during prolonged submaximum work to exhaustion, typical of some bodybuilding methods. Direct loading of the muscle, especially during the eccentric contraction phase, may cause muscle damage, which may then be aggravated by metabolic changes. Disruption of the muscle cell membrane is one of the most noticeable types of damage (swollen mitochondria, lesion of the plasma membrane, distortion of myofibrillar components, sarcolemmal disruption, etc.) (Friden & Lieber, 1992).

Eccentric contraction produces greater muscle tension than concentric contraction. Some coaches try to speed up the process of producing good athletes by employing the eccentric method. They disregard whether the athletes have enough strength training background to tolerate it or adequate connective tissue adaptation has occurred. The predictable results are discomfort and muscle damage. Eccentric contraction produces more heat than concentric contraction at the same workload. The increased temperatures can damage structural and functional components within the muscle cell (Armstrong, 1986; Ebbing & Clarkson, 1989).

Both mechanisms of muscle damage are related to muscle fibers that have been slightly stressed. When this occurs, the muscle fibers quickly return to their normal length without injury. If the stress is severe, however, the muscle becomes traumatized. Discomfort sets in during the first 24 to 48 hours following the exercise and is thus called *delayed-onset* muscle soreness. The sensation of dull, aching pain combined with tenderness and stiffness tends to diminish within 5 to 7 days after the initial workout.

For years lactic acid buildup was considered the main cause of muscle soreness, but recent research suggests that the actual cause is an influx of calcium ions into the muscle cell (Armstrong, 1986; Ebbing & Clarkson, 1989; Evans, 1987). Calcium, which is very important in muscle contraction, stimulates the fiber to contract and is then rapidly pumped back into the calcium storage area after the contraction has been completed. If calcium ions accumulate within the muscle fiber, however, it causes the release of protease, resulting in muscle fiber breakdown. The resulting soreness is due primarily to the formation of degraded protein components, or dead tissue. The body initiates a "cleanup" phase to eliminate the dead muscle tissue, and the muscles initiate a protective mechanism that produces stress protein, which stops further damage. This explains why muscle soreness is not felt every day.

Once the muscle has been traumatized, histamine, serotonin, and potassium accumulate. These substances are responsible for the inflammation following a muscle fiber injury (Prentice, 1990). When accumulation reaches a certain level, it activates the nerve endings. It takes a long time for the damaged muscle cells to accumulate all these substances, which may be why muscle soreness is not felt until 24 hours later (Armstrong, 1986; Ebbing & Clarkson, 1989).

The discomfort and soreness are felt most intensely in the region of the muscle-tendon junction since the tissue of the tendon is less flexible than that of the muscle and thus is more susceptible to injury from intense contraction.

As expected, greater damage is seen in FT fibers than in ST fibers, because a higher proportion of FT fibers participate in the intense contractions typical of heavy-load/high-intensity training.

Prevention of Muscle Soreness

The prevention of muscle soreness takes several forms, from training to medication. The most important preventive technique for a coach to consider is use of the principle of progressive increase of load in training. Furthermore, applying the concept of Periodization of Strength will avoid discomfort, muscle soreness, or other negative training outcomes.

An extensive overall warm-up will better prepare the body for work. Superficial warm-ups, on the other hand, can easily result in strain and pain. Stretching is also strongly recommended at the end of a training session. After extensive muscle contraction, typical of strength training, muscles are slightly shorter. It takes around two hours for them to return to resting length. Five to 10 minutes of stretching helps the muscles reach their resting length faster, optimal for biochemical exchanges at the muscle fiber level. Stretching also seems to ease muscle spasms.

Ingesting 1,000 milligrams of vitamin C per day may prevent or at least reduce muscle soreness. Similar benefits seem to result from taking vitamin E. Anti-inflammatory medication, such as Advil or aspirin, may help combat inflammation of muscle tissue. Massage is conventionally believed to relieve muscle soreness; however, both medication and massage provide only temporary relief. The best method for the relief of muscle soreness is prevention. The best prevention strategy is a progression in the use of eccentric contraction, especially at the beginning of strength training, such as:

- Week 1: use only concentric contraction (or 100 percent)
- Week 2: use 70 percent concentric and 30 percent eccentric
- Week 3: use normal concentric-eccentric ratios

Proper diet also helps athletes recover from muscle soreness. Athletes exposed to heavy loads in strength training require more protein, carbohydrates, and supplements. Inadequate carbohydrates may delay recovery of the muscle from injury and soreness.

Recovery From Strength Training

Various techniques are available for recovery from fatigue. Understanding how to use these techniques during training is just as important as knowing how to train effectively. New loads are constantly implemented in strength training programs, but the recovery methods used often do not keep pace. This can mean potential setbacks for athletes in peaking and regeneration following training. Approximately 50 percent of an athlete's final performance depends on the ability to recover. If recovery techniques are inadequate, adaptation may not be achieved.

Coaches must be aware of the factors that contribute to recovery. No single factor affects the body by itself; rather, it is the combination of these factors, all at varying degrees, that contributes to the recovery process. Among the main factors to be considered are age, experience, gender, environment, cell replishment, and emotional state.

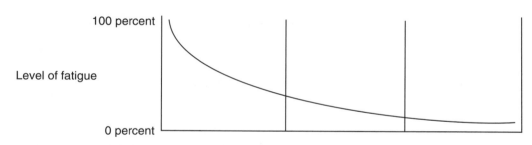

Figure 13.1 The dynamics of the curve of recovery.

Age affects the rate of recovery; older athletes generally take longer to recover. Better trained, more experienced athletes generally require less time to recuperate due to faster physiological adaptation to a given training stimulus. Gender may affect the rate of recovery, primarily due to differences in the endocrine system. Female athletes tend to have a slower rate of recovery. Environmental factors such as time differences, altitude, and cold climate tend to lessen the effects of the recovery process. Replenishment of nutrients at the cellular level has been shown to affect the recovery process. Restoration of proteins, fats, carbohydrates, and ATP/CP within the working muscle cell is required for cellular metabolism, as well as for the production of energy (Fox et al., 1989; Jacobs et al., 1987). Finally, negative emotions such as fear, indecisiveness, and lack of willpower tend to impede recovery.

Recovery is a slow process that depends directly on the training load employed. Similarly, the curve of recovery, which represents the body's ability to reach homeostasis, or its normal biological state, is not linear (figure 13.1). In the first third, the curve of recovery drops by 70 percent, whereas in the next two thirds, it drops by 20 and 10 percent, respectively.

The time interval for recovery depends on the energy system being taxed. Table 13.1 lists recommended recovery times for exhaustive strength training.

Table 13.1 Suggested Recovery Times After Exhaustive Strength Training (With Changes and Additions From Fox et al., 1989)

Recovery process	Recovery time
Restoration of ATP/CP	3-5 minutes
Restoration of muscle glycogen: *After prolonged exercise	10-48 hours
*After intermittent exercise (such as strength training)	24 hours
Removal of lactic acid from muscle and blood	1-2 hours
Restoration of vitamins and enzymes	24 hours
Recovery from overly taxing strength training (both metabolic and CNS to reach overcompensation)	2-3 days
Repayment of the alactacid oxygen debt	5 minutes
Repayment of the lactacid oxygen debt	30-60 minutes

The effectiveness of recovery techniques depends greatly on when they are employed. It is strongly suggested that they be performed during and following each training session (Fry et al., 1991; Kuipers & Keizer, 1988).

Recovery Techniques

Active recovery is the rapid elimination of waste products (i.e., lactic acid) during moderate aerobic recovery exercise. During the first 10 minutes of continuous light jogging, 62 percent of lactic acid is removed. An additional 26 percent is removed between 10 and 20 minutes. Thus, maintaining an active recovery period for 10 to 20 minutes after strength training seems advantageous (Bonen & Belcastro, 1977; Fox et al., 1989).

Complete rest, or passive rest, is perhaps the one necessity that all athletes have in common. To function at full capacity, most athletes require about 10 hours of sleep a day, a portion of which is usually gotten in the form of naps. Athletes should also have regular sleeping habits and be in bed no later than 11:00 P.M. Relaxation techniques should be employed prior to bedtime to put the athlete's mind in a more restful state (Gauron, 1984).

Massage, the systematic manipulation of soft body tissues for therapeutic purposes, is often the treatment of choice for most athletes (Cinique, 1989; Yessis, 1990). To achieve the best results from massage therapy, athletes are urged to use a certified specialist. The physiological effects of a massage are the result of mechanical intrusion and/or sensory stimulation.

The mechanical effects of massage include relief of muscle fatigue and reduction of excessive swelling. Massage can be especially beneficial when treating certain types of inflammation. Massage also stretches muscle adhesion. The mechanical pressure and stretching of tissue aids in mobilizing muscle adhesion for removal by the circulatory system. Massage also increases blood circulation. Squeezing relaxed muscles empties veins in the direction of the applied pressure. This stimulates the small capillaries to open and increases blood flow in the massaged area. At rest, approximately 4 percent of capillaries are open; this can be increased to 35 percent through massage (Bergeron, 1982). The end result is increased availability of "fresh" blood to the massaged area, allowing greater interchange of substances between capillaries and tissue cells.

Lymphatic circulation also increases. Massage assists circulation in the veins and the return of fluid (lymph) from the tissues. Unlike veins that have one-way valves, lymphatic vessels have no valves, so lymph can move in any direction, depending on external pressure. Gravity and muscle pump (including breathing activity) are the primary movers of lymph. Massage is the most effective external means of moving extravascular fluid into the lymph vessels and through these vessels into the circulatory system. This might be described as a cleaning-out action.

The sensory effects of massage are primarily reflexive in nature and are not fully understood. Massage may relieve pain and tenderness by slowly increasing the sensory input to the CNS. This necessitates massaging gradually into the painful area. Light stroking of the skin results in temporary dilation of capillaries. The stronger the stroking, the greater and more prolonged the dilation. Massage has only a local effect on metabolism that is due primarily to increased circulation throughout the massaged area. Breakdown of waste products and their absorption into the circulatory system may be increased up to 2.5 times above resting levels. Massage also relieves muscle spasm. Light stroking of an involuntary muscle contraction such as a muscle spasm may bring about relaxation through reflex mechanisms. Muscle spasms should first be stroked lightly in a direction parallel to the muscle fibers. If this fails, apply firm pressure to the muscle belly with both hands. If this also fails, apply deep thumb pressure into the muscle belly. In all cases, only gentle stretching of the muscle in spasm is recommended. Firm or deep pressure or sudden, violent stretching may increase the severity of the spasm.

Heat therapy in the form of steam baths, saunas, and heat packs can have a relaxing or regenerating effect. Although heat packs primarily heat the skin and not the underlying tissues, this modality is still useful. If applied long enough (at least 20 minutes), heat can be an effective way of increasing the circulation around the muscle. The only drawback is that the skin may become too hot before any muscle tissue has been heated. The best uses of heat may be to help athletes relax and to heat surface rather than deep muscle tissue.

Cold therapy such as ice, ice baths, ice whirlpools, and cold packs for 10 to 15 minutes may have important physiological benefits for recovery from fatigue. Rubbing ice on an excessively strained muscle may reduce swelling. In conjunction with heat, it may induce expansion (heat) or contraction (cold) of the damaged muscle tissue. Perhaps the best time to use ice is immediately following an intense training session where microtearing of the muscle tissue is likely.

Before discussing *diet and dietary supplementation*, a few words regarding caloric intake. Ideally, athletes should maintain an energy balance each day; that is, their daily energy expenditure should roughly match their energy intake. Athletes can judge rather easily whether their diet is adequate in calories. If they are losing weight while on a rigorous workout schedule, they probably are not consuming enough calories.

Even if they consume a "well-balanced" diet, athletes should not shy away from taking vitamin and mineral supplements. No matter how well balanced, a diet usually cannot replenish all the vitamins and minerals used during a training session or competition. Athletes typically experience a deficiency in all vitamins except vitamin A (Yessis, 1990). During periods of heavy training, supplements should be as much a part of the training table as any other nutrient.

In planning a supplement program, coaches and athletes should consider each period of training throughout the annual plan and adjust the supplements accordingly. For example, during the transition phase, the need for large doses of vitamins, particularly vitamins B6, B12, and C and certain minerals, will be much less due to the decreased intensity and volume of training. Planning for vitamin and mineral supplements can be made relatively easy by putting them in chart form with columns representing specific phases during the yearly training plan.

According to Clark (1985) and Yessis (1990), mealtime can affect the rate of recovery. These authors believe that it is much better for athletes to develop an eating pattern in which their daily intake is divided into at least four or five small meals a day, rather than three large meals. They reason that foods are better assimilated and digested with such a pattern. They recommend that about 20 to 25 percent of the daily intake be consumed for the early morning meal, 15 to 20 percent for a second breakfast, 30 to 35 percent for the midday meal, and 20 to 25 percent for the evening meal. Athletes should allow no more than 4 to 5 hours to pass between each meal of the day and no more than 12 hours between the evening meal and breakfast.

Clark (1985) and Yessis (1990) also believe that athletes should not eat immediately before a training session because a full stomach raises the diaphragm, forcing the cardiovascular and respiratory systems to work harder. Athletes should also avoid eating right after training, as few gastric juices are secreted during that time. Allow at least 20 to 30 minutes before eating a posttraining meal. During this time athletes should consume only fluids that contain carbohydrates and mineral supplements. Carbohydrates as well as foods rich in potassium are vital to normal muscle function (Clark, 1985; Fox, 1984).

Psychological recovery influences factors such as motivation and willpower and can be affected by stress from both physical and psychological stimuli. How fast the body reacts to various forms of external and internal stimuli greatly affects athletic performance. The more focused athletes are, the better they react to various training stimuli and the greater their working capacity. Lifestyle almost always has an effect on an athlete's rate of recovery. Poor relationships with a significant other, siblings, parents, teammates, and coaches can have a negative impact on the recovery process. If necessary, a sport psychologist can benefit athletes who are experiencing deep emotional problems that affect motivation and willpower.

Relaxation techniques can greatly improve an athlete's ability to focus. If the brain is relaxed, all other parts of the body assume the same state (Gauron, 1984). Perhaps the best time to employ such methods would be just before retiring for the evening. A warm bath or shower before bed might help induce a more relaxed state.

Recovery from short-term overtraining should start with the interruption of training for 3 to 5 days. Following this rest period, resume training by alternating each training session with a day off. If overtraining is severe and athletes need more recovery time, for every week of training missed, roughly 2 weeks will be required to attain their previous level of conditioning (Terjung & Hood, 1986). Repair of damaged muscle tissue falls under the category of short-term overtraining, requiring at least 5 to 7 days, whereas the regeneration of muscle tissue takes up to 20 days (Ebbing & Clarkson, 1989).

Recovery from muscle damage during the acute phase is best treated with ice, elevation, compression, and active or complete rest (depending on the extent of damage). After 3 days of this treatment, the coach should introduce other modalities such as massage. Alternation of hot and cold temperatures can also be an effective way of loosening the stiffness associated with exercise-induced muscle damage (Arnheim, 1989; Prentice, 1990).

According to Fahey (1991), diet may play a part in muscle tissue recovery. Aside from the obvious need for protein, in particular, animal protein, carbohydrates are also required. Recovery from muscle injury has been shown to be delayed when muscle carbohydrate stores are inadequate. Thus, from the standpoints of energy expenditure and recovery, it is vital that athletes pay strict attention to diet.

Appendix A: Training Log

No.	Exercise	Sets 1	2	3	4	5	6	7	8	9	10

Enter:

*Exercise

*Load and number of repetitions per set (i.e., 180 × 6)

Appendix B: Maximum Weight Chart

If for any reason (i.e., equipment) an athlete cannot lift the load necessary to calculate 1RM, but only 3RM, 4RM, or 5RM, and so on, it can still be calculated using the chart below. To calculate 1RM, perform the maximum number of repetitions with the load available (say 4 repetitions with 250 pounds), then follow the steps below:

1. Choose the column headed "4" (the number of repetitions performed).
2. Find the row marked "250 pounds"—the maximum load available.
3. Find the number where column 4 and row 250 meet.
4. This number is the athlete's 1RM at that given time.

Pounds	10	9	8	7	6	5	4	3	2
5	7	6	6	6	6	6	6	5	5
10	13	13	13	12	12	11	11	11	11
15	20	19	19	18	18	17	17	16	16
20	27	26	25	24	24	23	22	22	21
25	33	32	31	30	29	29	28	27	26
30	40	39	38	36	35	34	33	32	32
35	47	45	44	42	41	40	39	38	37
40	53	52	50	48	47	46	44	43	42
45	60	58	56	55	53	51	50	49	47
50	67	65	63	61	59	57	56	54	53
55	73	71	69	67	65	63	61	59	58
60	80	77	75	73	71	69	67	65	63
65	87	84	81	79	76	74	72	70	68
70	93	90	88	85	82	80	78	76	74
75	100	97	94	91	88	86	83	81	79
80	107	103	100	97	94	91	89	86	84
85	113	110	106	103	100	97	94	92	89
90	120	116	113	109	106	103	100	97	95
95	127	123	119	115	112	109	106	103	100
100	133	129	125	121	118	114	111	108	105
105	140	135	131	127	124	120	117	114	111
110	147	142	138	133	129	126	122	119	116
115	153	148	144	139	135	131	128	124	121

Pounds	10	9	8	7	6	5	4	3	2
120	160	155	150	145	141	137	133	130	126
125	167	161	156	152	147	143	139	135	132
130	173	168	163	158	153	149	144	141	137
135	180	174	169	164	159	154	150	146	142
140	187	181	175	170	165	160	156	151	147
145	193	187	181	176	171	166	161	157	153
150	200	194	188	182	176	171	167	162	158
155	207	200	194	188	182	177	172	168	163
160	213	206	200	194	188	183	178	173	168
165	220	213	206	200	194	189	183	178	174
170	227	219	213	206	200	194	189	184	179
175	233	226	219	212	206	200	194	189	184
180	240	232	225	218	212	206	200	195	189
185	247	239	231	224	218	211	206	200	195
190	253	245	238	230	224	217	211	205	200
195	260	252	244	236	229	223	217	211	205
200	267	258	250	242	235	229	222	216	211
205	273	265	256	248	241	234	228	222	216
210	280	271	263	255	247	240	233	227	221
215	287	277	269	261	253	246	239	232	226
220	293	284	275	267	259	251	244	238	232
225	300	290	281	273	265	257	250	243	237
230	307	297	288	279	271	263	256	249	242
235	313	303	294	285	276	269	261	254	247
240	320	310	300	291	282	274	267	259	253
245	327	316	306	297	288	280	272	265	258
250	333	323	313	303	294	286	278	270	263
255	340	329	319	309	300	291	283	276	268
260	347	335	325	315	306	297	289	281	274
265	353	342	331	321	312	303	294	286	279
270	360	348	338	327	318	309	300	292	284
275	367	355	344	333	324	314	306	297	289
280	373	361	350	339	329	320	311	303	295
285	380	368	356	345	335	326	317	308	300
290	387	374	363	352	341	331	322	314	305
295	393	381	369	358	347	337	328	319	311

(continued)

Pounds	10	9	8	7	6	5	4	3	2
300	400	387	375	364	353	343	333	324	316
305	407	394	381	370	359	349	339	330	321
310	413	400	388	376	365	354	344	335	326
315	420	406	394	382	371	360	350	341	332
320	427	413	400	388	376	366	356	346	337
325	433	419	406	394	382	371	361	351	342
330	440	426	413	400	388	377	367	357	347
335	447	432	419	406	394	383	372	362	353
340	453	439	425	412	400	389	378	368	358
345	460	445	431	418	406	394	383	373	363
350	467	452	438	424	412	400	389	378	368
355	473	458	444	430	418	406	394	384	374
360	480	465	450	436	424	411	400	389	379
365	487	471	456	442	429	417	406	395	384
370	493	477	463	448	435	423	411	400	389
375	500	484	469	455	441	429	417	405	395
380	507	490	475	461	447	434	422	411	400
385	513	497	481	467	453	440	428	416	405
390	520	503	488	473	459	446	433	422	411
395	527	510	494	479	465	451	439	427	416
400	533	516	500	485	471	457	444	432	421
405	540	523	506	491	476	463	450	438	426
410	547	529	513	497	482	469	456	443	432
415	553	535	519	503	488	474	461	449	437
420		542	525	509	494	480	467	454	442
425		548	531	515	500	486	472	459	447
430		555	538	521	506	491	478	465	453
435		561	544	527	512	497	483	470	458
440		568	550	533	518	503	489	476	463
445		574	556	539	524	509	494	481	468
450		581	563	545	529	514	500	486	474
455		587	569	552	535	520	506	492	479
460		594	575	558	541	526	511	497	484
465		600	581	564	547	531	517	503	489
470		606	588	570	553	537	522	508	495
475		613	594	576	559	543	528	514	500
480		619	600	582	565	549	532	519	505

Pounds	10	9	8	7	6	5	4	3	2
485		626	606	588	571	554	539	524	511
490		632	613	594	576	560	544	530	516
495		639	619	600	582	566	550	535	521
500		645	625	606	588	571	556	541	526
505		652	631	612	594	577	561	546	532
510		658	638	618	600	583	567	551	537
515		665	644	624	606	589	572	557	542
520		671	650	630	612	594	578	562	547
525		677	656	636	618	600	583	569	553
530		684	663	642	624	606	589	573	558
535		690	669	648	629	611	594	578	563
540		697	675	655	635	617	600	584	568
545		703	681	661	641	623	606	589	574
550		710	688	667	647	629	611	595	579
555		716	694	673	653	634	617	600	584
560		723	700	679	659	640	622	605	589
565		729	706	685	665	646	628	611	595
570		735	713	691	671	651	633	616	600
575		742	719	697	676	657	639	622	605
580		748	725	703	682	663	644	627	611
585		755	731	709	688	669	650	632	616
590		761	738	715	694	674	656	638	621
595		768	744	721	700	680	661	643	626
600		774	750	727	706	686	667	649	632
605		781	756	733	712	691	672	654	637
610		787	763	739	718	697	678	659	642
615		794	769	745	724	703	683	665	647
620		800	775	752	729	709	689	670	653
625		806	781	758	735	714	694	676	658
630		813	788	764	741	720	700	681	663
635		819	794	770	747	726	706	686	668
640		826	800	776	753	731	711	692	674
645		832	806	782	759	737	717	697	679
650		839	813	788	765	743	722	703	684
655		845	819	794	771	749	728	708	689
660		852	825	800	776	754	733	714	695

(continued)

Pounds	10	9	8	7	6	5	4	3	2
665		858	831	806	782	760	739	719	700
670		865	838	812	788	766	644	724	705
675		871	844	818	794	771	750	730	711
680		877	850	824	800	777	756	735	716
685		884	856	830	806	783	761	741	721
690		890	863	836	812	789	767	746	726
695		897	869	842	818	794	772	751	732
700		903	875	848	824	800	778	757	737
705		910	881	855	829	806	783	762	742
710		916	888	861	835	811	789	768	747
715		923	894	768	841	817	794	773	753
720		929	900	873	847	823	800	778	758
825		935	906	879	853	829	806	784	763
730		942	913	885	859	834	811	789	768
735		948	919	891	865	840	817	795	774
740		955	925	897	871	846	822	800	779
745		961	931	903	876	851	828	805	784
750		968	938	909	882	857	833	811	789
755		974	944	915	888	863	839	816	795
760		981	950	921	894	869	844	822	800
765		987	956	927	900	874	850	827	805
770		994	963	933	906	880	856	832	811
775		1,000	969	939	912	886	861	838	816
780		1,006	975	945	918	891	867	843	821
785		1,013	981	952	924	897	872	849	826
790		1,019	988	958	929	903	878	854	832
795		1,026	994	964	935	908	883	859	837
800		1,032	1,000	970	941	914	889	865	842
820		1,058	1,025	994	965	937	911	886	863
840		1,084	1,050	1,018	988	960	933	908	884
860		1,110	1,075	1,042	1,012	983	956	930	905
880		1,135	1,100	1,067	1,035	1,006	978	951	926
900		1,161	1,125	1,091	1,059	1,029	1,000	973	947
920		1,187	1,150	1,115	1,082	1,051	1,022	995	968

Table compiled by Strength Tech Inc., Box 1381, Stillwater, OK 74076, U.S.A.

References

Abernethy, P.J.; Thayer, R.; Taylor, A.W. 1990. Acute and chronic responses of skeletal muscle to endurance and sprint exercise. A review. *Sports Medicine* 10 (6): 365-389.

Abbruzzese, G.; Morena, M.; Spadavecchia, L.; Schieppati, M. 1994. Response of arm flexor muscles to magnetic and electrical brain stimulation during shortening and lengthening tasks in man. *Journal of Physiology London* 481: 499-507.

Appell, H.J. 1990. Muscular atrophy following immobilization: A review. *Sports Medicine* 10 (1): 42-58.

Armstrong, R.B. 1986. Muscle damage and endurance events. *Sports Medicine* 3: 370-381.

Armstrong, R.B.; Warren, G.L.; Warren, J.A. 1991. Mechanics of exercise induced muscle fiber injury. *Sports Medicine* 12 (3): 184-207.

Arnheim, D. 1989. *Modern Principles of Athletic Training*. St. Louis: Times Mirror/Mosby College.

Asmussen, E.; Mazin, B. 1978. A central nervous system component in local muscular fatigue. *European Journal of Applied Physiology* 38: 9-15.

Astrand, P.O.; Rodahl, K. 1985. *Textbook of Work Physiology*. New York: McGraw-Hill.

Atha, J. 1984. Strengthening muscle. *Exercise and Sport Sciences Reviews* 9: 1-73.

Baroga, L. 1978. Contemporary tendencies in the methodology of strength development. *Educatie Fizica Si Sport* 6: 22-36.

Bergeron, G. 1982. Therapeutic massage. *Canadian Athletic Therapist Association Journal* Summer: 15-17.

Bergstrom, J.; Hermansen, L.; Hultman, E.; Saltin, B. 1967. Diet, muscle glycogen and physical performance. *Acta Physiologica Scandinavica* 71: 140-150.

Bigland-Ritchie, B.; Johansson, R.; Lippold, O.C.J.; Woods, J.J. 1983. Contractile speed and EMG changes during fatigue of sustained maximal voluntary contractions. *Journal of Neurophysiology* 50 (1): 313-324.

Bompa, T. 1965a. Periodization of strength. *Sports Review* 1: 26-31.

Bompa, T. 1965b. Periodization of strength for power sports. International Conference on Advancements in Sports Training, Moscow. November 22-23.

Bompa, T. 1977. Characteristics of strength training for rowing. International Seminar on Training in Rowing, Stockholm. October 27-28.

Bompa, T. 1988. *Periodization of Strength for Bodybuilding*. Toronto: York University.

Bompa, T. 1993a. *Periodization of Strength: The New Wave in Strength Training*. Toronto: Veritas.

Bompa, T. 1993b. *Power Training for Sport: Plyometrics for Maximum Power Development*. Oakville-New York-London: Mosaic Press/Coaching Association of Canada.

Bompa, T. 1999. *Periodization: Theory and Methodology of Training* (4th ed.). Champaign, IL: Human Kinetics.

Bompa, T.; Cornacchia, L. 1998. *Serious Strength Training*. Champaign, IL: Human Kinetics.

Bompa T.; Hebbelinck, M.; Van Gheluwe, B. 1978. A biomechanical analysis of the rowing stroke employing two different oar grips. The XXI World Congress in Sports Medicine, Brasilia, Brazil.

Bonen, A.; Belcastro, A.N. 1976. Comparison of self-selected recovery methods on lactic acid removal rates. *Medicine and Science in Sports and Exercise* 8 (3): 176-178.

Bonen, A.; Belcastro, A. 1977. A physiological rationale for active recovery exercise. *Canadian Journal of Applied Sports Sciences* 2: 63-64.

Bosco, C.; Komi, P.V. 1980. Influence of countermovement amplitude in potentiation of muscular performance. Biomechanics VII Proceedings (pp. 129-135). Baltimore: University Park Press.

Brooks, G.A.; Fahey, T. 1985. *Exercise Physiology: Human Bioenergetics and Its Application*. New York: Wiley.

Brooks, G.A.; Brauner, K.T.; Cassens, R.G. 1973. Glycogen synthesis and metabolism of lactic acid after exercise. *American Journal of Physiology* 224: 1162-1166.

Bührle, M. 1985. *Grundlagen des Maximal-und Schnellkraft trainings*. Schorndorf: Hofmann Verlag.

Bührle, M.; Schmidtbleicher, D. 1981. Komponenten der Maximal-und Schnellkraft-Versuch einer Neustrukturierung auf der Basis empirischer Ergenbnisse. *Sportwissenschaft* 11: 11-27.

Burke, R.; Costill, D.; Fink, W. 1977. Characteristics of skeletal muscle in competitive cyclists. *Medicine and Science in Sports and Exercise* 9: 109-112.

Cinique, C. 1989. Massage for cyclists: The winning touch? *The Physician and Sportsmedicine* 17 (10): 167-170.

Clark, N. 1985. Recovering from exhaustive workouts. *National Strength and Conditioning Journal* January: 36-37.

Compton, D.; Hill, P.M.; Sinclair, J.D. 1973. Weight-lifters' blackout. *Lancet II*: 1234-1237.

Conlee, R.K. 1987. Muscle glycogen and exercise endurance: A twenty-year perspective. *Exercise and Sport Sciences Reviews* 15: 1-28.

Costill, D.; Coyle, E.F.; Find, W.F.; Lesmes, G.R.; Witzmann, F.A. 1979. Adaptations in skeletal muscle following strength training. *Journal of Applied Physiology*, 46: 96-99.

Costill, D.; Daniels, J.; Evans, W.; Fink, W.; Krahenbuhl, G.; Saltin, B. 1976. Skeletal muscle enzymes and fibre composition in male and female track athletes. *Journal of Applied Physiology*, 40: 149-154.

Councilman, J.E. 1968. *The Science of Swimming.* Englewood Cliffs, NJ: Prentice Hall.

Coyle, E.F.; Feiring, D.C.; Rotkis, T.C.; Cote, R.W.; Roby, F.B.; Lee, W.; Wilmore, J.H. 1991. Specificity of power improvements through slow and fast isokinetic training. *Journal of Applied Physiology: Respiratory Environment Exercise Physiology* 51 (6): 1437-1442.

De Luca, C.J.; LeFever, R.S.; McCue, M.P.; Xenakis, A.P. 1982. Behaviour of human motor units in different muscles during linearly varying contractions. *Journal of Physiology London* 329: 113-128.

Dons, B.; Bollerup, K.; Bonde-Petersen, F.; Hancke, S. 1979. The effects of weight lifting exercise related to muscle fibre composition and muscle cross-sectional area in humans. *European Journal of Applied Physiology,* 40: 95-106.

Dudley, G.A.; Fleck, S.J. 1987. Strength and endurance training: Are they mutually exclusive? *Sports Medicine,* 4: 79-85.

Ebbing, C.; Clarkson, P. 1989. Exercise-induced muscle damage and adaptation. *Sports Medicine,* 7: 207-234.

Edgerton, R.V. 1976. Neuromuscular adaptation to power and endurance work. *Canadian Journal of Applied Sports Sciences,* 1: 49-58.

Enoka, R. 1996. Eccentric contractions require unique activation strategies by the nervous system. *Journal of Applied Physiology* 81 (6): 2339-2346.

Evans, W.J. 1987. Exercise-induced skeletal muscle damage. *The Physician and Sports Medicine,* 15 (1): 89-100.

Fabiato, A.; Fabiato, F. 1978. The effect of pH on myofilaments and the sarcoplasmic reticulum of skinned cells from cardiac and skeletal muscle. *Journal of Physiology,* 276: 233-255.

Fleck, S.J.; Kraemer, W.J. 1996. *Periodization Breakthrough.* New York: Advanced Research Press.

Florescu, C.; Dumitrescu, T.; Predescu, A. 1969. *The Methodology of Developing the Motor Abilities.* Bucharest: CNEFS.

Fox, E.L. 1984. *Sports Physiology.* New York: CBS College.

Fox, E.L.; Bowes, R.W.; Foss, M.L. 1989. *The Physiological Basis of Physical Education and Athletics.* Dubuque, IA: Brown.

Friden, J.; Lieber, R.L. 1992. Structural and mechanical basis of exercise-induced muscle injury. *Medicine Science and Sports Exercise* 24: 521-530.

Fry, R.W.; Morton, R.; Keast, D. 1991. Overtraining in athletics. *Sports Medicine,* 2 (1): 32-65.

Gauron, E.F. 1984. *Mental Training for Peak Performance.* New York: Sports Science Associates.

Goldberg, A.L.; Etlinger, J.D.; Goldspink, D.F.; Jablecki, C. 1975. Mechanism of work-induced hypertrophy of skeletal muscle. *Medicine and Science in Sports and Exercise* 7: 185-198.

Gollhofer, A.; Fujitsuka, P.A.; Miyashita, N., M.-Yashita, 1987. Fatigue during stretch-shortening cycle exercises: Changes in neuro-muscular activation patterns of human skeletal muscle. *Journal of Sports Medicine* 8: 30-47.

Gollnick, P.; Armstrong, R.; Saubert, C.; Piehl, K.; Saltin, B. 1972. Enzyme activity and fibre composition in skeletal muscle of untrained and trained men. *Journal of Applied Physiology,* 33 (3): 312-319.

Gordon, F. 1967. Anatomical and biochemical adaptations of muscle to different exercises. *Journal of the American Medical Association* 201: 755-758.

Gregory, L.W. 1981. Some observations on strength training and assessment. *Journal of Sports Medicine* 21: 130-137.

Grimby, G. 1992. Strength and power in sport. In Komi, P.V. (Ed.), *Strength and Power in Sport.* Oxford, UK: Blackwell Scientific.

Grosser, M.; Neumeier, A. 1986. *Tecnicas de Entrenamiento (Training Techniques).* Barcelona: Martinez Roca.

Hainaut, K.; Duchatteau, J. 1989. Muscle fatigue: Effects of training and disuse *Muscle & Nerve.* 12: 660-669.

Häkkinen, K. 1986. Training and detraining adaptations in electromyography. Muscle fibre and force production characteristics of human leg extensor muscle with special reference to prolonged heavy resistance and explosive-type strength training. *Studies in Sport, Physical Education and Health No. 20.* Jyväskylä, Finland: University of Jyväskylä.

Häkkinen, K. 1989. Neuromuscular and hormonal adaptations during strength and power training. *Journal of Sports Medicine and Physical Fitness* 29 (1): 9-26.

Häkkinen, K. 1991. Personal communications on maximum strength development for sports. Madrid.

Häkkinen, K.; Komi, P. 1983. Electromyographic changes during strength training and detraining. *Medicine and Science in Sports and Exercise* 15: 455-60.

Harre, D. (Ed.). 1982. *Trainingslehre.* Berlin: Sportverlag.

Hartmann, J.; Tünnemann, H. 1988. *Fitness and Strength Training.* Berlin: Sportverlag.

Hay, J.G. 1993. *The Biomechanics of Sports Techniques.* Englewood Cliffs, NJ: Prentice Hall.

Hellebrand, F.; Houtz, S. 1956. Mechanism of muscle training in man: experimental demonstration of the overload principle. *Physical Therapy Review* 36: 371-383.

Hennig, R.; Lomo, T. 1987. Gradation of force output in normal fast and slow muscle of the rat. *Acta Physiologica Scandinavica* 130: 133-142.

Hettinger, T. 1966. *Isometric Muscle Training.* Stuttgart: Georg Thieme Verlag.

Hettinger, T.; Müler, E. 1953. Muskelleistung und muskel training. *Arbeitsphysiologie* 15: 111-126.

Hickson, R.C.; Dvorak, B.A.; Corostiaga, T.T.; Foster, C. 1988. Strength training and performance in endurance-trained subjects. *Medicine and Science in Sports and Exercise* 20 (2) (Suppl.): 586.

Hortobagyi, T.; Hill, J.; Houmard, A.; Fraser, D.; Lambert, J.; Israel, G. 1996. Adaptive responses to muscle lengthening and shortening in humans. *Journal of Applied Physiology* 80 (3): 765-772.

Houmard, J.A. 1991. Impact of reduced training on performance in endurance athletes. *Sports Medicine* 12 (6): 380-393.

Israel, S. 1972. The acute syndrome of detraining. *Berlin: GDR National Olympic Committee* 2: 30-35.

Jacobs, I.; Esbornsson, M.; Sylven, C.; Holm, I.; Jansson, E. 1987. Sprint training effects on muscle myoglobin, enzymes, fibre types, and blood lactate. *Medicine and Science in Sports and Exercise* 19 (4): 368-374.

Kanehisa, J.; Miyashita, M. 1983. Effect of isometric and isokinetic muscle training on static strength and dynamic power. *European Journal of Applied Physiology* 50: 365-371.

Karlsson, J.; Saltin, B. 1971. Diet, muscle glycogen and endurance performance. *Journal of Applied Physiology* 31 (2): 203-206.

Komi, P.; Rusko, H.; Vos, J.; Vihko, V. 1977. Anaerobic performance capacity in athletes. *Acta Physiologica Scandinavica* 100: 107-114.

Komi, P.V.; Bosco, C. 1978. Utilization of stored elastic energy in leg extensor muscles by men and women. *Medicine and Science in Sport and Exercise* 10 (4): 261-265.

Komi, P.V.; Buskirk, E.R. 1972. Effect of eccentric and concentric muscle conditioning on tension and electrical activity of human muscle. *Ergonomics* 15 (4): 417-434.

Kuipers, H.; Keizer, H.A. 1988. Overtraining in elite athletes: Review and directions for the future. *Sports Medicine,* 6: 79-92.

Lange, L. 1919. Über functionelle anpassung. Berlin: Springer Verlag.

Laubach, L.L. 1976. Comparative muscle strength of men and women: A review of the literature. *Aviation, Space, and Environmental Medicine* 47: 534-542.

Logan, G.A. 1960. *Differential Applications of Resistance and Resulting Strength Measured at Varying Degrees of Knee Flexion.* Doctoral dissertation, USC, Los Angeles, CA.

MacDougall, J.D.; Sale, D.; Jacobs, I.; Garner, S.; Moroz, D.; Dittmer, D. 1987. Concurrent strength and endurance training do not impede gains in VO_2max. *Medicine and Science in Sports and Exercise* 19 (2): 588.

MacDougall, J.D.; Sale, D.G.; Elder, G.; Sutton, J.R. 1976. Ultrastructural properties of human skeletal muscle following heavy resistance training and immobilization. *Medicine and Science in Sports and Exercise* 8 (1): 72.

MacDougall, J.D.; Sale, D.G.; Moroz, J.R.; Elder, G.C.B.; Sutton, J.R.; Howald, H. 1979. Mitochondrial volume density in human skeletal muscle following heavy resistance training. *Medicine and Science in Sports and Exercise* 11 (2): 264-266.

MacDougall, J.D.; Tuxen, D.; Sale, D.G.; Moroz, J.R.; Sutton, J.R. 1985. Arterial blood pressure response to heavy resistance exercise. *Journal of Applied Physiology* 58 (3): 785-790.

MacDougall, J.D.; Ward, G.R.; Sale, D.G.; Sutton, J.R. 1977. Biochemical adaptation of human skeletal muscle to heavy resistance training and immobilization. *Journal of Applied Physiology* 43 (4): 700-703.

Marsden, C.D.; Meadows, J.F.; Merton, P.A. 1971. Isolated single motor units in human muscle and their rate of discharge during maximal voluntary effort. *Journal of Physiology* (London) 217: 12P-13P.

Mathews, D.K.; Fox, E.L. 1976. *The Physiological Basis of Physical Education and Athletics.* Philadelphia: Saunders.

Matsuda, J.J.; Zernicke, R.F.; Vailn, A.C.; Pedrinin, V.A.; Pedrini-Mille, A.; Maynard, J.A. 1986. Structural and mechanical adaptation of immature bone to strenuous exercises. *Journal of Applied Physiology* 60 (6): 2028-2034.

McDonagh, M.J.N.; Davies, C.T.M. 1984. Adaptive response of mammalian skeletal muscle to exercise with high loads. *European Journal of Applied Physiology* 52: 139-155.

Micheli, L.J. 1988. Strength training in the youth athletes. In Bown, E.W., and Branta, C.E. (Eds.), *Competitive Sports for Children and Youth* (pp. 99-105). Champaign, IL: Human Kinetics.

Morgan, R.E.; Adamson, G.T. 1959. *Circuit Weight Training.* London: G. Bell and Sons.

Nelson, A.G.; Arnall, D.A.; Loy, S.F.; Silvester, L.J.; Conlee, R.K. 1990. Consequences of combining strength and endurance training regimens. *Physical Therapy* 70 (5): 287-294.

Ozolin, N.G. 1971. *Athlete's Training System for Competition.* Moscow: Phyzkultura i sports.

Piehl, K. 1974. Time course for refilling of glycogen stores in human muscle fibres following exercise-induced glycogen depletion. *Acta Physiologica Scandinavica* 90: 297-302.

Prentice, W.J. 1990. *Rehabilitation Techniques in Sports Medicine.* Toronto: Times Mirror/Mosby College.

Ralston, H.J.; Rolissan, M.J.; Inman, F.J.; Close, J.R.; Feinstein, B. 1949. Dynamic feature of human isolated voluntary muscle in isometric and free contraction. *Journal of Applied Physiology* 1: 526-533.

Sahlin, K. 1986. Metabolic changes limiting muscular performance. *Biochemistry of Exercise,* 16: 86-98.

Sale, D. 1986. Neural adaptation in strength and power training. In Jones, L., McCartney, N., and McConias, A. (Eds.), *Human Muscle Power* (pp. 289-304). Champaign, IL: Human Kinetics.

Sale, D.G.; MacDougall, J.D.; Jakobs, I.; Garner, S. 1990. Interaction between concurrent strength and endurance training. *Journal of Applied Physiology* 68 (1): 260-270.

Schmidtbleicher, D. 1984. *Sportliches Krafttraining.* Berlin: Jung, Haltong, und Bewegung bie Menchen.

Schmidtbleicher, D. 1992. Training for power events. In Komi, P.V. (Ed.), *Strength and Power in Sport* (pp. 381-395). Oxford, UK: Blackwell Scientific.

Scholich, M. 1992. *Circuit Training for All Sports.* Edited by P. Klavora. Toronto: Sports Books Publishers.

Staron, R.S.; Hagerman, F.C.; Hikida, R.S. 1981. The effects of detraining on an elite power lifter. *Journal of Neurological Sciences,* 51: 247-257.

Stone, M.H.; O'Bryant, H.S. 1984. *Weight Training: A Scientific Approach.* Minneapolis, MN: Burgess.

Terjung, R.L.; Hood, D.A. 1986. Biochemical adaptations in skeletal muscle induced by exercise training. Cited in Layman, D.K. (Ed.), *Nutrition and Aerobic Exercise* (pp. 8-27). Washington, D.C.: American Chemical Society.

Tesch, P. 1980. Muscle fatigue in man. *Acta Physiologica Scandinavica Supplementum* 480: 3-40.

Tesch, P.; Sjödon, B.; Thorstensson, A.; Karlsson, J. 1978. Muscle fatigue and its relation to lactate accumulation and LDH activity in man. *Acta Physiologica Scandinavica* 103: 413-420.

Tesch, P.A.; Karlsson, J. 1985. Muscle fibre types and size in trained and untrained muscles of elite athletes. *Journal of Applied Physiology* 59: 1716-1720.

Tesch, P.A.; Dudley, G.A.; Duvoisin, M.R.; Hather, M.; Harris, R.T. 1990. Force and EMG signal patterns during repeated bouts of concentric or eccentric muscle actions. *Acta Physiologica Scandinavica* 138: 263-271.

Thorstensson, A. 1977. Observations on strength training and detraining. *Acta Physiologica Scandinavica* 100: 491-493.

Thorstensson, A.; Larsson, L.; Tesch, P.; Karlsson, J. 1977. Muscle strength and fibre composition in athletes and sedentary men. *Medicine and Science in Sports and Exercise* 9: 26-30.

Verkhoshanski, Y. 1969. Perspectives in the improvement of speed-strength preparation of jumpers. *Yessis Review of Soviet Physical Education and Sports* 4 (2): 28-29.

Wathen, D. 1994. Agonist-antagonist ratios for slow concentric isokinetic movements. In Baechle, T.R. (Ed.), *Essentials of Strength Training and Conditioning.* Champaign, IL: Human Kinetics.

Wilmore, J.H.; Costill, D.L. 1988. Training for sport and activity. *The Physiological Basis of the Conditioning Process.* Dubuque, IA: Brown.

Wilmore J.H.; Parr, R.B.; Girandola, R.N.; Ward, P.; Vodak, P.A.; Barstow, T.J.; Pipes, T.V.; Romero, G.T.; Leslie, P. 1978. Physiological alterations consequent to circuit weight training. *Medicine and Science in Sports and Exercise* 10: 79-84.

Wright, J.E. 1980. Anabolic steroids and athletics. In Hutton, R.S., and Miller, D.I. (Eds.), *Exercise and Sport Sciences Reviews*: 149-202.

Yessis, M. 1990. *Soviet Training Methods.* New York: Barnes & Noble.

Zanon, S. 1977. Consideration for determining some parametric values of the relations between maximum isometric relative strength and elastic relative strength for planning and controlling the long jumper's conditioning training. *Athletic Coach* 11 (4): 14-20.

Index